LONDON COUTURE
AND THE MAKING OF A FASHION CENTRE

LONDON COUTURE
AND THE MAKING OF A FASHION CENTRE

MICHELLE JONES

The MIT Press
Cambridge, Massachusetts
London, England

The MIT Press would like to thank the anonymous peer reviewers who provided comments on drafts of this book. The generous work of academic experts is essential for establishing the authority and quality of our publications. We acknowledge with gratitude the contributions of these otherwise uncredited readers.

This book was set in Bembo Book MT Pro by New Best-set Typesetters Ltd. Printed and bound in the United States of America.

Library of Congress Cataloging-in-Publication Data

Names: Jones, Michelle (Design scholar), author.
Title: London couture and the making of a fashion centre / Michelle Jones.
Description: Cambridge, Massachusetts ; London, England : The MIT Press, [2022] | Includes bibliographical references and index.
Identifiers: LCCN 2021017749 | ISBN 9780262046572 (hardcover)
Subjects: LCSH: Fashion design—Great Britain—History—20th century. | Clothing trade—Great Britain—History—20th century. | Popular culture—England—London—History—20th century.
Classification: LCC TT504.6.G7 J66 2022 | DDC 746.9/20941—dc23
LC record available at https://lccn.loc.gov/2021017749

10   9   8   7   6   5   4   3   2   1

CONTENTS

INTRODUCTION: LONDON COUTURE—DESIGN COLLABORATION, NETWORKS AND NARRATIVES

In 1948 for an article entitled 'Tweed Returns', the British trade magazine *Fashion and Fabrics Overseas* included an image of a young woman posed in perfectly tailored day clothes, executed in wool, with one foot on a map of the London Underground (figure I.1). The clothing she wore, designed and produced by Victor Stiebel, a member of the Incorporated Society of London Fashion Designers, for his autumn/winter export collection, represented not only the work of this couturier but also a specific design identity for this trade group and more broadly for Britain's fashion and textile industry. In the same month, for British *Vogue*, the photographer Cecil Beaton staged similar examples of the Incorporated Society's daywear next to the Albert Memorial, another cornerstone of London iconography that, having survived the Blitz untouched, was an emblem of national endurance. In the garments selected, the London fashion designers' symbolic and commercial counters to the privations of the war years were made clear. In the softer silhouettes, small waists and long, pleated skirts, the design of the suits adhered to the fashion industry's search for a new post-war silhouette. As a measure of London's couture industry these were confident images. The skilfully tailored town and country wear, the Underground map and the Albert Memorial speak of movement, travel and heritage and promote London as an assured destination for luxury couture-based fashion design. The activities that led to this confidence, undertaken by a group of England's made-to-measure dressmakers throughout the 1930s and 1940s, provide the central preoccupation for this book. Today London is acknowledged, alongside Paris, New York and Milan, as one of the world's major fashion cities; this study examines the part the establishment of its small couture industry played in the development of London as an internationally recognised fashion centre.

Originally conceived in Paris and produced for consumption by a wealthy and fashionable elite, haute couture, the practice of creative

Figure I.1
Victor Stiebel suit, photographed by Zoltan Glass for the article 'Tweeds Return',
Fashion and Fabrics Overseas, September 1948.

made-to-measure womenswear, was internationally acknowledged as inherently French and the fashion industry's most prestigious and creative form. Paris-based couturiers were recognised not just as custom dressmakers who responded to the whims of elite clients but also as style dictators who created fashion. By the 1930s, when a small London couture industry began to emerge, French models were a main source of design inspiration throughout all levels of the international fashion industry. This was particularly the case for the lucrative American market, where French dictates operated as a major source of inspiration and style guidance not only through the sale of original models but also through their licensed reproduction and adaptation.[1] With such an established competitor in close geographical proximity, at a time when in Britain mass manufactured clothing could be a more lucrative investment, a London-based couture business was a questionable and tenacious business proposition.[2] With France so far ahead in this design field, the emergence of a recognised London couture industry, in an age that was also witness to intense economic and political instability, offers an interesting example of an attempt to shift power within the international fashion system.[3]

Since the 1860s the designation of haute couturier and the boundaries of this form of French production have been regulated and protected by the Chambre Syndicale de la Couture Parisienne. This body offered business protection and reinforced the Parisian couturiers' claims to creative supremacy.[4] It was not until 1942 that the Incorporated Society of London Fashion Designers (INCSOC), a similar but less official body, was established as a wartime measure to protect the interests of a number of London's creative couture businesses. In its first year the Society brought together nine designers and couture houses: Hardy Amies, Charles Creed, Norman Hartnell, Edward Molyneux, Digby Morton, Bianca Mosca, Peter Russell, Victor Stiebel and Worth (London). The INCSOC was to remain exclusive; indeed, between 1946 and 1962 it recruited only a further eight members: Angele Delanghe (1945), Giuseppe Mattli (1948), Michael Sherard (1949), Lachasse (1950), John Cavanagh (1952), Ronald Paterson (1953), Michael Donnellan (1953) and Clive Evans (1962). These designer-members financed the Society alongside small discretionary contributions from the textile export groups of the British wool, cotton, rayon, silk and lace industries.[5] Representatives from the export groups, alongside Lord Derby (Patron of the Cotton Board), acted as its vice presidents. In

1942 Margaret Havinden (the account executive of Crawford's Advertising Agency) operated as its first chairman.[6] Daisy Fellowes (the socialite and heiress to the Singer sewing machine fortune) was its first president.[7] Whilst it shrank in size and relevance throughout the 1960s, for a little over thirty years (it was officially dissolved in 1975) the Incorporated Society was the recognised nucleus of the British couture industry.[8]

The INCSOC's stipulations for membership rested on the production of made-to-measure garments based on original designs. This aligned with the expectations of 'Couture-Création' set out by the Parisian Chambre Syndicale, yet this Society did not impose the strict rules that governed all aspects of French haute couture production and distribution. These stipulated that to be considered 'Couture-Création' a designer had to twice-yearly create and present original dress models on live mannequins in a Paris-based couture house. In France there were specific guidelines that governed the production of the models; these covered aspects such as the number of in-house employees, the technical execution of the made-to-measure process, the number of fittings and even how these garments were presented and sold.[9] The structural difference between the Incorporated Society and the Chambre Syndicale was not just one of scale (there were seventy registered houses in Paris in 1946, in comparison to ten in London) but also of organisation. 'Half union and half guild', the Chambre Syndicale was a large administrative body with considerable industrial power. Supported by government subsidies drawn from the textile industry, it operated as a judicial and legislative body. It protected French couturiers from style piracy, whilst it also coordinated aspects such as foreign relations and press coverage.[10] In comparison, the Incorporated Society was self-appointed and regulated by its designer-members; its funds were limited; and its administrative team consisted of one secretary.

Unlike their Parisian counterparts, the Incorporated Society's members had to work together in a more collective manner. For the design historian, the small scale and ad hoc nature of this Society, formed and maintained by its designer-members without government support, offers a particularly interesting case study, a pertinent example of designer collaboration in a field that thrives on the celebration of individual visionaries. It is extremely rare within the fashion system for its designers to even acknowledge, let alone work with, a competitor. The reason for this extends beyond commercial rivalry and fears of plagiarism, which of course remain, to the professional identity of the fashion designer, which rests on originality and creative autonomy.[11] In recognition of this distinction it is therefore the atypical collective identity and the collaborative strategies of the London couturiers that fuel the critical exploration of this book.

Although created by a small number of London-based couturiers, without government funding, the idea that the Incorporated Society's objectives should be broader than merely the commercial concerns of its members' businesses was enshrined in its Articles of Association. Here, the two most fundamental aims were, first, to maintain and develop the reputation of London as a creative fashion centre and, second, to collaborate with manufacturers and others involved in the industry to 'increase the prestige' of British fashion and textiles and encourage their demand in foreign markets.[12] In 1942, such objectives were clearly dictated by the economic and political situation brought about by the Second World War; whilst Britain had to turn much of its industrial production over to the war effort, it still needed to maintain its exports to bring finance into the country. The period of study and rationale for this book are drawn from the Incorporated Society's original objectives to preserve the London couture industry and to operate as a vehicle for industrial design reform. Before the interwar period, while London was acknowledged as an important Imperial capital, this recognition was mainly as the 'city of business' in contrast to the notion of Paris as the 'city of pleasure', and it had not been particularly associated with women's fashion.[13] In terms of British high-level clothing production, this led to a gendered understanding, a binary, which historically saw London as the centre for elite male tailoring and Paris as the centre for creative women's dressmaking. It was not until the 1930s that the Incorporated Society's founder members gained recognition for the production of original women's fashions. Historians agree that this decade saw the emergence of a London couture industry and that by the 1950s, in part due to the creation of the Incorporated Society, London had achieved international acknowledgement as a fashion centre.[14] In recognition of the fact that the Incorporated Society was created to protect and develop an already established industry, this study spans the years 1930–1949. The 1930s began with an economic depression and ended with the declaration of World War II. Within the wartime and post-war economy of the 1940s the couturiers then had to react to and navigate a series of government restrictions imposed on clothing production; by 1949, when the system of clothes rationing finally ended, the identity, operation and boundaries of the London couture industry had in many ways been fully established. The temporal scope of this study therefore facilitates not only a consideration of the creation of a London couture industry but also the cultural politics of design practice throughout a difficult economic period of depression, war, and post-war reconstruction.

In terms of their professional identity the London couturiers operated within the conceptual and formal boundaries established in Paris. This led to their retrospective acknowledgement as merely a small-scale parody of their French predecessor and their practice as 'the synthetic drafting of Parisian style onto the London scene'.[15] In both contemporaneous and retrospective acknowledgement there was a tendency to describe London's couturiers as mimics of their French counterparts; for example, Victor Stiebel was declared 'London's Balmain' in 1957 (although Stiebel opened his business eight years before Balmain) and Michael Donnellan (in the catalogue to an exhibition on couture in 2007), its 'Balenciaga'.[16] The notion of individuality, authenticity and novelty and the designer as the instigator and conduit of these elements is a key part of the discourse of fashion: representative of a designer's individual creative agency.[17] The consistent suggestion of a mimetic and therefore inferior form of production demonstrates how comparison to their Parisian-based counterparts operated to undermine the professional standing and relevance of the English couturiers.

The Incorporated Society of London Fashion Designers represented the interests of the city's designated couturiers, yet even the name chosen points to a level of unease in the use of the French term. The specification that its members were *fashion designers* was a product of its time; wartime nationalism and egalitarianism ensured that the designation *couturiers* would have been not only foreign but also elitist. However, even before the war there was a notable uncertainty in the terms used to describe the London made-to-measure dressmakers' practice. Throughout the 1930s this fluctuated from court dressmaker to dressmaker or, alternatively, to dress or fashion designer. The first two terms were primarily used in relation to the production of garments for specific clients, the latter when the designers' models were reproduced or adapted by other fashion producers. In 1942, when the Society was created, the whole idea of a London-based couture industry was still very new. An alternate title, 'The Incorporated Society of London Couturiers' was something that was debated by its members in the early years of its formation. Yet, even by 1949, this nomenclature was still agreed to be 'unwise', although by this point the term 'couturier' was the main designation used for the Society's members.[18] In that year, Hardy Amies' response to the question, posed in a BBC radio interview, of whether he wished to be called a 'fashion designer', was that whilst he found this term appropriate he liked to be called: 'a *couturier*—a French word—but it does sort of mean that you do more than actually dress design which is in fact what I do'.[19] In his 1954 autobiography, *Just So Far*, Amies asserted that:

> What I have done is to found a *couture* house, which, so far as it can be in these difficult days, is now well-established. This achievement, of course, has in some measure been due to my taste as a designer, but equally so I consider it has been due to my skill as a *couturier*, in that I have been able to bring out the best in all the people who work for me; for I am a conductor of an orchestra . . . I invented a motto, which I rather pompously had translated in Latin. It is "less than art and greater than trade". I still think it is a good description of our business.[20]

Amies' association of his fashion business with art is now recognized as a tried-and-tested technique for 'conferring meaning on fashion products and of acquiring cultural capital for the occupation'.[21] Yet beyond promotional rhetoric his assessment of being a couturier positioned this form of creative practice as wider than that of either fashion designer or businessowner. For Amies the establishment of a craft-based dress house that twice-yearly produced seasonal collections of original designs placed it above, but not beyond, the concerns of commerce. The suggestion that couture lies in a space partly between cultural and commercial production points to the in-between status of the couturier within design discourse. 'Less than art and greater than trade' positions the craft of made-to-measure over machine-made manufacture, exclusivity and elitism over universality, creative integrity over commerciality; it blurs the separation between conception and execution so prevalent within design practice. This ambiguous design space and the grouping of these practitioners into a collective therefore opens the London couture to a nuanced design historical analysis.

A study of producers of luxury clothing for an elite market may appear out of step with the direction of current fashion scholarship, which has more recently turned towards considerations of everyday consumption and the internal mechanisms of industrial mass production.[22] Yet the rejection of the mass market by owner-designers such as Amies presents a pertinent historical case study for those interested in the establishment and maintenance of creative livelihoods. In the twenty-first century, as climate crisis sees a questioning of disposable fashion and unsustainable production, as a pandemic interrupts the unreflective consumption of globally mass-produced goods and governments adopt protectionist stances against world trade, the production methods and business structure of early twentieth century couture are a reminder that the current business model of the fashion industry is a precarious and recent paradigm.[23] With the release of her *Anti-Fashion Manifesto* in 2015, the influential fashion forecaster Li Edelkoort highlighted this instability; she declared the international fashion industry 'a ridiculous and pathetic parody of what it has been' and predicted the 'end of a specific industrial era' and the 'comeback' of couture; where the 'profession of couturier will become coveted' and offer 'a host of new ideas of how to handle the idea of clothes. And maybe from these ashes another system will be born'.[24] The couture she referred to is its historical rather than contemporary manifestation. Not the luxury brand version that has emerged since the 1980s, where a radical shift saw small- and medium-sized often family-owned companies pass to a few multinational conglomerates and groups.[25] Within this late capitalist structure long-established Parisian couture houses operate as prestigious cultural assets within luxury brand portfolios, a tool of spectacle to promote the sale of ready-to-wear, accessories, perfume and cosmetics at premium prices.[26] In July 2020, when the Queen's granddaughter, Princess Beatrice, rejected the new and walked down the aisle in a vintage Norman Hartnell wedding dress, Edelkoort's prediction of the comeback of 'old-school' couture appeared particularly prescient.[27] When looking back at the design practices of the London couturiers of the 1930s and 1940s, it must be recognized that they operated in a completely different market, where made-to-measure clothing dominated high-end fashion production and they could set up their businesses, unlike designers today, with relatively limited capital investment. However, they had to establish a professional identity in the shadow of Paris and negotiate huge shifts in the market during a time of economic depression, war and post-war reconstruction. In relation to the cracks emerging in today's fashion system, the collectivist structure of these small-scale craft-based fashion businesses and their navigation of a disrupted social, economic and political landscape consequently takes on a particular resonance.

Before this century, the fact that London had established a couture industry that operated for over forty years received limited acknowledgement within fashion history.[28] While many Parisian couture houses retained their cultural currency due to their relaunch as luxury brands for the contemporary market, the London houses (with the exception of Amies) remained dormant and sunk in obscurity.[29] At both an academic and popular level, it was the anti-establishment practices of British designers in the later post-war era that received focused study.[30] London's emergence as a world fashion city was positioned within the 1960s 'Youthquake' and the arrival of successful ready-to-wear designers such as Mary Quant, its success and distinction attributed to the creativity that emanated from Britain's art schools and its idiosyncratic youth styles.[31] Throughout the noughties, however, an academic focus on the implications of national identity within the fashion industry and in particular the power structures of fashion world cities witnessed a concurrent rise of scholarly interest in the English couturiers.[32] Much of this work came from London-based curators, who drew on the material objects and archival documents surviving within museum collections. This saw the INCSOC's work included in exhibitions and its individual designers become the focus of scholarship.[33] The culmination of much of this research can be seen in *London Couture 1923–1975: British Luxury*, edited by Amy de la Haye and Edwina Ehrman, which in 2015 finally brought full recognition to the couturiers. With the career of the Incorporated Society's members each the subject of a specific chapter, this beautifully illustrated book offers an in-depth documentation of the history and material culture of the London couturiers. The documentation of both the designers' biographies and the range of objects they produced provided a much needed and timely corrective, which resurrected the INCSOC's members from obscurity and firmly positioned them within fashion history. In so doing, it created the foundation to examine the topic through the lens of design history, which alongside the scholarship on Parisian couture has seen a disciplinary turn away from canonical figures and their objects.[34] Design history, due to its early 'heroic age approach', which positioned the designer at its centre, has had a tendency to 'overlook designers whose lives and work are less well documented and also ignores the collaborative nature of design'.[35] Similarly, studies of fashion design and its designers are notoriously uncritical and the collaborative element of practice primarily ignored as individual creativity is celebrated. A move beyond the individual couturiers to a focus on the Incorporated Society and its pre-war predecessor, the Fashion Group of Great Britain, allows this study to shift from viewing designers as autonomous artists or authors to the ways design practice can operate within a group structure.[36]

Although the term *design* in design history appears to be an inclusive one, as Jennifer Kaufmann-Buhler, Victoria Pass and Christopher Wilson pointed out in *Design History Beyond the Canon*, it is 'often used in ways that police and maintain disciplinary boundaries among the various types of design practice'. They note that even in 2019, 'commonly used design history textbooks and readers rarely include fashion in a substantive way' and that in particular it is 'rather rare to encounter scholarship that puts fashion into meaningful dialogue with other kinds of design'.[37] This is demonstrated, for example, in the introduction to Charlotte and Peter Fiell's 2016 overview *The Story of Design: From the Paleolithic to the Present*, which defines the history of design 'as the story of how all man-made things came into being', but excludes fashion from this definition as it 'has its own history'.[38] The INCSOC's specified aims—to assume design authority, elevate the level of design in British fashion and textiles, and thereby play an important role within the British export agenda—clearly positions the London couturiers within design history discourse. The role luxury fashion played within British design reform allows the Incorporated Society to be addressed specifically as a body of official tastemakers.[39] In 1997, Jonathan Woodham (highlighting an understanding that his work sought to challenge) stated that 'given the tendency of what might be termed "first generation" historians of design to focus on their workings and supposed import . . . there, has been an implicit assumption among many working in the field that the historical intricacies and significance of design organizations have already been explored in sufficient depth'.[40] Studies of design groups had however primarily focused on advocates and proselytizers for 'good design', which adhered to the tenets of Modernism and the search for a universal, egalitarian and rational style. In comparison, fashion design has typically been left out of this discourse, probably because its gendered, seemingly irrational, search for novelty rendered it incompatible to such ideals. In so doing, not only the Incorporated Society, but also fashion itself, remains firmly open to design historical research.

For its designer-members, despite the official declaration of an altruistic agenda, the INCSOC was a vehicle for professional recognition. Design history has shifted from its 'first generation' focus on groups of designer-tastemakers who promoted reform for both economic and ideological reasons towards the processes of professionalisation.[41] This has extended the discipline's scope and inclusivity, allowing it to address a broader range of practices, practitioners and research questions. In so doing, it has created space for the recognition of female designers and areas such as interior design, art direction, television design and amateur practice.[42] In line with such work, the Incorporated Society and its predecessor the Fashion Group of Great Britain are understood and positioned within the wider context of the professionalisation of design in Europe and America.[43] With a focus on the establishment of professional identity a number of central themes emerge that are centred not on production or consumption but on collaboration and the networks and aspirations that supported this field of design. Whilst not to deny the benefits of a focus on the consumption of couture clothing (so clearly demonstrated in Alexandra Palmer's exemplary scholarship of the retail and consumption of European couture in Toronto) this book responds to Jeffrey Meikle's claim that historians 'have no way of knowing with certainty how and why consumers at a given historical moment responded to particular products'.[44] Collaboration is explored not to question its benefits to sales and the couturiers' profitability but rather to understand how it facilitated and supported their professional standing within the Western fashion system's hierarchy.

Professional success, as the research of the business historian Pamela Walker Laird has shown, is a profoundly social process, dependent on access to circles that control and distribute opportunity and information. This encourages an interpretation of professional careers based not on individual skill and effort but on the ability to make connections within specific social milieu, and networks bound together by shared expectations.[45] As a design group the Incorporated Society's formation and operation occurred not in a vacuum but within a specific social, industrial and political network. The evolution of a London-based couture industry and its designers' official collaboration is therefore considered, and in large part explained, in terms of its interaction with other interest groups and fashion producers within Britain, for example, design reform bodies such as the British Colour Council, the Council for Art and Industry and the Council of Industrial Design and other trade associations such as the London (wholesale) Model House Group, and Textile Export Groups such as the Cotton

Board. Predictably, due to the time frame under consideration, when the couturiers were forced to react to an environment of economic instability and when industrial performance had a 'political edge', the British government and most specifically the Board of Trade constituted one of the most important elements within this network.[46] This approach recognises that within the collective structure of the Incorporated Society, design was formulated not just by the couturiers themselves or in response to consumer needs and demands, but also to the specifications of a broader network of producers, organisations and institutions.

The London couturiers are therefore positioned as tastemakers and intermediaries within a specific national network.[47] The business historian Regina L. Blaszczyk uses the term 'fashion intermediaries' to describe the internal network of professionals who operate between the producer and consumer, who studied the market, collected data about consumer taste and promoted products to meet public expectations.[48] She pointed out that 'focusing on these fashion brokers as the primary agents of innovation turns the canon of design history inside out and upside down'.[49] Her work has been instrumental in the recent direction of fashion history that has begun to acknowledge the internal culture of design practice and consider more fully the 'process of value creation in the fashion industry'.[50] Another business historian, Per H. Hansen, has also encouraged the adoption of cultural analysis, but offers a different nuance in the understanding of what constitutes a tastemaker. This is separate from Blaszczyk's reading of 'fashion intermediaries' and of the design historical discourse that surrounds the proselytisers of 'good design'. Hansen recommends that business be viewed through the perspective of external narratives, a move from 'merely understanding the wants and needs of consumers to exploring the construction of meaning and identity'.[51] As he points out, 'collective entities such as organizations and other communities, create order in and make sense of, the real world and the past by telling stories'.[52] This sees taste-making as a wider practice of external networks that construct a cohesive narrative around a range of goods.[53] He demonstrated this methodology in an article on 'Danish Modern' furniture, which explored the impact of a network of tastemakers on that particular design industry.[54] He concludes that this form of design succeeded through the creation of powerful narratives that framed consumer understanding and the development of a network of individuals and organisations who promoted and legitimised them.

This turn to external narratives aligns with a consideration of mediation, which Grace Lees-Maffei, in 2009, identified as the 'third stream' in design history.[55] The main current within this methodology has been an emphasis that continues the 'consumption turn' within the discipline by exploring the role of channels such as 'television, magazines, corporate literature, advice literature and so on in mediating between producers and consumers, forming consumption practices and ideas about design'.[56] This is an approach to design history that supports Hansen's claim that 'we cannot look into people's heads to see how they perceived and made sense of the world, but we can study the narratives they have left behind in order to see how they established, circulated and perceived meaning.[57] The Incorporated Society's members, as practitioners of an elite form of fashion production, never advertised in the traditional sense (except in the very early parts of their careers) but operated through a subtle manipulation of a system of representation offered by a particular national network.[58] The mediated narratives left behind by the London couturiers can therefore reveal the conflicts within competing agendas and also the limits of the designer in the ways meaning is made. The parameters for this study are therefore not restricted to the design activity and business strategies of the London couturiers but explore their external mediation particularly at the point of collaboration, not only in newspapers and magazines, museum exhibitions, films and theatre productions but, most importantly, in their collective showcases.

Within the framework of the INCSOC, which focused on export and the development of prestige, its members had to create an easily recognized international vision for British fashion.[59] This needed a clearly understood concept of London design, with certain meanings assigned to it, to cause consumers, at both a national and international level, to prefer garments designed and produced in Britain.[60] The narratives constructed around the couturiers therefore relied on a specific discourse of national identity and character.[61] The past decade has seen a decentering of scholarship away from the idea of a single fashion history emanating from Europe and North America, and the centrality of its fashion cities has also been opened to debate.[62] Yet the aspiration to fashion centre status was embedded within the INCSOC's constitution, and in the time frame under consideration the fashion system was a Western and nationally determined structure.[63] As a framing devise, the concept of the nation is also a tried and tested unit of analysis, one of the 'most pervasive of all cultural collective identities particularly within the field of cultural representation'.[64] As Kjetil Fallan and Grace Lees-Maffei have argued, for the design historian it is both 'premature and unwise' to reject this categorisation as 'the growth of global cultures makes the examination of national and regional cultures even more important'. An assertion perhaps supported by the 2019 declaration by *Vogue* (Hong Kong) of 'a new era of couture', where Chinese designers 'aspiring to establish a distinct identity' are 'making a name for themselves among fashion circles and society elites around the world' and 'represent a benchmark in Chinese craftsmanship and style, pivotal in developing the country's rapidly growing fashion scene'.[65] The study of the historical construction of a specific national fashion identity for London's couturiers, in an industry where France had an established hegemony, thereby acquires a particular relevance to today's global design perspectives.

Fallan and Lees-Maffei also acknowledge that national studies of design should be 'attentive to cultural exchange and international trade and influence'.[66] The fruitfulness of this approach can be seen in recent fashion scholarship on Parisian couture, for example, in Lou Taylor and Marie McLoughlin's work which considers its 'global diffusion' during World War II to challenge the understanding that France stopped its international dissemination of fashion during the Nazi occupation.[67] While the British colonies and dominions, alongside Europe and Latin America, were export markets for the Incorporated Society's designers, this study focuses on the London couturiers' specific appeal to North America.[68] This does not deny the wider global distribution network of London couture, but is dictated by the importance of the lucrative US dollar market for British trade policy and European couture production throughout the period under consideration.[69] This also responds to one of this study's main contentions: that the identity of the London couture industry was in many ways a reaction to the commercial dictates of the North American market and its democratization of fashion.

The book follows a chronological structure, which is separated into four chapters that give equal weight to an exploration of the development of the London couture industry in both the 1930s and 1940s. The first half of the book considers the factors that led to the creation of a London couture industry in the interwar period. This acts as the foundation for the subsequent chapters to offer a comparative understanding of the process of both continuity and transformation that took place in the wartime and within the immediate post-war period of reconstruction. The framing devise for the overall study, the Incorporated Society of London Fashion Designers, was not created until 1942; it therefore emerges as a point of analytical focus in the second part, so that the impetus towards and the objectives that underpinned this designer collaboration can propel the argument. While each chapter performs many functions in its use of primary material to explore the creation and maintenance of London's couture industry, they also address their own individual concerns.

At the analytical core of chapter 1, which explores the evolution of a London couture industry, is the process of professionalisation of design practice. Unlike the following chapters, which trace the chronological developments of the industry in a more linear manner, this chapter constructs the narrative around three often concurrent and overlapping themes: the commercial, social and political factors that facilitated the construction of the professional identity of the London couturiers.

Chapter 2 then looks specifically at the years 1935–1939 and is primarily concerned with designer collaboration and the activity of the Fashion Group of Great Britain. As a national body this Group brought together the London couturiers with a range of practitioners from other creative fields as part of the interwar process to promote the importance of design and the designer to industry. This positions the professionalisation of the London couture industry within the historical discourse of British interwar design reform. The fact that this group stemmed from developments in America extends the exploration into a broader transatlantic network to offer a historical example of an interconnected creative economy.

Chapter 3 then moves to the war years, 1939–1945, the period when the Incorporated Society was created. Whilst it considers examples of designer collaboration and how the war facilitated the design reform aspirations explored in the previous chapter, it also acknowledges that these activities were distorted by the social, political and economic changes brought about by the conflict. At a time of war, the production of elite, fashionable, made-to-measure dress could be seen as an unpatriotic frivolity and ultimately irrelevant. The creation of the Incorporated Society was a response not to a normal consumer society but to one that was constrained by social attitudes and governmental legislation particularly towards restraint and against conspicuous consumption. Wartime designer collaboration and the creation of the Society are therefore examined as strategies adopted to defend this form of luxury production.

Chapter 4 then considers the immediate period of post-war reconstruction, 1946–1949. It is at this point that the book can explore the operation of the Incorporated Society. It addresses not only why the INCSOC, a wartime strategy for business preservation, continued into the post-war period but also how it was shaped by shifting power structures in the national and international fashion industry. Within this time frame the need to increase exports and to reassert cultural and industrial strength became a political and industrial preoccupation, which saw the government's creation of the state-funded Council of Industrial Design. Yet, within design historical discourse there is little recognition of fashion within the design reform agenda of this period; this is particularly notable in its omission from the scholarship on the main design event, the *Britain Can Make It* exhibition of 1946 (even though dress and textiles constituted a quarter of its displays). Whilst the chapter addresses this oversight its primary concern is to question whether the Society fulfilled the aims set out in its constitution.

Despite the specific focus of each chapter they all address the construction of the fashion industry's hierarchies in relation to the highly specific social, economic and political conditions of Britain during the 1930s and 1940s. The networks and narratives that a collaborative body of designers used to sustain a specific form of luxury fashion production are examined to question whether by 1949, when the wartime controls over clothing production finally ended, the small body of London couturiers had fulfilled the Incorporated Society's stated objectives, established their professional identity and ensured London a position within the international fashion system.

LONDON LAUNCHES A MODE: THE DEVELOPMENT OF A MAYFAIR COUTURE

[In London's Mayfair] the very air announces that something important is about to happen. For, behind the hushed doors of Bruton, Grosvenor, Regent and Bond Streets, the new spring clothes are being born. First, we call on Madame Isobel . . . we marvel to ourselves at the enigma of an artist who is also an executive . . . her intriguing prophesies merely whet our appetite for more and we urge our oracle for news of colour and fabric. [From Norman Hartnell . . . Victor Stiebel . . . Glen Glenny . . . Madame Champcommunal . . . Peter Russell . . . Digby Morton] we gather a picture of what we shall wear next spring.[1]

In January 1935, *Vogue*, in an article entitled 'London Launches a Mode', informed its British readership that seven of its dressmakers now operated as an influential source of original ideas and fashion leadership. The article was notable, as this magazine had previously promoted Paris-based couturiers as the only source for the creation of new fashions. The following month *Harper's Bazaar* also claimed that these same designers (with the inclusion of 'Charlie' James and Eva Lutyens) had ensured that in London 'the pulse of fashion grows stronger day by day', and that the city was 'a sure competitor to Paris', particularly in the production of 'sensational new evening silhouettes'.[2] Whilst these claims, in British editions of American-owned publications, could be read as token gestures to the local culture, they are substantiated by their reproduction in their American editions and in a range of international news reports. The *New York Times*, a good barometer of transatlantic recognition, had previously highlighted many of these designers (with the addition of Edward Symonds, the owner of Reville Ltd, and Hardy Amies, the in-house designer at Lachasse) as the key protagonists in what it defined as London's 'new culture of dress design'.[3]

In his 1954 autobiography Norman Hartnell gave a brief explanation for this changed attitude towards London-based dressmakers, in his mention of the 'growth of a new school of English fashion'.[4] The practitioners he referred to all followed the approach and understanding of original

made-to-measure production created by the Parisian haute couture system
and adopted its policy of seasonal fashion-aware collections in discrete
salons for an exclusive clientele. Yet the use of 'couturier', the French
term, was not adopted by the members of this 'new school', who continued to refer to themselves as 'dressmakers' and their businesses as 'dress/
model' houses. This reticence is indicative of the 'widely felt uncertainty'
in the construction of professional identity for many designers in the interwar period.[5] Yet, from the middle of the 1930s, the idea that a number
of London's made-to-measure dressmakers were now operating as couturiers received constant endorsement. In terms of this acknowledgement,
1936 was the tipping point in London's recognition as a destination for the
consumption of creative dress design. In that year, for instance, the *Sunday Referee* newspaper declared that 'there is only a short history of British
dress designing . . . [and] this is the first year that London is hailed as an
individual fashion centre'.[6] This assertion was supported not only by the
notable upsurge in the amount and type of press attention given to specific
London dressmakers but also by the number of foreign buyers at its salon
presentation, which in 1936 suddenly increased in number and included
representatives from eighteen different countries.[7]

In the 1930s, London's elite dress culture was given clear definition by
Britain's established aristocracy, which, unlike much of Europe, had been
sustained into the twentieth century. The social structures that had evolved
around this titular elite, in both its idiosyncratic country-based sporting
activities and its court-based social arena, offered London's designers a
unique national platform for both the stimulation of consumption and the
display of fashionable dress. This, however, had not previously led to
the establishment of a recognizable London couture industry. Wealthy
Englishwomen either took their custom to Paris, bought imported
garments, or had their clothes made to their own (often conservative) versions of French models.[8] The design authority of Britain's made-to-measure
dressmakers was therefore restricted by both their clients' belief that Paris
was the only source of creative fashion and their characteristic reticence
in the consumption of obviously new and conspicuously styled clothing.
The traditional dress culture of the capital's social scene and its participants'
preference for French models therefore needed careful navigation by any
London-based designer who aspired to the creative autonomy and contemporary relevance of a couturier.

This chapter will question why the 1930s, an era of economic depression, was the formative decade for English creative fashion and the period when a range of London dressmakers established their professional identity and authority as couturiers. To do so, it breaks this down into three sections that explore the commercial, socioeconomic and political factors, in order to understand the infrastructure that supported London's evolution as a destination for the production and consumption of couture and the altered narrative that surrounded the 'new school' of English fashion designers.

FROM COURT DRESSMAKERS TO MAYFAIR COUTURIERS

In the interwar period London was at the centre of the political, social and economic life of Britain. An Imperial capital, it was the nexus of trade and governance for an Empire that still presided over one fifth of the world's population. The West End, in particular, had a long-standing status as a retail environment for new goods and novelties linked to the trading systems of the British Empire. The support this global exchange offered to the development of menswear in the nineteenth century has been documented by the fashion historian Christopher Breward, who has noted its impact on a plethora of men's tailors, shirt-makers and hatters that flourished in and around Savile Row and catered to an affluent and international clientele.[9] In the case of womenswear, a source such as Charles Pascoe's *Illustrated Handbook for the Season* from 1890 demonstrates that London's made-to-measure dress houses were equally numerous, although they have received only limited documentation.[10] This source cites an extensive range of elite West End dress houses to fully support its claim that for the female consumer in 'a city where fashion's votaries are so numerous and wealthy, there is abundant opportunity for gratifying every personal taste, caprice, or whim in respect of style, make and material'.[11] A tourist guide for those unaccustomed to London's commercial arena, the *Illustrated Handbook* outlines the clearly defined geographic space of elite female consumption. At the end of the nineteenth century, fashionable dress houses were located primarily in Piccadilly, Regent and Bond Streets, with the most elite around Hanover Square and Grosvenor Street. It is therefore of little surprise that forty years later members of the 'new school of English fashion' chose this area of Mayfair as their site of production. For example, Hartnell set up there in 1923, Stiebel in 1932 and Russell and Mattli in 1933. The business historian Andrew Godley has examined the benefits of an efficient local economy for the East End's mass-manufactured dress trade. He has shown that, in the interwar period, location and interdependence of production, with subsidiary merchants for fabric and accessories, skilled labour and clearly defined distribution channels, were key determinants to commercial success.[12] In a similar manner, the historical development of the West End and in particular the district of Mayfair allowed young made-to-measure dressmakers to operate from within a fully established site of elite women's clothing production, promotion and consumption.

In the history of London retail, the interwar period has often been portrayed as a depressed commercial phase for the West End, situated between the heyday of the Edwardian department store and Carnaby Street in the Swinging Sixties.[13] However, Bronwyn Edwards' reassessment of the 'shopping geographies' of London's West End in the pages of British *Vogue* has shown that, in the 1930s, Mayfair was a 'focal pull' within the network of expanded retail and consumption throughout the nation.[14] This allowed magazines and tourist guides to present a carefully defined geography of fashionable consumption, where, as Edwards points out, 'the precise location where shopping took place was as important as what was purchased'. The fact that throughout the interwar period Mayfair became a more important shopping destination and source of fashionable consumption is demonstrated through an analysis of Victor Stiebel's promotional adverts placed in British *Vogue* in 1933 which all place his salon's address in large font, recognising its effectiveness as an essential marketing device for a young designer setting out to establish his fashion credentials.

A key factor that supported Mayfair's ability to operate as the nation's central point for the consumption of luxury fashion goods was the relaxation of its tenancy agreements in 1928. This change in planning law saw the area swiftly move from primarily residential to commercial occupancy. The *London Post Office Directory* from 1936 demonstrates the impact of this development, as it evidences the establishment of a wide variety of luxury businesses.[15] On Bruton Street (where Hartnell and Stiebel opened their dress houses) this network of luxury trading ranged from the society decorator Sibyl Colefax to beauty salons, corsetieres, milliners, goldsmiths, art dealers, wine merchants, motor car showrooms, furriers, furniture dealers and a selection of court dressmakers and ladies' and military tailors. The presence of these luxury businesses supported and nurtured the emergent

London couture industry, as it encased its development within the 'micro-cosm of the fashionable consumers' bijoux world'.[16]

Mayfair's claim to fashion authority and attraction for consumers of couture was bolstered not only by a rise in luxury traders but also by the influx of Parisian-based couturiers to the English capital. Edward Moly-neux opened a branch on Grosvenor Street in February 1932, followed by Elsa Schiaparelli in 1934. Two smaller, newer, but nevertheless significant designers, Dilkusha and Karinska, opened businesses the next year and they were followed, by the end of 1936, by Robert Piguet and Jacques Heim.[17] Whilst all these couturiers remained firmly centred in Paris, an additional house in Mayfair was clearly a beneficial business strategy. The fact that all but one of these couturiers were not French is significant, as their presence in Paris was based not on national allegiance but on commercial dictates: it was the only recognised destination for couture production.[18] Their move-ment to London is an indication of Mayfair's ability to support the growth of a couture industry.

The transferral of Parisian couture houses to London was a response not only to the increased commercial viability of Mayfair as a source of luxury fashion but also to the era's economic situation. Prior to 1932, Paquin and Worth were the only Paris houses of note that operated in London. Paris' hegemony was such that its couturiers had been able to expect English cli-ents to come to them. However, since the stock market crash of 1929 and the ensuing worldwide depression the Parisian couture industry had lost a large proportion of its business.[19] French exports, which relied on wine and luxury goods, fell from 50.1 billion francs in 1929 to 14.7 billion in 1936, and the Parisian couture industry was put under financial pressure.[20] The French capital also experienced significant labour unrest between 1932 and 1936.[21] The loss of custom and production problems saw many Paris-based couturiers search for a wider market, and London's Mayfair presented a viable alternative.

By the middle of the 1930s, alongside the Parisian couture houses, there were also twenty-nine dressmakers of note with a Mayfair (W1) post-code.[22] The geography of London's elite fashion production was therefore developed on a village scale, with all these businesses located within a five-minute walk from 'bustling Bond Street' to 'sedate and wealthy Berkeley Square'.[23] Within this geographical arrangement Grosvenor Street became the fulcrum of creative fashion production. This was consolidated by the arrival of Edward Molyneux's business; as 'one of the most powerful names in international fashion', this motivated many established dressmakers with substantial businesses to undertake expensive relocations.[24] In March 1932 the dressmaker Eileen Idare moved her 500 employees to operate from this location. Mme Hayward, who became business partner with the couturier Karinska, also shifted from New Bond Street to 67 Grosvenor Street in March, followed by Worth (London) and also Digby Morton, who left Palace Gate in Kensington for number 63 in July. In September, Madam Isobel, who had operated from Regent Street since 1919, also moved her dress house to Grosvenor Street. Despite her original premises costing a reported £100,000, she now claimed that Regent Street's sheer popularity, crowdedness, rent rises and lack of parking space made this geographical position untenable for a dressmaker whose 'reputation rested on the recommendation of clients rather than shop windows'.[25] Whilst this relocation of her 320 workers was only a short distance, it was an important business strategy, for as Paul Cohen-Portheim (the émigré anglophile chronicler of interwar Britain) noted, Regent Street had begun to suffer from 'stolid respectability', whilst the streets closer to Berkeley Square were the space of the 'more novel dressmakers'.[26] The clustering of made-to-measure dressmakers in Mayfair, and particularly the opening of a London house by Molyneux, who headed an internationally recognised brand and held the 'status of one of the world's great couturiers', consolidated Mayfair's position.[27] By July 1936 *Vogue* declared that 'Grosvenor Street is becoming the street of *Haute Couture*'.[28] For producers of elite made-to-measure fashions, geographic proximity within the commercial vibrancy of Mayfair was thus a clear prerequisite for recognition, creative legitimacy and commercial success.

Prior to the 1930s, *couturiers* had remained in Paris and Mayfair-based *court dressmakers* operated at the pinnacle of London's system of elite clothing production. As the latter's name implies, whilst they also supplied bridal trousseaux, evening wear, corsets and sportswear, their reputations rested predominately on the creation of Lord Chamberlain–regulated court dress, presentation gowns and coronation robes. Their field of production focused on the activities that surrounded London's monarchy and its aristocratic social season, which ran from April (which coincided with the sitting of parliament) to the 'Glorious Twelfth' of August (the beginning of the shooting season). The Season began with the presentation of debutantes to the monarch at court and operated as an elite marriage market. Members of the political and social elite also held innumerable balls, dinner parties and charity events, the most exclusive being at the aristocracy's town palaces. The Season also incorporated sporting fixtures such as Ascot, Henley Regatta and Wimbledon, where status dressing excelled amongst the wealthy spectators. After 1935, Glyndebourne Opera House became another fixture, and particularly beneficial to London dressmakers as elaborate evening dress was regulation for the outdoor picnic between acts.

For women who participated in society, the Season was therefore a plethora of court-based activity, luncheons, cocktail parties, charity events, balls, theatre productions and sporting fixtures. These occasions demanded specific types of clothing, and many women 'with a significant income lavished considerable attention to their dress and its detail'.[29] Throughout the 1930s approximately 350 debutantes were presented to the monarch each

Figure 1.1
Margaret, Duchess of Argyll and her husband Charles Sweeny at Ascot 1938, gown by Victor Stiebel. *Source:* © National Portrait Gallery, London.

year at the Court of St. James, usually at the age of seventeen, with around one hundred of these being from America, the Dominions, India and the diplomatic corps. The Season followed this 'coming out' with around ninety debutante dances. The memoirs of the Duchess of Argyll ('Debutante of the Year' in 1930) demonstrate that for the wealthy socialite the excessive sartorial demands of the Season continued into the decade, as each year she commissioned 'at least a dozen evening dresses and many day outfits'.[30] Debutantes, 'young marrieds' and their mothers therefore provided not only established court dressmakers but also the 'new school of English fashion' with a reliable and sustainable market.

It is notable, for example, that in Victor Stiebel's adverts for his new dress house set up in 1932, he initially operated under the designation of 'court dressmaker', (a title that drew on his previous apprenticeship and training at the house of Reville-Terry); however, within a few months this was shortened to 'dressmaker'. This altered nomenclature should be seen in light of the traditional practice of court dressmaking, which may have ensured a ready market for made-to-measure dress but was not recognised as an incubator of contemporary fashion. The accepted view of London court dressmakers aligns with Pascoe's assertion in 1890 that they were not 'fashion designers in the true sense'.[31] This was because their output had some originality of design but primarily adapted Parisian styles to suit social conventions and their clients' more conservative tastes. In his autobiography Harry Yoxall (who as business manager of British *Vogue* had a professional knowledge of London's dress houses) separated London's high-fashion consumers of the 1920s into 'really smart women who went to Paris at least semi-annually for their clothes . . . [and] the patriotic (or un-enterprising) rich who preferred to be dressed at home and patronized establishments such as Court Dressmakers . . . [whose] designing had little to do with fashion'. In his recollection of this decade, London maintained only a small number of salons 'where the upper middle-class woman could find some originality of design (or should I say, some variety in copying?)'.[32]

Hardy Amies' recollection of Miss Gray Limited (the court dressmaking parent company of Lachasse) supports this assertion and highlights the unproblematic nature of adaptation. He pointed out that the company's owner 'always bought some models in Paris, and made others to her own design, which she never pretended were anything other than adaptations of Paris models, which she had seen either in reality or reproduced in the fashion newspapers'.[33] Advertisements for the services of court dressmakers demonstrate that copies of 'fashions direct from Paris' were often promoted as their unique selling point. Such adverts clearly show that for many court dressmakers their professional esteem emanated not from originality but from the production of affordable copies of French styles, with a perfect fit and finish. The couture houses of Paris were therefore seen as above and beyond competition for the conception of original women's fashion. This was an understanding that London's court dressmaking establishments did not challenge but instead used to their own commercial advantage.

What differentiated the 'new school' of Mayfair-based couturiers from their court dressmaking competitors was that many of them aimed to become creative designers rather than simply high-level dressmakers. To do this they shifted their focus to the creation of original models, which captured the dramatic element of fashion production rather than merely respond to customer specifications and the intricacies of construction. The creation of ball, debutante and presentation dresses often saw them operate in the same field of production as the court dressmakers, but they were differentiated by their refusal to adapt French models. In the cases of Norman Hartnell, Victor Stiebel and Peter Russell, for instance, the aspiration for creative design autonomy rather than accomplished dressmaking was to a certain extent a product of their backgrounds and routes into the fashion business. All three were drawn into the world of fashion through the creation of costumes for fancy dress parties and theatrical performances. Hartnell, for example, claimed he originally set out to work in 'art not trade', and to support this assertion recalled that Mainbocher (the American Paris-based couturier) declared of his 1927 collection that he had never seen 'so many incredibly beautiful dresses so incredibly badly made'.[34] In his unpublished memoirs Stiebel also noted that his first year of production contained badly constructed garments, 'where in the scramble to satisfy the snowballing of trade, customers' fittings were often rushed, workmanship suffered and several ladies complained bitterly'.[35] This admission is substantiated by an examination of the cut and construction of a dress from his first year of production (figures 1.2a and b).

The design is basic, the garment unlined and the stripes of each panel do not always line up at their seams. The construction of the dress both supports Stiebel's claim that production was rushed, whilst it also provides evidence that Stiebel's design focus was on the production of fashionable

Figure 1.2a
Victor Stiebel, cream rayon with blue stripe dress and velvet bolero and belt, 1932.
Source: © Museum of London.

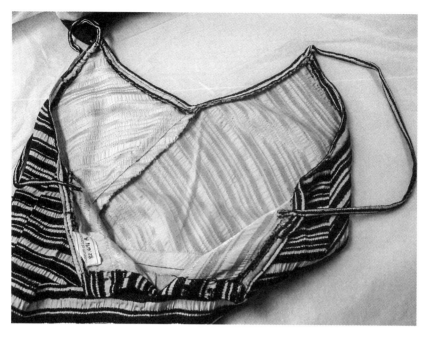

Figure 1.2b
Inside of Stiebel cream rayon with blue stripe dress. *Source:* Author's image.

dress, for an ephemeral moment and particular aesthetic, rather than the intricacy of skilful dressmaking. To a certain extent Hartnell's and Stiebel's move into the fashion industry was supported by the change of the style of dress towards simpler construction and less ornamentation; which is clearly seen in the latter's designs for his first collection. (figure 1.3a–c) However, it should be noted that by 1936, when the London couturiers began to produce more tailored ensembles, the poor quality of construction was reduced by an influx of experienced (often Jewish) tailors and dressmakers from the Continent.

In order to develop design authority as couturiers, it was also imperative that the new generation of London dressmakers convince wealthy clients (those with a yearly income of at least £3,000) to switch their allegiance from Paris, or at the very least encourage them to buy original models from both cities.[36] However, this was difficult to implement, as they had to negotiate with what the dressmaker Madame Isobel, in a BBC radio broadcast of 1928, described as their customers' 'fixed belief that original

Figure 1.3a
Victor Stiebel's design for his first collection 1932. *Source:* Reproduced courtesy of
Adrian Woodhouse.

Figure 1.3b
Victor Stiebel's design for his first collection 1932. *Source:* Reproduced courtesy of
Adrian Woodhouse.

Figure 1.3c
Victor Stiebel's design for his first collection 1932. *Source:* Reproduced courtesy of
Adrian Woodhouse.

fashions needed the French capital for their creation'.[37] In his autobiography Norman Hartnell also pointed out that when he first went into business in the 1920s he 'suffered from the unforgivable disadvantage of being English in England', as clients would often 'reject his models, as they were not of French origin'.[38] Throughout the early 1930s contemporary press reports continued to use the similarity to Parisian styles as a measure for any English designer's fashion credentials. However, this type of reportage began to dissipate throughout the decade as many articles in both British and international newspapers began to congratulate London dressmakers, as the *Daily Express* put it, 'for having the courage of their own convictions . . . [and] not even bothering to get inspiration from Paris'.[39] In 1936, the *New York Times* contained one of the first references to the London dressmakers' new creative identity when it singled out Hartnell as an important European 'couturier' and claimed he had finally destroyed 'the idea that all designing must have a French tag'.[40] Although French modes were still dominant, London-based dressmakers received credit for the originality of their work, and this in turn led to their acknowledgement as couturiers. It is also notable that although Norman Hartnell set up his business in 1923, he claimed he did not achieve any considerable profit until 1934. This success can be understood as a result not only of his developing reputation but also of the commercial transformation of Mayfair in the early 1930s and its heightened recognition as a site for the consumption of not only elite made-to-measure clothing but also original fashions.

Acknowledgement as a London couturier was therefore dependent on the ability to produce original designs and also on the setting up of a dress house within a tightly defined area of Mayfair. The interior design of these premises was also an important element within the shift towards the dressmakers' recognition as couturiers. Traditionally, the city's elite dressmaking was an arena particularly noted for the gendered ownership of the many West End establishments, which were predominately opened 'by ladies for ladies'.[41] This gendered practice was made apparent within the interior decoration of the 'atmospheric premises' of London's dressmakers, which were reliant on what has been described as 'set dressing . . . often linked by observers to the cult of domesticity with which English feminine culture was internationally associated'.[42] In comparison, the interior decoration of the 'new school' dress houses, designed in the early 1930s, was light, modern and professional. For instance, Hartnell and Stiebel both rejected the dark boudoir-like interiors that many female dressmakers had copied from Lucile (at this point the most internationally successful English dressmaker) and the solid Arts and Crafts tradition adopted by male court dressmakers such as Redfern.[43] In 1932, Hartnell commissioned the young innovative architect Gerald Lacoste to redesign his interior architecture. This resulted in a space that utilised a vast expanse of bevelled mirror panels which has since been recognised as a perfect example of '*moderne* pre-war commercial design' (figure 1.4).[44]

This style was also evident in Stiebel's millinery department situated at the top of his four-floor premises, whilst the ground floor interior, designed by Syrie Maugham, featured oatmeal walls, mock French furniture, chandeliers and an Adam mantelpiece.[45] Stiebel's subtle fusion of classicism and modernism reflected the Georgian Revival, a style of interior decoration popular in fashionable circles at the time.[46] This was a particularly relevant aesthetic choice for a modern fashion house as it was associated with both youth and class. The architectural historian Peter Mandler has shown that in the 1930s this style 'acted in clear opposition to the old meaning and identities of the Arts and Crafts aesthetic as it trickled down to the masses. By embracing the Georgian, the younger generation could simultaneously reject the feeble, romantic aestheticism of their elders and the mean, fussy Englishness of bourgeois suburbia'.[47] Mary Lynn Stewart has also acknowledged the ability of this style, which she calls 'hybrid modernity' and shows was widely evident in Paris salons, to act as a commercially successful arena 'in which to peddle the designers' claim to contemporary relevance'.[48] The interior of both Hartnell's and Stiebel's premises therefore presented an astute retail environment and visually aligned their practice with Parisian couturiers rather than English court dressmakers. In so doing, these designers transformed their impressive eighteenth-century town houses into discrete yet vibrant, modern retail environments for the 'smart set' of fashionable society. In these hybrid-modern interiors, young male dress designers such as Hartnell and Stiebel created a seemingly less-feminine environment in which to present not only their claim to creativity but also a new professional identity.

In his retrospective assessment of the changes in London's fashion arena in the 1930s, British *Vogue's* business manager claimed he was witness to 'a new and rather un-British phenomenon . . . university graduates were

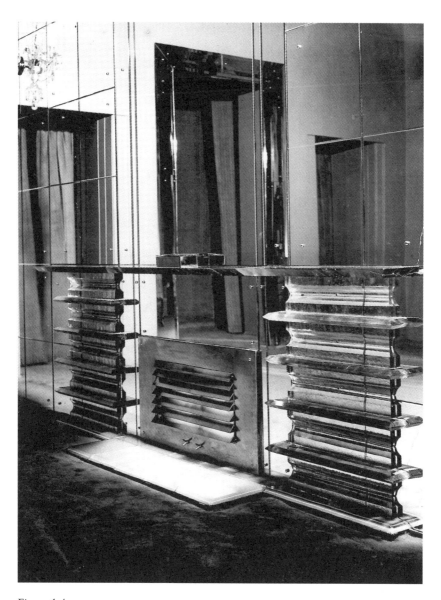

Figure 1.4
Norman Hartnell's salon, c. 1936. Designed by Gerald Lacoste. *Source:* Reproduced courtesy of Michael Pick.

going into fashion designing! . . . [and] they had a genuine creative taste'.[49]
With university graduates commonly recognised as male, Yoxall's statement highlights that the production of fashion by young educated men
was an important component in the recognition of these practitioners as
couturiers rather than dressmakers. In the context of the professionalisation of this field of design, the presence of young men, particularly those
who moved from university to dressmaking, brought a new sensibility to
the London dress scene. Whilst the main fashion showings of 1932 may
have seen an equal representation of both female and male dressmakers, by
1936 as London gained increased recognition as a fashion centre, two thirds
of the dress houses were operated by male designers.[50] Newspaper reports
that refer to the creativity and design autonomy of London's dressmakers,
such as the *Sunday Referee*'s typical article of 1936 entitled 'These Four Men
Dictate Designs for Women: Hartnell, Stiebel, Russell, Symonds', demonstrate that the gender of these producers was often an important factor
within their acknowledgement as couturiers.[51] This was in opposition to
Paris at this point, where it was often female couturiers, such as Vionnet,
Chanel and Schiaparelli, who 'set the [fashion] agenda after the First World
War'.[52] This reflects the gender bias in British design circles in the interwar period. The design historians Suzette Worden and Jill Seddon, in their
consideration of the relationship between women and the redefinition of
professional design at this point, highlight the manner in which the social
construction of production saw the creative autonomy of male designers
receive more recognition than their female counterparts. This they argue
was because it was a moment when the economic depression intensified
accusations that women who worked outside the home deprived 'men,
who had families to support, opportunities for employment'.[53] In the formation of a London couture industry, this suggests that male designers may
have found it easier and more socially acceptable to establish their creative
design autonomy and construct a professional identity as a couturier. Thus,
the process of professionalisation of London's made-to-measure clothing
production, from court dressmaker to Mayfair couturier, was to a certain
extent a gendered affair that aligned with social expectations.

The change in the culture of the city's dress design, whereby the dressmakers were often (but not exclusively) male, operated under their own
names and produced innovative and creative clothing without obvious
adaptation of Parisian models, was an important element in many young

London dressmakers' designation as couturiers. In order to validate their professional identity and differentiate themselves from court dressmakers, a cluster of young dress designers drew on Mayfair's vibrant commercial infrastructure and aligned this with a shift in intent to be bespoke originators rather than adapters of French styles.

VICTOR STIEBEL AND THE COMMERCIAL MANIPULATION OF LONDON'S HIGH SOCIETY

> In the way these things happen, smart, fashion-leading English women began to discover that some of our young home-grown designers were making beautiful, wearable, stunning clothes, which were not only grand to look at but which had behind them a complete understanding of the British feminine character. . . . Well, the sort of Englishwoman who began buying and wearing these clothes around, usually belonged to what is known as the gay international crowd. They did not sit at home in their drawing rooms. They travelled. And everywhere they went, it was noticeable that their English-designed clothes had another quality besides smartness. This they had had, of course, in their French-designed clothes. Now . . . they were beginning to look right as well.[54]

In 1937, a patriotic *Daily Mail* article entitled 'London Is the World's Fashion Centre' pointed to a key element in the steady growth of creative English dressmakers by recognizing that this was in large part attributable to changes in their clients' dress culture and social life. In the assertion, that the city's smart set had begun to 'look right' in their English-designed clothes, Lady Elizabeth Murray (the article's author), suggested that London had the capacity to both support and champion its aesthetic leadership. The article also highlighted the increased patronage offered to 'home-grown designers' by society's fashion leaders. This was a particularly important factor for the establishment and development of any new fashion business, as the custom of the 'right' fashion-conscious people from within high society was a fundamental component for the commercial viability of any designer, as it brought them prestige, facilitated investment and reinforced their claims to creative authority.

In order to explore how London couturiers began to compete with Paris and define their practice as modern, creative and original, this section will explore how the city's social arena was manipulated by Victor Stiebel to promote his professional identity as a couturier. This designer is particularly relevant because he began his operation in 1932, at the age of twenty-five, and quickly achieved both recognition for his creativity and business success. So much so, that within two years, he went from employing 30 to 200 people and within four years the Paris editor of *Women's Wear Daily* (the American trade newspaper) could claim with some confidence that in 'London's dressmaking world . . . he is an Establishment with a capital E'.[55] Although South African by birth, Stiebel created a couture house deeply rooted within the context of London and in the 1930s was instrumental in the production of a new set of meanings for English dressmaking. This analysis of Stiebel's practice will therefore consider how his business responded to changes in London's social sphere and manipulated a number of promotional platforms in order to support his professional identity as a couturier.

Victor Stiebel's practice provides evidence that the shift from court dressmaker to couturier was facilitated by changes in the constitution and habits of London Society. Social historians acknowledge that whilst the traditions of the Season (which supported court dressmaking) continued, the First World War had irrevocably changed much of its character and social composition. Ross McKibbin has argued that its 'exclusively aristocratic and august behaviour' prior to 1918 was replaced throughout the next twenty years 'by a kind of New York Café Society', which encouraged the notion that it was in some sense 'open' and therefore appropriate to a democratic age.[56] For Barbara Cartland (the novelist and Hartnell client), this openness saw society become a 'pot pourri of the titled, the beautiful, the famous and notorious, all welded together with money'.[57] McKibbin also points to the 'slippery concept' of the constitution of society in the interwar period, where 'discerning too close an affinity between Society and the Upper Class is hazardous'. Whilst many within Society remained upper class, many in the 'old' upper class did not 'move in Society'; membership was based on 'how money was spent rather than how it was earned' but also required a mix of breeding, education, wealth and cultural assumptions.[58] This social change also coincided with an unprecedented growth of nightclubs, restaurants, and large modern hotels built to encourage and accommodate an increase in wealthy visitors such as the Grosvenor in 1929 and the Dorchester in 1931. When the Season opened, these environments provided an extended arena for public display, in which the numerous entertainments were more open to moneyed newcomers.

Historians have noted that the members of this new form of Society
predicated themselves on glamour, fashion and wit, rather than title and
duty, and flaunted their wealth with what David Cannadine, the eminent
historian of the British aristocracy, describes as 'opulent and irresistible vul-
garity'.[59] The altered constitution and extension of London's social arena
therefore gave dress designers with aesthetic flair a specific commercial and
promotional platform that could be manipulated to support their credentials as creative couturiers. The new 'social verve' amongst London's rich,
which 'encouraged the upper classes to reconstitute themselves along more
glamorous American lines', also allowed London dressmakers to produce
clothes that did not compromise their claim to international relevance.[60]
This aspect, particularly for the American market, became an important
component within the promotional narrative constructed to authenticate
the London couturiers' aesthetic authority. When Stiebel presented his
collection in the United States in 1934, in a tour backed by a number of
prestigious department stores, he constantly reiterated the fact that he did
not cater to 'dowdy aristocratic debutantes, but quite the opposite . . . especially since London has become a great social center; very gay, very smart
and very amusing'.[61] He thereby used the changes in society to support his
fashion credentials. The main image for *Life* magazine's coverage of the
tour (figure 1.5) in its depiction of the young designer in a simple, contemporary setting, surrounded by eight youthful models, presented what could
be seen as a democratic view of London's dress culture. Six of the ensembles were evening wear: streamlined and slim fitting with fashionable capes,
butterfly sleeves, corsages and bows. The daywear consisted of bright, deli-
cately printed silks with jaunty 'Robin Hood' hats. Such designs challenged
American expectations of English tailored daywear and formal evening
dress, particularly the latter's traditional association with the grandeur of
stiff satins and low décolletage to show off the jewels of society ladies. An
understanding of London as a modern, vibrant and international social centre therefore became an important promotional narrative that underpinned
Stiebel's design aesthetic and authority in America. In turn, he used this to
support his representation as a creative fashion designer whose work was
applicable across a wide market.

In the lectures Stiebel delivered whilst in America he both challenged
Paris' design hegemony and drew on the rhetoric of originality to present
a romantic notion of his artistic creativity. He represented himself as a

Figure 1.5
Victor Stiebel and his head fitter and models, *Life* magazine, September 1934. *Source:*
© Getty.

fashion creator who gained inspiration not from others but from his personal siphoning of the modern world. This is demonstrated in the *New York
Times* article, 'An Englishman's Idea', from November 1934, which quoted
Stiebel's declaration that due to an international 'smart set' of women there
was now:

> No nationalism in dress for the truly modern woman, her individualism finds
> expression in the same way in all countries. There is nothing strictly English,
> nothing strictly French . . . just the smart woman selecting her apparel with
> intelligence and good taste according to the style of the day. And in turn, we
> who design these for her are influenced by the times in which we live—the
> youth, the excitement, and the movement of present-day life. All this shows
> itself in rhythm of line, beauty of texture and subtlety of coloring.[62]

In the interwar period the narrative of internationalism, just as it was in architectural debates, was a key component within the dissemination of not only English but also French couture. For example, three years earlier, Lucien Lelong (the French Couturier), in a question-and-answer session with the American Fashion Group, in response to whether he designed and thought about the American buyer and the American point of view, promoted a similar narrative in his claim that 'the chic woman has no nationality . . . I am influenced by what I see today'.[63] The narrative of fashion promoted by these designers and magazines such as *Vogue* therefore rejected national inflections, which in turn allowed scope for the recognition of the London couturiers' creative autonomy and broadened the market scope and applicability of their design style.

The 'smart' or 'chic' woman, promoted as the archetypal couture client, was clearly a member of what Lady Elizabeth Murray referred to as the 'gay international crowd', a rising phenomenon in the interwar period, given particular agency not only by developments in the speed and reliability of transatlantic travel but also by the growth of newspaper gossip columns and fashion publications with international editions, such as *Vogue* and its rival *Harper's Bazaar*. The world of fashion that such magazines constructed was one of independently wealthy pleasure seekers that stretched across national boundaries and united wealthy consumers. Their pages were dominated by fashionable international figures such as Lady Mendl, Daisy Fellowes, Lady Diana Cooper, Wallis Simpson, Mrs. Leo d'Erlanger, Lady Jersey and Edwina Mountbatten. These were wealthy women, who by the 1930s not only socialized but also purchased their clothes in London, Paris and New York. Caroline Seebohm (the biographer of *Vogue's* publisher Condé Nast) has pointed out that one of the key strengths of the magazine's three international editions was their ability to chronicle such 'celebrity socialites on seemingly permanent vacation in page after page of photographs and chatter about Americans abroad and Europeans in New York'.[64] This constructed an understanding of the fashionable woman as 'equally at home in an English country house, a Paris salon, or a New York nightclub'.[65] Society women, with the money and leisure to predicate their lives on travel, therefore acted as conduits that connected these separate fashion arenas and the designers of London, Paris and New York through a shared community of standards, tastes and interests.

The role such magazines and their depiction of fashionable society played in the construction of the high fashion industry and the connection of separate markets in Britain, France and America cannot be underestimated. *Vogue*, for example, was the first publication to create international editions tailored to foreign markets, which thrived not as export magazines but as native periodicals.[66] By the late 1920s it was one of the top three magazines read by upper- and middle-class British women; not just society women read *Vogue* but also clothing producers and department store buyers.[67] It had therefore become a 'byword for fashion and key stakeholder able to both shape and influence the international fashion industry'.[68] Business historians posit the source of this success in *Vogue*'s innovative business model; the 'class publication', which revolutionized the British magazine industry in the interwar period and made *Vogue* not only highly profitable, but also 'able to authentically influence British women's fashion decisions . . . [as its management and editorial departments] went from being passive commentators to active participants in the fashion and apparel industries'.[69] The idea of a 'class publication' was based on the production of a low volume, high quality consumer magazine, which drew revenue from advertisers rather than sales. Commercial success was based not on large circulation figures but on advertising revenue, which in turn depended on the magazine's ability to link advertisers of high-end goods to an affluent target market. The marketing strategy of the 'class publication' therefore relied on the ability to understand and reach a select readership. *Vogue* maintained a strict policy that separated advertising from editorial, as its unique appeal rested on its seemingly authentic and unbiased knowledge of fashion. Throughout the interwar period *Vogue* was consequently dependent on access to fashionable society in order to verify its own relevance. This strategy is exemplified in both the magazine's editorial policy, which ensured that each edition contained a minimum of two 'society' photographs, and in the predominance of the 'Our Lives Day to Day' column, which documented the lives and fashions of a select elite. As a result, an internationally constituted social elite, which was both fashion conscious and highly visible, performed an integral role not only within the validation of fashion journalism and its images but also within a city's designation as a fashion centre.

What can be seen as *Vogue*'s process of authentication of its fashion authority is made particularly obvious in the work of the English photographer Cecil Beaton, whose gossip columns, drawings and romantic portraits of society women were ubiquitous in this magazine throughout the 1930s. What separated this photographer from many of his contemporaries, and made him indispensable to *Vogue*, was his insider knowledge of the idiosyncrasies of fashionable society. A similar mechanism operated within the validation of the creative agency of Victor Stiebel, who found it equally important to trade on his links to high society. For example, in 1933 to mark the start of the Season, he held a 'Midnight Party' at his dress house, where he also presented a small collection of his latest models to a carefully selected group of invited guests, which included Nancy Mitford, Lady Oppenheimer and Anne Armstrong Jones. This event was reported across a range of publications, with *The Sketch* (the weekly illustrated that focused on high society) producing a full-page feature on the event (figure 1.6). *Vogue* reported it as a 'charming, intimate affair' hosted for 'intelligent Mayfair'.[70] Intimate it may have been, but as with many such ventures, this was a public and commercial display of intimacy and belonging. It not only allowed a sense of voyeurism into an elite world, but the informality of the richly attired guests, seated on the floor or perched on sofa arms, further legitimised the fashion credentials of both Stiebel and *Vogue*.

The documentation of Stiebel's 'party' alongside the escapades of London society effectively blurred the line between fashion and gossip writing. The cultural theorist Kristen Hoganson has argued that this form of journalism 'not only made the imagined world of fashion seem more tangible by providing distinctive personas to emblematize it, . . . [but also] enabled the women who followed the fashionable world to buy the connotations along with the clothes, and foremost among the connotations were aristocracy and wealth'.[71] Caroline Seebohm has also shown that, in the interwar period, the editors of *Vogue* considered the English 'the height of fashion, particularly if they had titles'.[72] In the context of the magazine's business model, which was based on social aspiration, it is unsurprising that the English aristocrat and her social circle constituted an integral part of the fashion industry's authentication process, as a title automatically transferred the influential connotations of status, wealth and belonging. Thus, within the representational world of fashion magazines, which exerted considerable influence over the fashion industry, Britain's traditional social structure gave both London and its designers a symbolic niche.

In the interwar period the British aristocracy and its social sphere therefore maintained a strong representational appeal, despite its decline in terms

THE NEW MIDNIGHT AMUSEMENT:
DRESS-PARADE PARTIES.

The HON. SHEILA BERRY, second daughter of Lord Camrose, is here seen with the HON. TOM MITFORD, Lord Redesdale's heir. Her picture is on view at the Royal Academy.

MME. ALICE DELYSIA is listening to MR. RANDOLPH CHURCHILL. In the background, on the left, CAPTAIN and MRS. JOHN LASCELLES may be distinguished.

The MIDNIGHT DRESS-PARADE PARTY is the new society amusement. Last week there was a particularly important one; with Nina Mae McKinney to entertain the company after the mannequins had departed. This shows a group including Mrs. Vreeland, Mr. Walter Payne, Mme. Florence de Peña, Lord Howard of Effingham, Mrs. Charles Graves, Mrs. Madge Garland, Mr. Derek Patmore, and Mr. Leon M. Lion, admiring a white evening dress, adorned with a bouquet of field flowers, displayed by a mannequin.

(Right)
MRS. CARL BENDIX is the central figure in this group. MISS OLGA LYNNE is right in front, and MR. PHILIP KINDERSLEY on the extreme left. In the back row, on the right are MISS ANITA LESLIE (chin in hand), LADY GRANT, and her daughter, ESTHER. The group also includes MRS. ARCHIE CAMPBELL, MISS BETSAN HORLICK, and MISS LISA MAUGHAM.

Figure 1.6
'Victor Stiebel's Midnight Party, 22 Bruton Street', 1933. *Source:* Mary Evans.

of real economic and political power. Those with titles were influential, but they also had to have a developed sense of celebrity and be well disposed to public scrutiny. Consequently, for the London couturiers it was advantageous that many of the titled members of society were more open not only to fashionable dress but also to placing themselves and their wardrobes on public display. It has been argued that the final element in the transformation of London society in the interwar period was this reconstitution of 'old money into new celebrity'.[73] This was facilitated by the ubiquitous interest paid to its members not only by class publications such as *Vogue* and *Harper's Bazaar* but also throughout all levels of the national magazine and newspaper industry. As Paul Cohen-Portheim in his chronicles of London life noted, in comparison to continental Europe, where those in society 'remain private individuals', he had witnessed an 'astonishing' spectacle in England where 'people in Society are public characters. Every newspaper tells you about their private lives, every illustrated paper is perpetually publishing photographs of them and they are as much popular figures as cinema-actors are. Their parties and their dresses, their weddings, christenings and funerals, their houses and their travels are all described and depicted. Its great public simply demands it . . . the first duty of society is to be a show for the masses'.[74]

At the centre of the increased publicity that surrounded elite society was the young debutante. In the 1930s this was supported by the propensity of the daughters of the aristocracy and their peers to put themselves on display as never before. Many of these young women were also not averse to the use of public interest for commercial gain. For example, Lady Marguerite Strickland (a debutante in 1931) promoted 'everything from Kirby grips to Gordon's gin' and became one of the key models for the British off-the-peg fashion brand Matita.[75] Margaret Whigham (the 'Debutante of the Year' in 1930) pointed out that, before this generation,

> [T]he prevailing image of the debutante was that of a painfully shy mouse, lacking both make-up and conversation. Suddenly and unaccountably, all this changed. The girls of 1930 had good looks; they knew how to dress; and they had far more self-confidence than their predecessors. The Press were quick to swoop on this new development. Suddenly newspapers began to "feature" us. For the first time, debutantes became front-page news along with royalty, politicians and actresses.[76]

The interest taken in Whigham and her contemporaries may have appeared sudden, but with the blurring of the boundaries of elite society and the interest taken in it by an expanding publishing industry, it was certainly not unaccountable. The fact that debutante clothing was one of the main components within Stiebel's practice was therefore fortuitous, as a main impulse within fashion design in the interwar period was the ability to capture an element of youth and modernity. In his memoirs, Stiebel went so far as to credit the patronage of Margaret Whigham, the 'most beautiful woman of her generation', for the 'sudden success' of his business.[77] Daughter of George Whigham, the self-made founder of the British and Canadian Celanese Corporation, she was launched as a debutante in an extravagant coming-out ball in 1930. In the early 1930s, she was one of London's youngest and most fashionable socialites and a particularly popular and influential personality in newspaper gossip columns. In 1933, when she married Charles Sweeney in a Norman Hartnell gown, the *Sunday Dispatch* reported that in the crowd of 3,000 spectators who gathered outside Brompton Oratory were 'scores of young women who had obviously modelled their appearance on hers. They had long earrings, full, rich cupid bow lips, and tiny hats aslant, as "The Whigham" wears them'[78] (figure 1.7). The attention Whigham received within the national press made her style a source of fashion authority not simply for her own peer group but also for a broad market, and by extension brought authentication to the creative autonomy of the designers she patronised.

Before her marriage, *The Bystander* reported that Whigham was 'quite the smartest *jeune fille* London has seen for a long time. Her clothes are original, do not depend entirely on their cost, and she wears them with great chic'.[79] This acknowledgement of the price paid for her clothes was an indication of her patronage of English designers, who charged considerably less for their models than those from Paris. Whigham's patriotic consumption habits were therefore well documented in the press. She also had a developed sense of the value of her personal endorsement: after his first collection Stiebel claimed she 'struck a deal' with him that 'if he gave her his personal attention, if she had the best fitters and was never overcharged she would buy his clothes, and tell her friends about them'.[80] The fruitfulness of this client endorsement is clearly demonstrated in an article taken from *The Sun* newspaper from later that year, which described Whigham as 'dressed almost exclusively by Stiebel, whose fashion salon in Berkeley

Figure 1.7
Wedding of Margaret Whigham to Charles Sweeney. Dress designed by Norman
Hartnell, February 1933. *Source:* © National Portrait Gallery, London.

Square is the rendezvous for London's smartest and loveliest women'.[81]
Stiebel's recollection of this collaboration was that afterwards 'everyone
wished to know where "The Whigham" shopped and as soon as she wore
my clothes, women stampeded to my collections'.[82] This was however a
simplification of the process of emulation, as it concealed the business acu-
men behind this endorsement, which was a far more complicated public
relations exercise. This is illustrated by one of the first garments Whigham
purchased from Stiebel's second collection: a distinctive striped dress worn
with a beret hat, seen in figure 1.8, which demonstrates how this backing
was engineered for its maximum commercial impact. In the same month
that she appeared in the dress socially and was photographed in it, Stiebel
not only used this model in his advertising campaign but also supplied it
to both the daughter of the First Lord of the Admiralty for a *Vogue* photo
shoot and for the leading lady's costume in a much-publicised theatre

Figure 1.8
Margaret Whigham in Victor Stiebel ensemble, photographed by Bassano, October
1932. *Source:* © National Portrait Gallery, London.

production. This promotional activity is an indication of how Stiebel as a young designer manipulated this particular client's patronage and newsworthiness to achieve maximum publicity. The suggestion that wealthy women chose Stiebel's clothes merely because Whigham was a client disguises the industrious and multifaceted nature of this carefully executed promotion. The marketing strategy that surrounded Whigham's patronage is also indicative of the importance of not only a fashionable clientele and social arena for display but also a sophisticated network of mediation that incorporated fashion magazines, newspaper reports, advertising campaigns and theatre productions.

London not only presented a viable market for the consumption of fashionable goods but also offered a distinctive and effective platform for the display and promotion of its designers' products. For that reason, it was fortunate for both purveyors of luxury goods and services and those involved in the marketing of fashion that the interwar period saw a rise in highly visible socializing, and society was defined by itself and others for 'its public display'.[83] Nowhere was this epitomized more than in the increased extravagance of the parties organised by competitive social hostesses, which supported the growth of an array of luxury businesses that catered to society's propensity for display. The biographer Sue Shephard has shown that in the case of Constance Spry (the florist who dominated the market for flower decorations for London Society in the 1930s), her 'artistic' business 'relied on the wealth of patrons; on their glamorous lifestyle, their tight knit milieu and their competitive socializing'.[84] In a talk given to the American Fashion Group in 1939, Spry pointed out that she had never felt the need to advertise her business as it 'was made successful by my friends'.[85] She claimed that the only purely promotional work she ever undertook was a combined show with Stiebel called 'Flowers and Clothes' in 1935, where the dresses and their textiles were inspired by her floral displays.[86] The 'friends' she referred to were not her clients but an interconnected group of creative practitioners in the fields of fashion, theatre, photography, magazine publishing, interior decoration, architecture and catering whose commissions and recommendations garnered her clients and prestige. Stiebel was also firmly ensconced within this network of aesthetic businesses. This is demonstrated not only by the prevalence of Spry's flower arrangements at his dress shows, but most specifically by the fact that in 1935 he and Spry became reciprocal directors of each other's companies.[87] It is also evident that personal contacts allowed Stiebel to construct a mutually supportive network that validated his claims to creative agency. Much of this stemmed from his initial friendship with the interior decorator Syrie Maugham, who designed both his salon and his home, and also introduced him to Spry and many other contacts, such as the textile designer Marion Dorn, who designed the rugs for his showroom, Cecil Beaton, who featured his clothes in his society portraits and the theatre and events designer Oliver Messel, who facilitated important commissions particularly for costume balls.

Alongside the extravagant parties devised by socially ambitious hostesses, the charity fancy dress ball, a ubiquitous phenomenon between the wars, provided many creative practitioners with an extremely visible platform for extravagant and spectacular display. Whilst usually devised by an upper-class committee, this type of event has been described as one of London's more 'genuinely democratic institutions . . . [as] social mixing was part of the appeal of such functions'.[88] Charity balls can thus be taken as representative of the modernization of London society. These were fundraising events where formality was removed, frivolity and social mixing encouraged and visual flamboyance and public display the expectation. Such charity balls allowed London's creative dressmakers not only to garner publicity and new clients but also to extend and display their creative talents. For example, in November 1933, a number of publications included an image of the costume Stiebel created for Lady Warrender for an Edwardian Ball held in aid of Queen Charlotte's Maternity Hospital. *The Bystander* magazine also included a feature on this event entitled 'Which Period Do You Prefer?' where an image of Stiebel's reproduction of a 1903 gown for the Countess of Warwick was placed next to one of a model from his latest collection[89] (figure 1.9). Whilst the sketches and photograph of his current fashion designs were streamlined in comparison to those of his ball costumes, elements of Edwardian dress clearly informed his contemporary designs. Many press reports of Stiebel's spring/summer collection of 1934 comment on how he then went on to use 'the colours and stylistic tropes of the past in his modern dresses'. As one provincial journalist put it, 'we should have been incredulous a year or two ago if we had been told . . . material and colours, which are ghosts of the nineteenth century—would make a modern frock'.[90] Newspaper commentators may have feigned surprise at Stiebel's aesthetic mixture of the past and present, yet what they

Figure 1.9
'Which Period Do You Prefer', *The Bystander*, 13 December 1933. Left: Stiebel model and sketches for his 1933 collection; right: the Countess of Warwick, in her Stiebel gown for the Edwardian Ball. *Source:* © Illustrated London News Ltd/Mary Evans.

saw as his unconventional approach was taken as an indication of his ability to innovate new styles. In this way, costume balls not only provided women 'with an opportunity, however fleeting, to transcend the limits, which the dictates of their dress culture imposed', but also allowed scope for London's fashionable dressmakers to extend their design repertoire and creative range.[91]

Gowns worn at costume balls and historically informed modern fashions obviously responded to a different mood in London's interwar social scene, which at times seemed to be haunted by the past. Yet the fashions these produced supported rather than undermined the English couturiers' claim to contemporary relevance. These styles of dress can be seen to align with what the historian Alexandra Harris describes as the 'romantic modern' aesthetic prevalent in England in the interwar period, an idiosyncratic brand of nostalgic modernity, which she argues was characteristic of the age.[92] Rather than a deferral of the modern, Harris sees the tendency

of artists and designers to refer to the past as a quintessential and defining element within English modernity. She argues that the nostalgic aesthetic of the 1930s was neither anachronistic nor conventional, but was
recognised at the time as novel, young and non-conformist. In particular,
she points to the safeguarding of eighteenth-century heritage that characterised fashionable English style at this point where 'the experts in the
distinctive art of Georgian re-creation, such as Cecil Beaton and his circle,
young aesthetes, people of extremes, flaunted both their modernity and
their anachronism'.[93] Stiebel's position within this distinctive aesthetic circle, which was representative of a specific fashionable upper-class youth and
their modernity, is clearly demonstrated by the clothes he produced for his
'friends' in the short-lived Eighteenth Century Equestrian Group, which
included Beaton, Lady Castlerosse, Lady Weymouth and Nancy Mitford,
which went on to feature in many magazines (figure 1.10). Similarly, the

Figure 1.10
The Eighteenth Century Equestrian Group in costumes by Victor Stiebel. Left to
right: Hon. Nancy Mitford, Mr Cecil Beaton, Lady Castlerosse and Lady Weymouth,
The Bystander, 17 May 1938.

celebration of Victoriana, which Harris contends was another example of young modern rebellion, gained no greater prominence than in the clothes Norman Hartnell created for the Queen's 1939 state visit to Paris[94] (figure 1.11). The renowned 'White Collection' may have adopted the style of the most romantic and sentimental of Victorian painters, Franz Winterhalter, yet as Harris maintains the appropriation of styles from the Victorian era was not seen as conservative or a rejection of modernity.[95] It is in such hybrid-modern designs, where late Victorian styles constituted modern dress, or designs were informed by a bygone aristocratic age, that English designers were able to tap into a wider elite, fashionable aesthetic that correlated with the impulses of English modernity. The combination of romantic, historical styles mixed with modern elements may also have been an aesthetic that dominated many Parisian designers' collections in the 1930s; however, when such clothes were produced in England, they and their designers demonstrated a nationally specific, culturally astute, class-based design authority.[96] In so doing, the clothes produced positioned designers, such as Stiebel and Hartnell, within a definable aesthetic network that endorsed their cultural capital and claims to fashion innovation.

The vibrancy of the theatre in London's West End, alongside social events such as charity balls, offered yet another platform for the demonstration of a designer's cultural relevance and creativity. Whilst today, costume and fashion are often seen as distinct forms of design, in the 1930s they were inextricably linked. The showcase of new fashions had become paramount within many theatre performances and costume design became an integral component within the business practices of many in the 'new school of English fashion design'. It is therefore unsurprising that when Stiebel opened his dress house he immediately wrote to London's main theatre impresario Sir Charles B. Cochran to offer his services as a costume designer.[97] Over the next two years he went on to design costumes for at least six of Cochran's stage productions, many of which transferred to New York and brought the designer a large amount of transatlantic attention. Cochran's productions were extravagant, popular and lucrative; Norman Hartnell, Stiebel's more established competitor, had already costumed many of his performances. A main element of Cochran's repertoire was the elegant and stylish Revue: a medley of sketches and musical numbers based on wit, charm and pace. These productions were an important site of female-centred amusement, which indulged their audiences' need for

Figure 1.11
Queen Elizabeth in Hartnell's 'White Collection' designed for the state visit to Paris, arriving for lunch in the Hall of Mirrors, Versailles, with Mme Lebrun, wife of the French President, July 1938. *Source:* Topfoto.

pleasure and escape and became an integral part of the social season. In the interwar period Cochran also acted as a fulcrum within a specific network of cultural producers. His shows attracted some of the era's best creative talents, such as Ivor Novello, Cole Porter, Paul Nash, Lovat Fraser, Frederick Ashton, Oliver Messel, George Balanchine and the Diaghilev ballet company. Stiebel's work for Cochran, within the particularly vibrant field of London theatre, further ensconced him within an important network of creative practitioners and allowed him to publicize his clothes and name to prospective clients, whilst it also supported his claim of aesthetic autonomy.

The costumes Stiebel created for Cochran productions such as *Music in the Air* (which opened in May 1933, with set designs by Oliver Messel), with their oversized gathered sleeves, bows around the neck and gauntlet gloves, were exaggerated and distinctive (figure 1.12). Through performance and the associated publicity, these designs were quickly disseminated though a range of media, to become a design motif associated with Stiebel across a broad market.[98] Mary Ellis (the leading lady of *Music in the Air*) was featured in her Stiebel costume, with its exaggerated fur shoulders, on the front cover of *Tatler* magazine in June 1933. She also wore another of his flamboyant designs for a nationally disseminated advert for the breakfast cereal Shredded Wheat. Many magazines, such as *The Sphere* and *The Bystander*, which were read by fashionable society, also carried production shots and long reviews. The publicity generated by this particular theatre production successfully disseminated Stiebel's name and fashion authority beyond the West End and across an extended consumer market not only in Britain but also (when it transferred to Broadway) in America.

These designs, particularly their heavy butterfly shoulders, have clear similarities with ones seen the previous year in both Paris and Hollywood. They are comparable to those shown in 1932 in both the Parisian couturier Mainbocher's collection and the Hollywood designer Adrian's costume for Joan Crawford in the film *Letty Lynton*.[99] However, when Stiebel transferred elements of these costume designs into his fashion collections, despite such obvious similarities, they operated as a validation of his creative autonomy as press reports on his designs no longer compared them to the work of others. The theatre presented a dynamic and creative environment, so while Stiebel's designs may not have been entirely original, they captured and exaggerated a modern aesthetic of the day and demonstrated his design versatility and contemporary relevance. The provision of theatre costumes

The Bystander, May 24, 1933

Fashion Calling . . .

A Few Camera Studies of Victor Stiebel's
Striking Clothes designed for "Music in the Air"

*Enormous gathered sleeves of white organdie form a startling
contrast to the dress of scarlet shantung which Margaret Neeson
wears, while June Spencer-Dyke looks charming in a gown
of turquoise blue and a coat of white piqué which has
exaggerated shoulder-width achieved by huge sleeves. Her
gloves are also of white piqué and both dresses have trains*

*Left : Stephanie Insall
looks enchanting in a
blue dress with sleeves
of fitch fur and a
sash and bow of white
organdie. As you will
note, Victor Stiebel
makes a great feature
of large gauntlet gloves*

*White piqué is the leading material in
this group which shows Angela Litolf
in a costume of black flamisol and white
piqué coat and hat, and Winifred
Talbot in a purple shantung dress
which is accompanied by white piqué
accessories — belt, bow, and gloves*

*Left : white crêpe with
black and green striped
panels make a striking
combination ; so does
navy blue and white
ciré satin with cape
sleeves of blue and
white organdie*

*Right : the fair good
looks of Margaret
Neeson are shown
to advantage by her
white dress and blue
coat which has a
yoke and sleeves
of a material
printed in stripes
to resemble zebra fur*

Photos by Dallison

Figure 1.12
'Fashion Calling . . . A Few Camera Studies of Victor Stiebel's Striking Clothes
designed for "Music in the Air"', *The Bystander*, 24 May 1933. *Source:* Mary Evans.

was not only a promotional strategy but also allowed Stiebel to extricate himself from the production of conservative, socially specific dress, which in turn extended both his sartorial field and authority.

To further authenticate their creative authority it was also crucial that London's couturiers became well-known personalities in their own right. This was a clear element within Stiebel's promotional activity where his personality, youth and charm, as an embodiment of his practice, became an integral component of his marketing strategy. From very early in his career the publicity surrounding his business focused not only on his design work and the lives of his clients but also on his personal identity. An indicative example was a *Manchester Daily Sketch* journalist's claim that 'this young designer is the most interesting man I have ever met with his witty, frighteningly-bright conversation, he is able to charm everyone . . . when he arrives, a dull party becomes electrified'.[100] Stiebel carefully manipulated his own personality to encourage this type of coverage. For example, images of the designer at leisure, such as of him exercising on the roof of his business premises, were disseminated throughout the press and, by no small measure, helped to align his creations with a clear, youthful identity. When British *Vogue* launched its *House and Garden* supplement in February 1936, Stiebel was one of the first 'personalities' to invite the magazine into his home to discuss not only his clothes but also his own taste and lifestyle. This aspect of personality advertising mirrors the practice of stage actresses and movie stars who, as part of their carefully constructed public persona, also displayed their residences and by association their implicit good taste. This was also part of a public relations shift seen in New York and Paris to brand fashion products with a clearly identified designer. In this way, Stiebel's presentation of himself as a creative couturier involved full engagement in the twentieth century's growing celebrity culture, part of an individualizing project that brought validation to many forms of production within a rising mass culture that was seen to destabilize social structures. It is therefore significant that many London dressmakers gained professional recognition as couturiers at a time when a major increase occurred in mass production and consumption. The case study of Victor Stiebel highlights that his recognition as a creative London couturier brought prestige and cultural validation to his own practice, as well as his clients and other fields such as the theatre and fashion publications. In the 1930s this was further supported by a range of idiosyncratic social and cultural platforms that could be manipulated to validate young dressmakers' professional status as couturiers.

PROPAGANDA, PROTECTIONISM AND THE PROJECTION OF ENGLAND

> Just imagine how excited everyone in London must be, and how gay the town is. I can hardly believe it . . . how dull it used to be before the war, just grand parties for the aristocracy and no fun and pleasure at all for the masses. But now London is Europe's merriest capital, with everyone sharing in the fun. And as for the clothes . . . it is incredible. No buyer ever dreamed of going over to London even to look at the models except for tailor-made suits, in which the English always excelled. But now every buyer from America takes in all the London openings as a matter of course, and dress models by Hartnell, Stiebel and other designers command as much respect, as do those of the French houses.[101]

In 1937, an American syndicated newspaper column, entitled 'Diary of a Fashion Model', recognised London's newly established position as an international fashion centre. This particular editorial worked on the premise that the writer, 'Grace', was a mannequin in the dress shop of 'Madame' and wrote about the exclusive fashions she encountered. In this account, London was modern, exciting and fashionable, and this impacted on the representation of its young dressmakers who in turn gained creative credibility. The article (just one example of many produced in America at the time) may have reformulated the image of the internal workings of the country's social sphere and linked the rise of English couturiers to a democratizing ethos in London, yet it was produced in response to the heightened interest of the world's press caused by the run-up to the lavish coronation of King George VI.

In an article for *The Studio* three years earlier, the dress historian James Laver, in his consideration of the growing influence of the 'English Contribution' to dress design, claimed London dressmakers had become 'conscious of their power' not only because of the changes that had taken place in modern British society but also because of the stability of its social traditions:

> We who live in England are apt to see nothing but the changes, which have taken place in our social life. To us England is in a state of rapid and alarming flux. To the rest of the world we hardly seem to have moved at all; we are a solid rock in the midst of a torrent, a point of permanence in a changing world. . . .

It is inevitable that the foreigner should come to look upon the place where evening dresses are worn as the place where evening dresses can be bought.[102]

In this account Laver posited England's perceived 'stability' and 'conservatism' as a key stimulant behind the London dressmakers' market advantage. This highlights the inherent contradictions evident within the representation of London dress design in the 1930s. In one way it celebrated both the modern and open attitude of society, whilst in another it utilised the continuation of the country's traditional class and monarchical structures to authenticate the production of fashionable dress. To a certain extent these articles can be explained by the instability in continental Europe brought on by the rise of totalitarian politics, which meant that in comparison Britain, whilst still an imperial class-based nation, was seen as a democratic country that was culturally and politically closer to the United States.[103]

The way in which London society and its fashions were reported is equally indicative of the propaganda that emanated from Britain throughout the 1930s. At its basis, this had a particular agenda to present the country, in line with American social ideals, not as class-riddled and imperialistic but as stable, modern and inclusive. Having shown how the designers' move to creative autonomy was supported by the commercial infrastructure of Mayfair and London's specific platforms for display and dissemination, this section now turns to the role the economic situation played in the establishment of London's couture industry. It recognises that the city's acknowledgement as a fashion centre came at a time of worldwide economic depression and in response explores the role political propaganda and protectionism played in supporting the development of London's couture industry.

Throughout the interwar period propaganda increased in importance as the British government became aware that, for reasons of trade and peaceful relations with other nations, it needed to take positive steps to make its country better understood abroad.[104] An important guide to this process, produced in response to the onset of economic depression and a decrease in British exports, was Stephen Tallents' 1932 pamphlet *The Projection of England*. In his work as secretary of the Empire Marketing Board, Tallents had noted the growth of anti-British state-subsidized propaganda by foreign governments and was alarmed by its impact on British cultural and commercial relations. He argued that to maintain Britain's prosperity and to promote both trade and diplomacy it was essential to engage in what he called the 'new art of national projection'. This practice aimed to dispel the myth being constructed by foreign propaganda that the nation was in decline and replace it with a more positive modern image of British society and culture. The government's response to Tallents' call for cultural propaganda was the establishment of the state-sponsored British Council in 1934, with a Mission Charter (which remains the same today) aimed at 'promoting abroad a wider appreciation of British culture and civilization . . . [by] encouraging cultural, educational and other interchanges between the United Kingdom and elsewhere'.[105]

The following year Rex Leeper (the British Council's first director), in an article for *Contemporary Review*, used Tallents' ideas in his claim that 'in an age of instability England alone is stable. . . . It is time that this nation of shopkeepers did a little stocktaking to see how far our contribution to civilization is understood elsewhere and to decide how best we can satisfy this new demand for fuller information about almost every aspect of our national life, character and institutions'.[106] In an increasingly unstable political and economic world, the British Council presented Britain as modern, but also secure, peaceful and civilised. Interestingly, there are striking similarities evident in both Leeper's account and James Laver's claim that the 'power' of the English dressmakers was due to the country's recognition as 'a solid rock in the midst of a torrent, a point of permanence in a changing world'. Both articles, released within four months of each other, are examples of the dissemination of a specific discourse of cultural propaganda that had become increasingly prevalent by 1935. Laver's account is therefore an indication of the role fashion could play within the narratives of national projection.

Magazine articles and newspaper reports were the dominant medium for national projection; however, in line with government attitudes such reports had to avoid the appearance of blatant political propaganda.[107] Unlike many of its continental counterparts, it was this aspect that gave British propaganda the appearance of being simply positive publicity. In 1931, the Department of Overseas Trade issued guidance on the formulation of official propaganda, which was 'to a large extent a matter of creating an appreciative background for the seller of concrete goods . . . [therefore] sporting records and stories of national prosperity and efficiency, the Boat

Race and the Grand National are influential. Almost any topic which magnifies British institutions comes within this sphere'.[108] The type of events that were used within national projection, such as sporting fixtures and presentations at court, were typical platforms for the display of the London couturiers' wares. Internationally distributed images and reports of the latest gowns worn at such 'British institutions' were a pertinent yet discrete way to document and magnify the civilised nature of modern Britain. The juxtaposition of traditional events and fashionable dress demonstrated both the country's stability and capacity to adapt to the modern world. Creative fashion and the idea of London as a modern fashion centre was a particularly effective challenge to the assertion of foreign propaganda that Britain was 'down and out'.[109] Fashion reports, with their gendered focus and outward superficiality, whilst apparently innocuous, were able to project a positive national image. Within the interwar policy of concealed propaganda, fashion as a design form and embodied practice was therefore an effective visual and seemingly apolitical way to convey its designated ideals.

By the middle of the 1930s, the mechanisms of national propaganda were fully operational and undertaken by a range of official and semi-official organisations established to 'project' Britain abroad. This was achieved not only through the establishment of the British Council and Tallents' employment as the head of the BBC's public relations, but also by the unprecedented growth of a foreign press corps in London. The British Official News Service, which supplied information directly to foreign newspaper offices and news agencies, was at the centre of this network of mediation. One of the main aims of its overseas representatives and press attachés was to secure 'good copy for the British point of view' in the foreign press.[110] In 1936, the government suddenly increased the News Service's funding and in order to remove suspicion about the integrity of the information supplied also instructed the Foreign Office 'to expand the covert supply of British news to private channels of distribution'.[111] This call for positive propaganda, and the sudden increase in the dissemination of favourable news about Britain, explains why 1936 was the tipping-point in London's mediated recognition as a fashion centre. The effectiveness of fashion reportage within national projection also accounts for the incongruity of the rising profile of London's luxury fashion businesses at a time of world-wide economic depression.

The 'great slump', which followed the Wall Street crash in 1929, had paradoxically caused further social, economic and political changes that proved beneficial to London's creative dressmakers. Victor Stiebel, for instance, recalled that setting up his business in the worst year of the depression was ironically fortuitous. In his memoirs he pointed out that:

> In '32 the economic situation in Great Britain was disastrous. Ever since the Wall Street crash in '29 money has been scarce and there was a strong disinclination to spend it. All my friends and my solicitor and accountant had tried to dissuade me from opening a luxury business at such an inopportune moment; gloomily they said that it would need a turnover of £20,000 to make the thing pay. That first year we did a turnover of £40,000, what they did not realise (and neither did I) was that the very fact of opening a business during those economic doldrums would be a spark of interest, not only to the National Press . . . but also for potential customers who for so long had been preached at about the sinfulness of extravagance. The timing of my first collection was therefore lucky.[112]

By the end of 1933 London's economic recovery was underway and between 1934 and 1937 Britain sustained growth that extended through most sectors of the economy, particularly in the South East. Economic and business historians agree that consumption rose steadily throughout this period, particularly for fashion goods.[113] While the type of quantitative evidence used to support these assertions may demonstrate the growth and vitality in the consumption of fashion, it does not account for the move of consumer patronage from Paris to London. This is explained more readily by the qualitative impact of three specific governmental policies instigated in response to the rapid fall in export revenue: the Buy British campaign, devaluation and the imposition of protective tariffs. These key developments in economic policy, a depression-induced retreat from the capitalist free market, were to have a positive impact on the English fashion industry through their appeal to consumers' patriotism and financial prudence.

In February 1932, the month Stiebel and Molyneux launched their London houses, Hartnell flew his mannequins and models to Paris and informed *Pathé News* that as 'several of the big French dressmakers are coming over here, I go in the spirit of friendly rivalry, though I admit that my main objective is to make people buy British abroad'.[114] In that same month *Vogue* opened with an advert to encourage its readers to consider

their fashion consumption in terms of a patriotic act and ensure that the
clothes and accessories they bought were British. Hartnell's comments and
this advert were a response to the Buy British campaign initiated by the
Empire Marketing Board in November 1931, a highly visible component
of trade protectionism.[115] The *Vogue* advert was only one amongst 1,400
items that were disseminated in over 500 newspapers and magazines to
ensure that this campaign received extensive national coverage.[116] J. H.
Thomas (the Secretary of State for the Dominions) called this drive 'the
largest example of government propaganda undertaken in peacetime'.[117]
This push for patriotic consumption was to prove beneficial for London's
made-to-measure womenswear as the campaign had particular resonance
with many couture clients. First, as the Prince of Wales made clear in his
public radio address that launched the campaign, this was because women
were its main target; it was an 'opportunity for every woman, in a simple way and in her own way, to help her country in her hour of need'.[118]
Second, whilst the actual success of the Buy British message has proved
difficult for historians to accurately measure, research indicates that the
more affluent end of the market (particularly those who bought couture)
'appeared to be most susceptible to the propaganda'.[119] For the London
dressmakers the Royal Palace's decree that 'their majesties have expressed
the wish that ladies attending court should as far as possible, wear dresses
of British manufacture', was particularly beneficial.[120] In line with the campaign, 1932 also witnessed many newspapers change their attitude towards
the London dress designers and the narrative they used in their reviews. At
February collection time, for example, the *London Evening News* began to
use the language of battle in its fashion coverage, as it purported to have the
news from the 'Fashion Front . . . [in] London's campaign to oust Paris as
the world dictator of what women will wear'.[121]

   At one level this promotion of nationalistic consumption supported the
development of English couture and the viability of the new businesses created in 1932 and 1933 such as those of Victor Stiebel, Digby Morton and
Peter Russell. Yet the allure of French clothing was deeply ingrained and
difficult to counter by a jingoistic call to patriotism. Lady Elizabeth Murray, for example, would later point out in the *Daily Mail* that the national
consumer may well 'wave a flag for England, die for her if necessary' but
they would not 'buy dowdy clothes for her'.[122] Alongside the creativity
apparent in many London collections it was the implementation of two

politically contentious government policies that helped the acceptance
of London as a centre for couture consumption. The first was Britain's
withdrawal from the International Gold Standard and the devaluation of
the pound in 1931, which gave the dress houses an advantage by making
French products more expensive for British and American consumers.[123]
This ensured that when the value of the dollar also fell in 1933, 'the American habit of coming to England for her clothes was already established'.[124]
The French franc remained overvalued in terms of the dollar and pound
and this continued to curtail its fashion exports until it was finally devalued
in October 1936. The English dressmakers were also given the opportunity
to build up their market position as the economic situation saw the British
government reverse its long-established policy of free trade and introduce
import tariffs.[125] In 1932, this enforced a levy of 15 per cent on French
couture and textiles, which in conjunction with the weakness of the pound
against the franc, particularly in the home market, strengthened the position of London's made-to-measure dressmakers.[126]

In 1931, the American Smoot-Hawley Act had also introduced trade
tariffs to protect American producers and discourage the import of foreign
luxury goods. This imposed a 90 per cent ad-valorem tax on imported garments 'embellished with embroidery, tulle, spangles (lame) or lace'.[127] As
these fabrics were key components within imported dress, the tariffs led to
'a freeze in the international garment trade', which destabilized the relationship between the French producers of luxury goods and the lucrative
American market.[128] In the case of the fashion industry, a noted response
to this protectionist stance was the 'American Designer Movement' initiated, the following year, by Dorothy Shaver at the New York department
store Lord & Taylor, which was a coordinated promotion of American
fashion designers. At the time of the Wall Street crash, the American fashion industry was heavily reliant on the understanding of Paris as the only
source of fashion creation. To support American-made fashion based on
French styles, transatlantic retailers, mass-market producers, advertisers,
magazines and dressmakers had worked together to promote and solidify
the Parisian hegemony in fashion design. American department stores, in
particular, had made an enormous capital investment in the promotion of
French couturiers.[129] However, with the onset of the economic depression
and the introduction of trade tariffs, the American industry needed to promote its own designers and bring flexibility to the belief in a French-style

monopoly. The protectionist dismantling of this promotional rhetoric ironically also benefitted London couturiers, for as the American fashion industry took steps to undermine French trade and promote both New York and Hollywood as fashion centres, London also became part of this extension of the international fashion system.

Established in 1928, but not fully formalized until 1931, the powerful American Fashion Group was at the centre of this realignment of the fashion trade, setting out to professionalize women's roles in the fashion industry and act as an important source of fashion information for the nation's producers and retailers.[130] One of the Fashion Group's fundamental objectives was to encourage an increase in the annual consumption habits of American women and offer the industry a concrete forecast for the future direction of fashion. The latter was demonstrated in 1935 when the Fashion Group organised the first of its influential *Fashion Futures* dress shows which brought together a selection of 'one hundred perfect ensembles . . . representing those fashions most likely to meet the principles of good taste and to accord with the desires of American women'.[131] The *Miami News* declared that this 'exciting style symposium' was 'a distinct innovation' and 'for the first time gave the women of America and those who cater to their wishes, a composite picture of coming fashions edited by America's foremost authorities from the multitude of early season trends found in the world's fashion centres'.[132] *Fashion Futures* included Parisian couturiers, yet their designs constituted only half of those on display, with equal attention then paid to the style forecasts of designers from New York, Hollywood and London.[133] To bring full authority to *Fashion Futures'* predictions the Fashion Group also made sure that the London couturiers received increased recognition within the American market. For example, in 1935 after setting up Stiebel's aforementioned promotional visit the previous year, the American Group also sponsored and coordinated tours for Hartnell, Isobel and Madame Enos, ensuring the success of the English designers by linking them to prominent journalists and specific retailers.[134] The wider political and industrial implications in the American promotion of English couturiers were made transparent in many of the press reports of these tours, with the *Chicago Illustrated*, for example, proclaiming that they were there to 'shatter the myth that only Parisian designers know how to make beautiful clothes'.[135] *Women's Wear Daily* in an article entitled 'Victor Stiebel Hopeful of Establishing London as a Couture Centre for U.S.' also pointed out that London couturiers were 'not restricted to sports types in woollens, as in the past, but are also extending to the formal fashions of afternoon and evening which have been rapidly developed'.[136] In order to protect the American fashion industry and promote American designers, fashion journalists, retailers and the influential Fashion Group therefore gave full endorsement to the idea of London as a fashion centre and source of original fashions in order to challenge the popular consumer belief that the creation of new styles was the monopoly of Paris.

★   ★   ★

In the 1930s, London's 'new school of fashion design' positioned and promoted their fashion statements as expressions of luxury and authority steeped in the cultural politics of Britain's wealthy elite. To promote the internationalism of their designs, these creators of original fashions subverted the traditional meaning of court dressmaking to sell new notions of British aristocratic theatricality by carefully aligning these traditions with the international and commercial elements of London. In so doing, they were able to move away from an atmosphere of 'cold hard business', to position their products between culture and commerce, between art and trade, shifting their practice from dressmaking to the production of creative couture. These designers therefore capitalized on social change and reacted to the commercial and cultural shifts of the 1930s in order to give their businesses, and London itself, the requisite cultural capital and cachet of an international fashion centre.

Yet for the city to be cast as a fashion centre it needed not only creative practitioners who produced original designs at a competitive price and an elite fashion-conscious consumer base that bought and displayed their wares, but also a changed attitude in the international fashion industry. A number of interrelated economic and political objectives supported the growth of a defined and visible London-based couture industry. In the 1930s, as producers of material and cultural forms sought to construct clear hierarchies within a developing and competitive marketplace, the acknowledgement of the professional identity of a number of London's dressmakers as couturiers became important to the cultural authentication of a network of separate creative industries. Scholars have often described the workings of an interconnected creative economy as a relatively recent phenomenon,

yet the case study of Victor Stiebel's business, which highlights the importance of a creative network in the development of this designer's professional identity as a couturier, illustrates its historical dimensions. To explore
this further, the following chapter will investigate the role performed by
designer collaboration in the recognition of London as a creative fashion
centre. It will therefore consider the creation and operation of the Fashion
Group of Great Britain, as a specific example of an interconnected network
where art and industry met, to shed new light on the mechanisms of British
interwar design reform.

MADE IN ENGLAND: PRE-WAR COLLABORATION AND THE PURSUIT OF THE AMERICAN MARKET

Fashions from England; British fabrics and British fashions; London as a fashion centre. All those are new sounds in our ears, but constantly recurring sounds. Only a few years ago when the cry was raised "why not London as a fashion centre?" the very idea seemed nonsense. There were not the designers in the capital to make of it a fashion centre. But things have greatly changed within the last five years. The eyes of the world have turned to this country . . . and stayed turned. Young men have arisen as dress designers whose names are mentioned with those of the Paris dress creators . . . The Fashion Group of Great Britain. Five years ago that would have meant nothing but blah, would have had no substance.[1]

In December 1936, when the fashion advisor and journalist Alison Settle claimed that London was now a recognised fashion centre she credited this achievement to the Mayfair dressmakers who had cultivated a reputation for the production of original made-to-measure clothing. She also acknowledged the role of the Fashion Group of Great Britain, particularly its recent organisation of the first collaborative collection of original London couture, which in May 1936 had been taken to New York on the maiden voyage of the RMS *Queen Mary*. The ship's launch had provided the perfect ambassadorial vehicle for the demonstration of London's claim to fashion authority, whilst the support offered by the creation of a British branch of the influential American Fashion Group ensured that when the onboard showcase reached New York it achieved its full promotional potential. The American Group issued invitations to 'socialites and the British colony' (key couture clients) to a glamorous onboard supper dance and fashion show.[2] An estimated 10,000 people saw the collection when it was then shown in two separate presentations to the country's main fashion buyers and transferred to a number of department stores in New York, Cleveland and Philadelphia.[3] *Draper's Record* (the British trade journal) claimed the voyage had 'without doubt, proved the artistry of the English fashion creators'.[4] Yet, if this was so, it was primarily demonstrated not by the work of the individual designers but by a number of competitors being brought together into a collaborative showcase.

In the 1930s, there were many made-to-measure fashion producers throughout Europe; however, it was unusual for individual cities or their designers to achieve international fashion authority and recognition. This chapter will demonstrate that to present an alternative to Paris, there was a need not only for a substantial number of autonomous design-originators but also for these businesses to be linked into a clearly defined network of fashion production and promotion. The collective couture showcase on the *Queen Mary* is therefore an important indication of the role designer collaboration played in the recognition of London as a fashion centre. It also demonstrates a move towards an effective network of specific London couturiers that came together to attract the attention of the North American market. The previous chapter, which considered the inception of London's couture industry, pointed to the importance of an interconnected network of creative practitioners and a general move towards the professionalisation of creative design practice. This chapter now extends the analysis beyond the creative autonomy of individual dressmakers to offer a fuller examination of the role collaborative networks played in the development and transatlantic appeal of Britain's couture industry in the 1930s.

As the number of London-based creative dress houses grew, so too did the need to expand demand. Mayfair dressmakers had only a finite consumer market; their clothes were sold in a high price bracket and they needed to preserve the exclusivity of their made-to-measure models so could not risk their sale for adaptation by British wholesalers. In England a social anxiety surrounded individuality in dress, an impulse clearly indicated in a *Daily Mirror* article in August 1936, which reported on the arrival in Southampton of the American actor Douglas Fairbanks and his wife (formerly Lady Ashley) being met by the English actress Heather Thatcher. Unfortunately, despite purchasing their clothes on different continents, both women had chosen to wear the same Stiebel dress. The text that accompanied the image of the women, under the heading 'Identical Dresses!' took immense pleasure in the social embarrassment of this sartorial faux pas (figure 2.1). Yet it was in this duplication that Stiebel's move from a court dressmaker to international couturier is made most apparent, a visual indication of the commercial reality of couture production, which Nancy Troy calls 'the logic of

Figure 2.1
'Identical Dresses', *The Daily Mirror*, August 1936. *Source:* Mirrorbix.

fashion', the tension between originality and reproduction that increased in the early twentieth century in response to developments in the ready-made clothing industry.[5] Whilst the seasonal couture model was never intended to be a one-off original, in England each model's copy was carefully limited or adapted for individual clients. However, when sold to foreign buyers it was destined for serial reproduction either made to order or ready to wear in department stores and elite dress shops, or for further adaptation by clothing outlets that catered to a broader consumer market. Thus, during the interwar period the couturier's role was to cater to an elite clientele and also to act as a fashion authority to authenticate the serial reproductions of foreign, and most specifically American, clothing producers.

In America, at the start of the twentieth century, middle-class women had been reluctant to wear ready-made clothing due to its perceived lack of quality, individuality and status. At this point, many women still had items that were readily available off-the-peg (such as blouses and skirts) made-to-measure by their own dressmakers or professionally at department stores and dress shops.[6] The first quarter of the century, however, was pivotal for the American clothing industry, when new and efficient production methods led to competitive prices and increased quality and accuracy in fit and sizing. These advances were supported by the expansion and improvement of the country's transport and communication networks and innovations in retail, such as the growth in department stores and mail order. These helped both to ensure the acceptance of off-the-peg clothing and to create a market where standardisation in dress gained cultural acceptance. In America, the advances made in the production and retail of ready-made clothing challenged the boundaries between elite and mass consumption and elite and mass taste and led to a different attitude towards exclusivity in dress. This saw the idea of standardisation, rather than as a negative, gain cultural acceptance as an indication of the American aspiration for democratic universality.[7] For example, as Victor Stiebel publicly stated in 1934, 'the women of New York are the great copyists because they all wear the same clothes at the same time'.[8] In a speech given to the American Fashion Group, he commended the American market for its appreciation of novelty and new ideas in modern dress, but also offered a critique of the lack of individualism caused by a strict adherence to the dictates of fashion:

> It makes such a difference to find that one's newest and most exciting ideas are accepted and criticized constructively, instead of just being ignored as is so often the case in England. . . . I think the standard of chic in America, or rather in New York, is unbelievably high. . . . [However,] American women are much too willing to accept a new idea. They will follow faithfully whatever fashion dictates . . . but there is a complete lack of individuality. Ninety percent of the women look the same.[9]

What Stiebel saw as the American attitude to dress was the antithesis of the exclusivity and individuality inherent within European made-to-measure production. French couturiers, however, had already adapted their practice to take full advantage of the opportunity for serial reproduction that this outlook facilitated. So much so, that by the interwar years, with the decrease in actual couture clients, the sale to American buyers of both original and 'bonded models' (where designers sold toiles, rather than garments, to be made up abroad and thereby avoid import tariffs) was a key component within the economic viability of the Parisian couture industry.[10]

Amidst the copious publicity that accompanied the Queen Mary show-case when it arrived in the US in May 1936, only *Women's Wear Daily* made clear the main business objective and stimulus for this collective endeavour; the collection had been created to demonstrate the 'originality of design of Britain's leading couturiers . . . [and the] great possibilities in the inter-change of American ready-to-wear for British styles and fabrics'.[11] For London's elite dressmakers the business opportunities presented by the vast American market, with its consumers' seemingly homogeneous attitude to dress and its mass-market producers' need for clear fashion guidance, could not be ignored.[12] The showcase on the *Queen Mary* was the first example of the English couturiers working together to create a joint collection. It offers a good starting point to consider the extent to which, in the 1930s, the needs of the American market provided the stimulus not only for designer collaboration but also for the development of a London couture industry.

The Queen Mary collaborative export collection was one of the first activities facilitated by the Fashion Group of Great Britain. This previously little-considered branch of the American Fashion Group was established in 1935 and disbanded in 1940 and contained seventeen of London's creative dressmakers.[13] Most accounts of the formation of the Incorporated Soci-ety of London Fashion Designers have always seen it as an unprecedented instance of collaboration. Taylor and Wilson's work is indicative of this in its contention that 'it took a world war to force British couturiers to work together'.[14] More recently, Edwina Ehrman has updated this under-standing, noting that the 'INCSOC was not the first group to represent Britain's fashion interests. Many of its members had belonged to the Fash-ion Group'.[15] In his 1954 autobiography, Hardy Amies pointed out that although the Incorporated Society and 'the whole idea of an established and organised *haute couture* in London is very new . . . [and the impetus to collaboration was] the encouragement of export during the war . . . [this had already begun by] the year of the Coronation of George VI in 1937'.[16] In 1942, just after the Incorporated Society was created, the designer Digby Morton also told an interviewer from Mass Observation that it was not a new idea, but a 'continuation' of the collaborative activity of the Fashion Group of Great Britain.[17] This Group, however, has received only limited discussion within fashion history and remained unacknowledged until 1997.[18] In Robert O'Byrne's consideration of London's construction as a fashion capital, where the British Fashion Group is briefly considered as the foundation for the development of the city's designer fashion, he asserts that this example of designer collaboration was 'fatally flawed by a problem that would hamper the development of the high fashion industry in Britain for a long time to come: lack of unity'.[19] This chapter will therefore focus on the Fashion Group of Great Britain, in order to question this 'lack of unity' and posit an exploration of this embryonic interwar collaboration as the most important foundational point for understanding the development of both London's couture industry and claim to fashion centre status.

THE FASHION GROUP OF GREAT BRITAIN: 'THE MOST CHARMING ATTEMPT TO ALLY ART AND INDUSTRY'

You are here [at the Fashion Group of Great Britain's inaugural lunch], a gathering of leaders practically speaking, a miniature Who's Who. You are a cross section of the taste of Great Britain and you represent between you most of the great industries of the country and the country's prosperity rests to a large extent on your shoulders. Call it if you will a coordinating link between designers, creators, manufacturers, wholesalers, and retailers down to the public. Call it if you will a group that exists to coordinate the brains of fashion. Call it, if you will not only an exchange of ideas, but also an exchange of personalities. Call it a collecting together of the key people in each branch of fashion. In fact, in Mr. H. G. Wells' words call it the "shape of things to come".[20]

In November 1934 the American Fashion Group informed its members that, 'under the leadership of Alison Settle who has kindly consented to be our Regional Director', it now planned to create a British branch.[21] After seven years as editor and director of British *Vogue*, Settle was an ideal choice to lead this new organisation, as she had procured and also learnt to manipulate a broad range of contacts across a spectrum of cultural, industrial and commercial production. This is made obvious by both the calibre and number of people she convinced to join and actively participate within the Fashion Group of Great Britain, with its initial membership of around one hundred creative practitioners who had reached prominent positions in their respective fields. Documentation of those present at the Group's inaugural lunch shows that by October 1935 Settle had indeed brought together an impressive 'Who's Who' of members. The opening speeches were given by H. G. Wells (England's most famous author of the time), René Clair (the French film director) and Hubert (the Hollywood costume designer) to a room of 140 people that included Cecil Beaton, Norman Parkinson, Edna Woolman Chase, Sir William Crawford, Ashley Havinden, Edward McKnight Kauffer, Oliver Messel, Sibyl Colefax, Elsa Schiaparelli, C. B. Cochran, Edmund Dulac, Constance Spry, James Laver and Elizabeth Arden.[22] Sir Herbert Morgan (author of many guides on British business efficiency and organization) proposed the main toast 'to this possibly the most intelligent and certainly the most charming attempt to ally art and industry'.[23]

The Group's first president was Lady Ivy Chamberlain (sister-in-law of the Chancellor of the Exchequer); Norman Hartnell and Alison Settle became vice presidents; Victor Stiebel the chairman; Ronald Fleming, the interior decorator, as vice chairman; and Margaret Havinden of Crawford's Advertising Agency as secretary. The main committee members were the milliner Aage Thaarup and the magazine editors Joyce Reynolds of *Harper's Bazaar* and Geoffrey Holme of *The Studio*. Thus the Group's main board was headed by a president with political influence and brought together key players from the fields of creative dress and textiles with representatives from 'the twin engines of modern consumerism': advertising and marketing.[24] Key members such as Settle, Havinden and Reynolds were intermediaries whose careers were based on the creation of 'extraneous interventions into the market in order to stimulate demand for consumer goods, regularise output, and flatten the booms and slumps of the trade cycle'.[25] This ensured that the aspirations underpinning the Fashion Group of Great Britain were fully informed by the new promotional culture under expansion in the 1930s.

Settle's speech at the inaugural lunch set out the Group's strategy: to build 'friendly contact', to break down 'barriers of reserve and custom . . . to hold meetings, small meetings between this person and that; between designers and manufacturers; between people who have something in common, in order that they may pool their difficulties and their interests'.[26] The Group was therefore presented to its new members as an informal forum where aesthetic leaders could communicate with one another. There was, however, an altruistic agenda behind the Group's formation that went beyond the establishment of individual business contacts: it was hoped that the shared knowledge of a cooperative network of fashion leaders and tastemakers could be harnessed to increase the stylistic appeal and commercial viability of a range of British products. Such goods had been traditionally sold by their quality and price and supported by the Empire's favourable trading system. However, in a period of economic depression, their market, both at home and abroad, had been reduced not only by trade tariffs but also by an increase in foreign competition. One area where the latter was particularly noticeable was in the sale of imported cotton dresses in the home market, where American models vastly outperformed their British equivalents. So much so, that by 1939 a Board of Trade survey demonstrated that these American products, despite 20 per cent trade tariffs, represented 47 per cent of total UK imports.[27] In the 1930s US government–backed initiatives supported the American apparel industry's developments in the standardisation of dress sizes, in engineering that helped the section method of construction (where garment makers worked on individual sections rather than the whole) and in spun rayon that could be used on machines set up for cotton. Such innovations increased production by 25 per cent and gave American manufacturers a competitive product that increased its market share in both French and English markets.[28] Cotton was the British industry that had registered the most dramatic collapse in the interwar period, and the sale of imported dresses was a particular source of anxiety for both Britain's textile industry and its government.[29] Reports produced to address this market weakness by both the Man-Made Fibres Federation and the Board of Trade concluded that the American products maintained their position not only because of their accurate sizing and fit but also, and most importantly, because of the appeal of their fashion-conscious designs.[30]

The concept of fashionable styling in order to raise the 'eye appeal' of industrial products was a fundamental component of the American approach to design. Since the late 1920s, American manufacturers had fine-tuned strategies that used product styling in order to stimulate sales and counteract the problem of under-consumption that afflicted mass production. Through the process of 'built-in obsolescence', design was used to both anticipate and encourage changes in consumer taste in order to limit mass-market saturation. This can be seen most clearly in the American profession of design consultancy, which emerged during the Depression when industrial design entrepreneurs such as Raymond Loewy and Henry Dreyfuss, with backgrounds in advertising, were employed by many companies as styling experts in order to increase profits.[31] At the British Fashion Group's inaugural lunch Settle pointed out that in comparison to American production, what she referred to as this 'element of fashion, the greatest trading influence in the world . . . on which more money is spent than on anything else, is unsupported in Britain because producers with common causes do not communicate with each other'.[32] She therefore presented the Fashion Group as a meeting point for creative practitioners that would correct this problem. Although it was not made explicit to its members, the Fashion Group of Great Britain was therefore underpinned by the belief that the adoption of American commercial strategies was imperative for Britain's future economic vitality.

The appeal for creative practitioners to share their knowledge also drew on another concept developed within American interwar political and commercial culture: cooperative associationism. This brought to Britain a business model that promoted the dissemination of ideas for the benefit not only of commerce but also the country as a whole: a key component within the system of progressive reform implemented throughout the 1920s by the US Department of Commerce. Under the leadership of Henry Hoover, this system drew on the ideas of 'scientific management' and brought together many different interest groups in order to increase industrial efficiency and productivity and thereby improve the standard of living for all American citizens.[33] This created business cultures that valued and promoted networks of cooperation and 'the progressive idea that businesses could set aside their differences and use trade associations to advance the common good'.[34]

Cooperation in order to improve industrial efficiency was a founding ideology behind the American Fashion Group. Alongside its initial aim to professionalise the role of women within the industry, its main rationale was to analyse new styles and consumer preference in order to forecast the direction of consumption, then to share this knowledge throughout the industry to direct and coordinate supply and to ensure demand. The business historian Regina Blaszczyk, in her work on colour forecasting, claims that this form of business interaction was a thoroughly North American phenomenon whereby only there 'did collaboration among experts generate fashion forecasts that could be applied across a broad range of style industries'.[35] In Britain the idea of businesses working in cooperation for the trade benefit of others was new and needed acclimatisation.

The explanatory tone of the Fashion Group of Great Britain's first quarterly magazine shows that in 1935 its definition of both fashion and its main objective to disseminate trend forecasts were foreign concepts to many

of its members. So much so, that Settle's first editorial had to take time
to define and explain both the meaning of 'fashion' and the concept of a
'trend'. The term 'fashion', she claimed, was used 'in its entire sense and not
the word "fashions" as not all fashions become fashion'. In this definition
fashion depended on the creation of and adherence to definable trends. Settle explained this process to the Group's members in the following manner:
'the grand idea you have inside your own head, that is an inspiration; then
when you carry it out and materialise it, that is the expression of your idea;
but it doesn't become a trend until it influences other people and moves in
a general direction'.[36]

From December 1935 onwards, to ensure that the members' ideas could
be immediately translated into definable fashion forecasts, the Group began
to hold regular meetings where ideas were converted into clear trend predictions. At these 'trend luncheons' members were encouraged to write down
their style forecasts and give either short talks or produce 'trend boards' that
were pinned around the walls for discussion. The findings of these events
were then published in the Group's *Bulletin* for dissemination to members
in both Britain and America.[37] Although many of the Group's dressmakers
initially participated in these meetings, they were particularly guarded in
the discussion of their latest ideas. For example, Norman Hartnell's address
at the initial trend luncheon (which he claimed was the first public speech
he had ever given to an audience) was particularly opaque. This meeting
may have taken place at a time when his new collection was almost ready
for presentation, yet he declared, 'I cannot tell you much about my own
trends in the fashions that I am making at the moment because I am busily
engaged on them and it depends how the pencil moves on the paper as to
what the silhouette for my next collection will be'. He did give a vague
indication, however, that 'lines ought to be completely concurrent with the
times in which they live, and with that in view I am designing along a pencil silhouette'.[38] The caution apparent in this speech is an indication of the
problematic nature, for creative practitioners, of the Fashion Group's idealism of 'breaking down barriers' and the 'exchange of ideas'. Dressmakers,
such as Hartnell, needed to safeguard the originality of their new designs,
so the spirit of cooperation that could be found in American commercial
culture, with its vast market and economies of scale, was difficult to trans-
pose to Britain. Despite the trade structures of its empire, Britain's limited geography and home market had created clandestine business cultures

that curtailed this cooperative idealism. It should also be noted that whilst many of the 'trends' disseminated throughout the American Fashion Group were taken from Paris, alleviating the commercial antagonism of American producers, in comparison London's creative dressmakers were expected to share their ideas with their domestic competitors.

The British branch of the Fashion Group therefore had to negotiate a number of cultural and commercial differences. It may have operated under the aegis of an American organisation, but communication with both its members and the British public was carefully presented as an inherently national body, independent of American control and commercial standardisation. To a certain extent, at a time of increased national protectionism, this could well have been an attempt to alleviate the anxiety that surrounded the American influence on British culture and commerce in the interwar period.[39] One of the only public documentations of the aims of the British Group was written by Settle, in December 1936, for *Tit-Bits* (a weekly mass-circulation magazine) under the heading, 'The Story of the British Fashion Group: Women's Whims Bring Work'.[40] In this account of the Group's first year of operation, Settle, whose title was subtly changed from 'regional director' to 'vice president', omitted the fact that it was a branch of a New York organisation and promoted the idea that it should be seen as 'a national body that operates in the friendliest affiliation with the New York and Paris groups'. The need for the British branch to demonstrate a sense of national sovereignty was also made apparent in her discussion of two specific modifications that separated it from its American counterpart. She pointed out that the British Group had vetoed the American idea of 'a women-only organisation, as not to include men as leaders equally with women in this country, as in Paris, was seen as unthinkable'. It also changed the stipulation that the membership be limited to those involved in the design, manufacture and merchandising of dress and fabric. Unlike its American prototype the British Group's definition of the 'branches of fashion' was extended to 'any informed design activity that responded to or forecast changes in public taste'. This included practices such as interior decoration, design for the stage and cinema, elements of the beauty industry such as hairdressing and cosmetics and restaurant food and décor. Settle could therefore draw the patriotic conclusion that the British Group was more inclusive, far-reaching and defined by a belief 'that the country's future economic health lies in it becoming a leader of the "world of fashion" not just clothing related—but in dictating fashionable tastes in many fields'.

For its members, the British Group's quarterly magazine also avoided overt references to American business strategies and commercial objectives. Instead, it promoted both the personal and altruistic benefits received from the annual membership fee, which, as Margaret Havinden pointed out, could not 'be reckoned in money—it is what you as an individual put into the Group that makes everybody's five guineas worth more valuable'.[41] For the individual, she claimed, membership offered the opportunity to make 'personal contacts with key people in your own and allied businesses, . . . [and] the backing, if you use it, of a whole organisation of experts in furthering your own particular interest . . . [and] the fun of knowing famous people personally and not just by repute'.[42] On a more philanthropic level, in her inaugural lunch address Settle asked the members to put their influence into the Group not only for personal gain, but also as an 'opportunity to take part in a movement to improve public taste . . . to further the cause of good design and offer a representative voice for the creator and the designer. . . . [To thereby] challenge unimaginative British manufacturers and retailers whose business approach is to give the public what it wants! Well, the public wants what obviously it can get. Therefore, give it the best that there is and it will want it!'[43] In this light, the British Fashion Group was cast as a form of design consultancy that could act as a mouthpiece for the transmission of good aesthetic practice amongst 'the country's best creative practitioners'. In turn, it was hoped that this would encourage design reform as these ideas were filtered to British manufacturers, who would then educate mass consumer taste rather than merely respond to it, increase aesthetic discernment and modify demand towards products that could compete in the international marketplace. The 1930s were formative within the development of mass-market provision, when rapid change stimulated cultural and political anxiety around the consumption habits of the masses and the Fashion Group of Great Britain was obviously motivated by a desire to drive and transform this demand cycle towards changes in elite taste.[44] Its philosophy was therefore underpinned by the idea of the passive consumer and a paternal top-down manipulation of the market.

The suggestion that creative dressmakers held the key to design reform for all sectors of British industrial design saw the Fashion Group position

London couturiers as the most important conduits of informed design activity. Business success for these practitioners was based not only on originality but also on a thorough knowledge of the fluctuations in their clients' tastes and preferences. The couture saleswoman performed a crucial role in the design process; at dress fittings she interacted with and observed the clients and then informed the design studio of changes in their taste. Thus, made-to-measure dress was produced through a symbiotic design process because the original model was often adapted to the clients' favourite colours, shapes, forms and decorations. Consequently, for the British Fashion Group's design reform agenda the foresight gained in the intimacy of the dressmakers' fitting room, a unique space in which to gather information on the fashionable whims of elite society, brought specific agency to the London couturiers' design knowledge.

The preoccupation with the role creative practitioners could play in elevating the standards of public taste gave the British branch of the Fashion Group a specific national inflection. This aligned its aims with the design reform aspirations of many other groups, organisations and societies that rose to prominence in Britain in the 1930s, in particular, the Council for Art and Industry (CAI), which was set up by the Board of Trade in 1933.[45] This organisation had a brief to educate consumer taste, improve creative training and encourage good design within British manufacture.[46] The link between the aims of this government-sponsored body and the Fashion Group was not accidental. For example, in 1936, in response to 'the large and increased importation of factory-made women's dresses from the Continent and America, largely on the score of design', the CAI established a Dress Committee to consider how to improve the standard of design in the women's clothing industry and make Britain 'of more consequence as a creator of original design and less dependent in that respect upon Paris and other foreign sources'.[47] The spur behind this research, as with most government-backed movements towards design reform, was clearly the growth in mass-market consumption and the increase in imports. Under the chairmanship of Sir Frederick Marquis (the future Lord Woolton), the Dress Committee included ten members, four of whom (Alison Settle, James Laver, Joyce Reynolds and Lady Chamberlain) were taken from the Fashion Group; the remainder were employees from the Board of Trade or those involved in education.[48] The Dress Committee's research, meetings and communications were constantly informed by the Fashion Group's activities and agenda. This influence is made clear in the CAI's resultant report, *Design and the Designer in the Dress Trade*, in the references it makes to the creative autonomy recently achieved by a number of Mayfair dressmakers and its recognition of their practice as a paradigm for design reform throughout the British clothing industry.

The Fashion Group's promotion of the role elite dressmakers could play in the improvement of the products of mass production both mirrored and challenged the discourse of interwar design reform. The utilisation of the couturiers' practice, in order to solve industrial problems, aligned with the taste-elevating aspirations of many such proselytisers, who looked towards the aesthetic choices of the more elite and affluent sectors of the market. Where it differed, however, was fundamental, as it positioned fashion, rather than the functionalist philosophy of the Modern Movement, as the key agent of improvement for the industrial marketplace. At its source, the British modernist polemic, clearly demonstrated in Noel Carrington's influential *Design in Civilisation* of 1935, had a concern with notions of decay within civilisation and culture due to the rise of unrestrained mass consumption. The concept of fashion, which led to the prevalence of change and revivalist styles within the products of mass production, was often used as a clear indication of this decay. The architectural historian Julian Holder has pointed out that the concept of designers, and in particular of architects, 'as guardians of civilisation, engendered a cultural superiority not only towards the construction and aesthetic of design but also to its separate forms'.[49] Within this structured hierarchy the transitory nature of fashion, which did not adhere to a functionalist philosophy, was often situated as the antithesis of the ideals of modern design. By the 1930s the critical discourse that surrounded ideas of reform, evidenced for instance in periodicals such as *The Studio* and *Architectural Review*, demonstrated an increase in the 'preoccupations, priorities and prejudices of an increasingly prescriptive and hegemonic Continental modernism'.[50] The design historian Cheryl Buckley asserts that from the 1930s onwards:

> There was a strong emphasis on utility, fitness for purpose and 'form follows function'. Decoration and historical styles became anathema, along with fashion and the transient, which were rejected in favour of the universal and the timeless. As a consequence, at the very moment that modernist ideas from the Continent were gaining ground, alternative modernisms already evident in British design began to be attacked or effaced from critical discourse. Thus craft,

decoration and eclecticism, integral to modernist practices in Britain before 1930, were estranged after it.[51]

The ambitions of the Fashion Group provide evidence of not only a continuation of pluralism but also hybridity within British interwar design reform. The Group merged British design discourse with the modernity of American commercial capitalism; however, in its aspiration to harness and disseminate elite taste to the masses rather than simply adhere to the dictates of the market, it fused elements of American industrial design together with European social idealism. To a certain extent this was a counteraction to the unrestrained commercialism of American design practice where, under the slogan of 'styling follows sales', it operated as a marketing device in which aesthetic judgment was based on mass rather than elite taste.[52]

Unlike other groups established in the interwar period to bring together elite design with mass manufacture, the Fashion Group of Great Britain has not left a legacy of exhibitions, catalogues and publications. Its operation as a meeting point for creative practitioners meant that the majority of the Group's activity was business to business. It therefore worked primarily through connections with a cross section of the creative establishment rather than through engagement with the general public. For the historian, the outcomes of this collaborative network are therefore often hidden; however, an example of its activity can be seen in Alison Settle's Advisory and Efficiency Service, which she set up in 1936, after she left the editorship of *Vogue* and became regional director of the British Fashion Group.[53] The business model of this Service was based on the American practice of fashion consultancy and demonstrates that Settle's time at *Vogue* (a magazine that both documented and guided developments in the international fashion industry) had ensured that she was versed in American salesmanship and marketing strategies.[54] Her first commission for the Wedgwood ceramic company, which employed her as a consultant to increase sales, demonstrates how the Fashion Group's theoretical intentions were put into practice.

At a key meeting with Wedgwood in 1937 Settle informed the company that if it wanted to become a market leader its products had to change consumer taste. To do this they had to 'get by the [retail] buyer, whose taste and partiality decides what stores sell and how it is displayed'.[55] She therefore suggested that the ceramic company operate 'along similar lines' to the

London couture houses; 'because the public does not know their own taste until it is visualised for them . . . [she recommended that they] hold a press show each season in order to dictate the season's new colours, designs, and high fashion models'.[56] To facilitate this process her consultancy sent regular trend forecasts to help guide the company's designers. In April 1938, for instance, Wedgwood was informed that 'the change in dress taste' had influenced all the major interior decoration firms towards an 'Edwardian' aesthetic and that:

> This dress tendency is to put to their side the clean and simple lines of the past decade, above all to reject every form of angularity . . . what is most significant is richness. . . . West-end decorators . . . have no doubt in their mind that the dress fashions are prophetic and that the rich gold embroidery used upon pockets, collars, the fronts of jackets and round the necks of dresses, determine the use of gold and other embroideries on cushions, curtains and coverings.[57]

It is interesting that in the preceding Fashion Group London dress collections, Teddy Tinling was the only designer particularly noted for a major use of gold embroidery.[58] Yet this incongruity allows Settle's advice to Wedgwood to be viewed as a clear attempt to use the Fashion Group's activity to coordinate and manipulate the market. Tinling's collection was atypical as it used only British fabrics due to the fact that his collection was produced in collaboration with the Fashion Group's Dress Fabric Subcommittee, which in December 1937 had Tinling organise a display of creative British fabric to encourage its use by his fellow dressmakers.[59] These fabrics were produced in direct response to the findings of the Fashion Group's trend luncheons, which had specified the use of gold embroidery. Tinling, however, was the only dress member to use these fabrics, purportedly because the timing of this particular textile showcase was too close to the January collections to ensure the 'cooperation of the [other] designers'.[60] The trend forecast that Settle sent to Wedgwood was not an unbiased reflection on the aesthetic dictates of the London dressmakers but rather a strategic commercial manoeuvre to control the market. This example of the use of the creative dressmakers' supposed choice of form, fabric and decoration as a template for the styling of contemporary ceramic tableware also challenges the typical discourse of interwar design reform, as it rejected 'form follows function' in order to promote the idea that form should follow fashion and fluctuations in elite dress.

So far, this chapter has demonstrated that the Fashion Group of Great Britain brought together many of the country's creative practitioners in order to construct a network of official tastemakers. This example of collaborative activity both extends and challenges the understanding of British interwar design reform and also demonstrates a larger formalisation of the private networks of creative production that, as chapter 1 illustrated, supported the business viability of London's couture houses. What has become clear is that within the creative network constructed by the Fashion Group a recognisable body of London couturiers was a key determinant in the validation of Britain's ability to create competitive products.

COLLABORATIVE FASHION SHOWS AND THE BRITISH COLOUR COUNCIL: 'THE POOLING OF PRIDE'

I cannot too strongly emphasise that the question of the American market is one of paramount importance. America is not only willing but also eager to buy from us, but they must be humoured and their whims must be indulged. . . . Let us lay ourselves out to capture the transatlantic customer and keep her. Practically the whole of the model houses could be kept by American trade. . . . A society for promoting the interests of British dress designers would be a splendid start.[61]

In 1928, the Mayfair dressmaker Madame Isobel in a BBC radio address contemplated how London could support both its creative fashion houses and those who aspired to a career in dress design. She concluded that any future development or success needed coordination and depended entirely on an ability to appeal to the American market. However, it was not until the middle of the next decade that the Fashion Group of Great Britain was to answer her call for a 'society' that would both support and give transatlantic endorsement to London's dressmakers. Whilst the majority of this Group's activity was obscured from public view, the most evident was its coordination (between January 1937 and the outbreak of WWII) of a twice-yearly showcase of London couture for foreign buyers. These exhibitions were effectively trade shows that required the creative made-to-measure dressmakers to present together and edit their collections to appeal primarily to the expectations of the American market. The fact that these were highly visible and well-documented publicity events explains why, within the historiography of British design, the Fashion Group of Great Britain has only been acknowledged as 'a promotional body for British fashion' whose primary aim 'was to develop sales in the United States'.[62]

The first action taken by the British Fashion Group to promote the interests of the Mayfair dress houses took the form of a cocktail party given just before the presentation of the January collections in 1936. To determine what action was needed to ensure optimum publicity for the London dressmakers, this event brought together the Fashion Group members 'concerned with the designing and selling of clothes and those members of the press whose business it was to report them'.[63] This call for the support and favourable promotion of the city's emergent couture industry was fortunate to coincide with the recently instigated political policy of positive propaganda discussed in chapter 1. However, it was this specific meeting that had an immediate effect on the positive reports given to both the designers' work and London's claim to fashion centre status. For instance, two weeks after the party British *Vogue* released the aforementioned article 'London Launches a Mode' and by February its editorial policy was altered to include reports of the London couture collections alongside those of Paris.

In many ways this recognition was also a response to the Fashion Group's proposed 'calendar of events' for January 1936. This was a coordinated schedule of 'private-view' showroom presentations that did not clash, by eleven Mayfair dressmakers, alongside milliners and fabric manufacturers, specifically for foreign buyers.[64] Up until this point, competition amongst the London dress houses, due to the limited number of clients and the ease of plagiarism, saw many choose to show at exactly the same time as their domestic rivals. The 'calendar of events' was suggested by the American Fashion Group and organised by Norman Hartnell, who convinced his competitors that, in order to increase publicity and export potential, coordinated presentations to the press and foreign buyers made perfect business sense. Hartnell may well have operated England's largest and most internationally recognised dress house, suggesting that he had little need to cooperate with his rivals; however, he was now only London-based, as he had ceased showing his collections in Paris the previous year, and so had a vested interest in encouraging cooperation amongst the London dress world. In July 1935 showing only in London he had found that his presence was not enough to draw American buyers away from Paris. London dressmakers needed to present a united front; as he pointed out to his competitors, 'the American public will never see or be aware of London fashion if the store buyers do not come, en mass, to London during their Parisian buying trips'.[65]

In Paris, the Chambre Syndicale ensured that foreign buyers' visits were smooth and uncomplicated, organising elements such as the show times, the preparation and dissemination of press releases and the models' shipping dates. This coordination, as a *Tobé Fashion Report* from 1940 illustrates, allowed Paris to give American manufacturers 'snob appeal for the least financial expenditure and effort' and American buyers went there because they received 'a great deal for their money. It was easy, it was organised, and it was fun'.[66] A ten-day trip to Paris for a buyer would cost approximately $1,000, according to this source, and in that time they would be able to see around 4,000 original models. This carefully coordinated and mutually beneficial system had ensured that the American fashion industry (until the economic depression of the 1930s) was happy to remain dependent on Paris for model design and inspiration.[67] London, in comparison, was small-scale and unorganised. To secure a much sought-after place on the American buyers' schedule and present a beneficial detour the city needed a couture industry that not only produced original fashion designs but was also clearly defined and ordered.

The American Fashion Group scheduled the London showroom presentations to precede those held in Paris in January. It also ensured that news of the 'calendar of events' was widely disseminated to its members and that London was included in the American buyers' itinerary and travel arrangements. British press reports may have claimed that the timing would allow London to 'have the first go at the dollars' and sell its clothes before its French counterpart, yet this was not really the case as few buyers would purchase London models until after they had seen everything Paris had to offer.[68] The proposed schedule for the English collections may have been governed by the travel itinerary of the American buyers but it also ensured that they allocated part of their budget for London models and did not spend it all in Paris. The timing was also symbolic, as up until this point, the London dressmakers had shown their small collections after Paris, which left them open to the accusation that they merely copied French dictates. The earlier schedule therefore acted as a sign of London's design confidence.

Unfortunately, the death of King George V within days of the scheduled private showings threw the first concerted effort to present London as

a coordinated fashion centre into chaos.[69] Full court mourning was instigated, which continued until July and half mourning until October; the
dressmakers were inundated by orders from their regular clients for appropriate clothing. Despite the arrival of a substantial number of foreign buyers, many of the London couturiers had to cancel their shows or withdraw
certain creations. For example, Hartnell received many orders from royalty
and his entire show was abandoned, whilst Stiebel went ahead with a private view for buyers as planned but as a sign of respect withdrew all court,
wedding and formal occasion dresses.[70]

Two months earlier at the British Fashion Group's first Dress Subcommittee meeting, when the editor of *Harper's Bazaar* had requested a
collaborative dress show, 'on the lines of the recent New York "Fashion
Futures" . . . showing the quintessence of the English idea of fashion', all
the dressmakers present had rejected the idea. The Secretary, Margaret
Havinden, even offered reassurance that this form of event would misrepre-
sent the aims of the British Fashion Group as it would 'lose sight of the fact'
that it was 'wider than one for dress fashions only'.[71] The death of the king,
however, left many dress houses with unsold models and out-of-pocket
expenses as it disrupted the presentation of London fashion to American
buyers. This meant that there was a need to demonstrate what the city had
to offer to ensure these industry representatives returned for the next season's collections. Four months later, as a direct consequence, ten London
dressmakers provided original models for the joint showcase onboard the
Queen Mary's maiden voyage. The first joint collection of London couture,
which contained many of the models created for the American buyers but
not displayed as a consequence of national mourning, was therefore initiated by a particular series of events and business decisions that swiftly took
the Fashion Group's couturiers from coordination to collaboration.

In January 1937, after the Queen Mary collection had eroded some of
the Dress Subcommittee's reservations towards group presentations, thirteen London couturiers agreed to produce a twice-yearly design showcase
exclusively for foreign buyers initially held at Claridge's hotel, with each
dress house restricted to the presentation of six models.[72] The decision to
present a joint show in one public venue, rather than coordinate the showings at the separate dress houses, was taken despite the geographic proximity of these businesses, which, except for two members, operated premises
in Mayfair — half of which were on Grosvenor Street. Industry and press

reports took the joint shows as a clear demonstration of the London couturiers' readiness to accommodate and indulge the American buyers: *Draper's Record*, for instance, reported the fashion industry's appreciation of this
'pooling of pride', whilst the *News Chronicle* pointed out that it had taken
'modest English creators of fashion some time to discover that faint hearts
never won fair American buyers'.[73] A collaborative showcase, despite such
support for the idea, was a very different proposition to coordinated time
slots at each dress house. Although reported as a prelude to the 'full collections for invited guests in the participants' own showrooms', dressmakers
such as Norman Hartnell, Edward Symonds at Reville and Peter Russell
did not participate.[74] In a collaborative collection it was difficult for designers to differentiate their models from those of their competitors, negating
their design autonomy and identity. A joint parade also exposed them to
plagiarism by their closest competitors, making many of the participants
withhold their most creative garments. *Women's Wear Daily*'s review of the
first showcase highlighted these problems, for although it congratulated
the London 'couturiers for their joint initiative' and for 'attracting the
majority of the American model buyers', it also criticised the design of
the clothes on display as 'patchy' and claimed that there were only 'one or
two originators worth watching'.[75]

Despite initial difficulties the collaborative shows were an informed business reaction to America's modern commercial culture, which demanded
speed and efficiency. Participation saw the elite dressmakers shift their practice to operate as designers for a foreign fashion industry rather than simply for individual clients. In so doing, they had to imagine not only the
needs of American consumers but more importantly the judgments and
discriminations of their buyers. Whilst in Paris these industry representatives, sent by manufacturers, department stores and dress houses, often had
to view thousands of models each season, only a small minority of these
were selected and only a fraction of those found popular acceptance in the
American market.[76] The edited joint collection in London was an attempt
to speed up this process and to a certain extent do the buyers' job for them.
The ideas of one innovative couturier were not enough to stimulate, guide
and authenticate a clear fashion trend; this evolved through the mechanism of collective selection, when fashion intermediaries, such as magazine editors and department store buyers, detected and promoted similar
ideas within the separate collections. London's collective couture showcase

therefore offered to condense this process, which the sociologist Herbert Blumer called 'the fashion mechanism'—the intense process of collective selection, where buyers made well-informed choices from the individual designer's competing styles in order to 'preordain as yet indistinct and inarticulate newer tastes'.[77]

Control of the 'fashion mechanism' was a central objective for the British Fashion Group, so that its country's creative practitioners, rather than foreign buyers, would act as the 'agents of the incipient tastes of a fashion consuming public' and through their choices 'set the fashion'.[78] To present a discernible directive to industry the Fashion Group needed the London couturiers not only to show their collections together but also to agree to coordinate their design output. This process was noted by *Draper's Record*'s review of the first London showcase, which recorded 'a higher degree of unanimity in line, colour and style than there has been for years', a factor it claimed would help the industry by 'simplifying the job of wholesaler, designer, and manufacturer'.[79]

This design synchronisation was the direct result of a link established with the British Colour Council (BCC), an independent, not-for-profit body, with no official government connection, created in 1930 and supported by the subscriptions of just over 800 members.[80] The Council's main purpose was to manage chromatic change, standardise and forecast the use of colour, remove confusion and variation from its nomenclature and replace with a degree of certainty the speculative element in colour decisions. A year before he joined the British Fashion Group, Robert Wilson (the general manager of the BCC) informed *Draper's Record* that while 'the power' to authenticate the seasonal 'fashion-first, prestige colours' still emanated from Paris it was his conviction that Britain's 'future fashion plan should begin with better class firms . . . [and] above all the present need is for dressmakers, brilliant people with ability to bring out the full beauties of colour and make it famous'.[81] For the BCC a creative, highly visible and coordinated London couture industry was an important element within the authentication of its work, and the Fashion Group's network of creative practitioners presented an opportunity that Wilson could not afford to ignore.

The Colour Council's main output was its *Dictionary of Colour Standards* which recorded, named, numbered and coded 220 colours. The *Dictionary* then informed *Colour Cards*, which sponsored a specific number of colours each season. These were created to guide designers, producers and retailers and were applicable not only to dress but also to a range of design industries such as ceramics, furnishings and even domestic appliances. Seasonal shade cards were not a new idea, as they had been produced in Paris and distributed abroad since the late nineteenth century.[82] However by the 1930s, particularly across the American market, colour management had reached a new level of control and regulation. For an unstable industry guided by seasonal demand, the dissemination of authoritative guidelines for future colour trends was a commercial imperative. It alleviated one of the main risks faced by manufacturers and distributors of fashion stock where 'fully one third of all price "markdowns" in the ready to wear and accessory lines was due to color alone'.[83] The American Fashion Group constantly promoted the idea that 'an ensembled color coordinated supply of merchandise in the market' was the most successful way to increase retailers' profits. With colour management an important component within the market coordination strategies of the American Fashion Group it was swiftly transposed into its British branch.

Historical accounts of the British Colour Council are unaccountably missing from the documentation of the British fashion industry. Yet it not only went on to play a fundamental role in the Fashion Group of Great Britain but also exerted considerable influence over a broad spectrum of the British textile and fashion industry. In March 1940, for example, Donald Barber (secretary of the powerful Retail Distribution Association) told Mass Observation that the British fashion industry was 'in dire need of organisation' and that in his opinion, the only body that had 'any real influence' was the Colour Council.[84] The recollections of Alan Saville, an employee in the interwar silk trade, also highlights the importance of the Council's guidelines in his claim that 'in those days the Paris fads and the dictates of the British Colour Council had to be followed'.[85] Much of this influence can be attributed to the beneficial service the BCC offered to the commercial market. For both producers and retailers, authoritative colour forecasts removed an element of speculation from the system of supply and demand and facilitated continuous and increased production and distribution, which in turn raised profit margins. From its inception, the Colour Council also received substantial support from the national and trade press, which provided a vital link between fashion industry producers and consumers.[86] The BCC's *Annual Report* produced in May 1936 attributed much of its success not only to this network but also to a change in design aesthetic, as it claimed the simplicity of modern design demanded an increased knowl-edge of the correct use of colour. The report also referred to the recent expansion, particularly in London, of specialist dyeing companies, which thereby improved the skills of English dyers and the implementation of the BCC's directives.[87]

The Colour Council's influence and success can therefore be attributed to the fact that its work enhanced the commercial objectives of industry and responded to changes in both design and production. It also linked the members of the Fashion Group to an industrial, political and social net-work with particular influence. For instance, through the social connec-tions of the Colour Council's patron Lord Derby (who was also patron of the Cotton Board and the future patron of the Incorporated Society), it was even able to use the royal family to 'inspire confidence' in its colour forecasts and 'discerning' taste.[88] In 1935, Derby persuaded the Duke and Duchess of Gloucester to support two official colours for their marriage ('Gloucester Green' and 'Kenya Red'). Whilst for the previous year's British Industries Fair, Queen Mary christened a colour 'Jubilee', the Duchess of York named one 'Margaret Rose' and the Duchess of Kent gave her name to 'Marina Green'.[89] The future Queen Elizabeth also accompanied Derby to a BIF parade of cotton dresses produced in these colours, which gener-ated an 'unprecedented level' of press and consumer interest.[90]

The *Spring Colour Card* released in January 1936 was the first range of colours the Council promoted after it joined the British Fashion Group. The eight 'Chinese colours' it contained offer a pertinent example of how this network operated in order to control the market and influence the direction of fashion consumption. These colours were derived from the subtle glazes of the ceramics on display in the Royal Academy of Art's *International Exhibition of Chinese Art* held in London in November 1935. The BCC therefore used informed speculation that this cultural event could be used to stimulate future aesthetic taste. Unfortunately, these colours were launched just as state mourning commenced; however, the Colour Coun-cil quickly activated a network of influence to bring stability to the mar-ket. To alleviate the impact the King's death had on this particular set of colour forecasts, Lord Derby secured a statement from the Palace that after a short official period of mourning the general public should wear 'subdued colours rather than black'.[91] Eleven days after the death, this decree was then released to and disseminated across the national press, which reassured the trade that their expensive outlay in stocks produced in 'the greyed hues of that season's Chinese Colours' would not be 'surplus to requirement'.[92]

The 'Chinese colours', released four months after the Fashion Group's inaugural lunch, offer a clear example of the Group's activity to authenticate and direct production, promotion and consumption. This is particularly apparent in British *Vogue*, which throughout 1936 consistently promoted these colours. This was initiated in February when it informed its British readers that 'the greyed half-tones of the new Chinese colourings might have been specially evolved for this moment, so much in keeping are they with the subdued spirit of the times'.[93] One of its main articles in this edition, 'Chinese Fashion Moves', also featured miniature dolls produced by members of the Fashion Group that were carved by the artist Angus McBean and clothed by the Motley Couture House in fabrics of greyed blue, green and lavender shades from Harrods and Courtaulds. In the same month, the magazine's first House and Garden supplement extended these colours to designs for the interior (produced yet again by Fashion Group members) and pointed out that 'the Chinese exhibition at Burlington House already shows signs of influencing the new trend in decoration'. This continued in March when 'a square shouldered wool suit in the cool, greyed celadon green of Chinese pottery' by the wholesale model house Ferndern Sports moved the authentication of these colours onto the magazine's influential front cover. Even five months later, these colours were still apparent in the August cover's use of a 'crepe dress of the blue of Chinese porcelain'. This cover also promoted Elizabeth Arden's 'newly arrived Chinese makeup', thereby demonstrating the transference of these colour forecasts into the field of cosmetics by an international member of the Fashion Group. A full year after these colours were released, the evening wear Stiebel and Motley produced for the finale of the first Fashion Group joint show were also both produced in 'celadon' green.

The next joint dress show in July 1937 was accompanied by the release of *The Colour Chart of the Fashion Group of Great Britain in Cooperation of the British Colour Council* and a display of fabrics by the Dress Fabrics Sub-Committee that were 'dyed to the eight sponsored fashion colours'.[94] The designated colour palette of green and browns, overlaid with plums and blues and in many cases bright flecks and strips of purples and pinks were incorporated across the couturiers' separate collections and also left the industry 'in no doubt that plaids are in for a great burst of popularity'.[95] The most noted

Figure 2.2
Victor Stiebel, colour matched ensemble with tweed woven in cyclamen and violet checks over green base, July 1937. *Source:* Reproduced courtesy of Adrian Woodhouse.

aspect of these shows were the rich colour combinations, particularly the tweed daywear, which was woven in colourful flecks or checks (figure 2.2). American newspaper reports used the couturier's adoption of a brighter colour palette to promote a new sensibility in London dress design. The *New York Times* described the suits as 'a welcome change from the Oxford grays, the tans and dull browns one used to expect the well-tailored English woman to wear . . . now the tweeds are overlaid with rainbow checks'.[96] The Colour Council produced this bright and vivid palette specifically to appeal to the American market where they were 'taken up with enthusiasm'.[97] In the realm of British class distinction, bright colours were often considered vulgar and the social elite traditionally demonstrated their taste through a preference for subtlety, what the American Fashion Group *Bulletin* criticized as 'the gray scotch heather type of thing'.[98] The clothes produced for the joint showcase, however, were destined for consumption not by the London dressmaker's British clients but by foreign buyers. The bolder use of colour was an illustration of not only the dressmakers' but also the Colour Council's compliance with the needs and dictate of the American mass market, where the noted preference for 'punch' (the use of bright colours and strong contrasts) was a prevalent taste.[99]

In July 1937, the adoption of bold colours was also discernible in many of the concurrent Parisian collections of Molyneux, Chanel, Maggy Rouff, Creed, Lelong and Lanvin.[100] Schiaparelli (a key international member of the Fashion Group who attended meetings in London, Paris and New York) produced the most famous example of that season's colour dictates with many models in 'Shocking Pink'. When these collections are considered alongside the 'rainbow' colours of the London dressmakers a preordained fashion trend coordinated across national boundaries by the separate branches of the Fashion Group is made apparent. The use of vivid colour in both London and Paris was neither indicative of an inexplicable convergence of fashion designers' ideas nor a coincidental example of a dress artist's ability to capture the essence of the zeitgeist. Instead, it represents a level of fashion coordination that can ultimately be traced back to the needs of the American consumer market. The focus on the use of colour offers a clear example of how in the 1930s the Fashion Group of Great Britain established a network of official tastemakers that began to guide production, promotion and consumption not just at the mass level but also at the elite level of the fashion market. The couturier's participation in the joint showcase saw their designs become part of a broader system of fashion production, which in turn increased their industrial relevance. In so doing, London gained credibility as a destination for not only original but more importantly coordinated fashion design.

DESIGN SYNCHRONISATION AND A NARRATIVE FOR ENGLISH COUTURE: 'THE SPORTING NATION'

Like America, England is developing fashions of her own. Long famous for wonderful tailoring and a way with rugged sports clothes, London is now invading the French field of more feminine dressmaking creating many models of cosmopolitan smartness. [In the Queen Mary showcase] there was great emphasis on the tailored type of evening costume . . . which would indicate that London is bidding for some of the American dress business. For it has long been noted that the tailored evening costume—popular in Paris and even more popular in this country—has very little acceptance in London. Englishwomen like dressier, fussier clothes. It is to be assumed, then, that such frocks as those illustrated here were designed solely for American admiration and American dollars.[101]

When the first collaborative collection of London couture arrived in New York onboard the *Queen Mary* many newspaper reports were quick to congratulate their adherence to the taste of the American consumer. To promote London as a fully-fledged fashion centre that both understood and could cater to the needs of the American market, this collection included a range of garments from 'hard' sportswear to 'soft' evening wear. Press reports, which claimed that the models were designed specifically for the current taste of the North American market, suggest that intermediaries within the Fashion Group had guided their design. For example, the tailored evening dress, which the *Baltimore Sun* highlighted as the most obvious concession to American taste, was particularly prevalent in Stiebel's contribution. One of the most publicised of the showcase's outfits was his simply cut, black silk dinner dress, with a multicolour striped satin jacket, fitted to the waist with leg-of-mutton sleeves and large belt tied in a bow. The simplicity of the dress coupled with a distinctive jacket gave it an element of fashionable adaptability as it could be worn together or separated and mixed with other clothes from the consumer's own wardrobe. This type of outfit was 'much admired by an American audience who were versed at placing individuality, through adaptation of models in their dress sense'.[102] In terms of daywear, the outfit that was given the most exposure was 'Before October', a two-tone mohair tweed suit by Hardy Amies at Lachasse. The novel cut of this suit is an indication that it was also designed as a deliberate appeal to the American buyer, particularly its large suede belt that was worked into the construction of the jacket. This design feature offered a distinctive model for reproduction and, as the waistline could be pulled in for a better fit, assisted the sizing of ready-made models.[103] Both Stiebel's evening wear and Amies' suit exemplify the English couturiers' attempt to design specifically for the needs of the American market.[104]

However, to support London's claim to fashion centre status the city's dress designers also needed to imbue their work with a specific national identity. This is made evident in the reports on the London designer Edward Symonds' designs, which were all for debutante dress and promoted as inherently English. As president of the British Fashion and Fabrics Bureau and former vice president of the British Colour Council, Symonds was a prolific promoter and supporter of the collaborative links between innovative fashion designers and fabric manufacturers. At the House of Reville he operated as a specialist dealer in original and exclusive designs for both dress models and fabrics, and his belief that if London led 'in fashion' it could then 'lead in fabric' was often reported.[105] When invited, as organiser of the Queen Mary showcase, to give a talk to the New York Fashion Group's board and officers, he therefore made it clear that the uniqueness of British dress came specifically from its use of British fabric. He made particular reference to the fact that all his gowns were created in British velvet in 'traditional coronation colours' that took skilled workers 'a week to weave a yard'. This promotional narrative saw Symonds astutely align his work with both British pageantry and craftsmanship.[106] In consequence, he emphasized the idiosyncratic nature of London dressmaking and used the forthcoming coronation to give a national inflection to this promotion of British fashion and textiles.

Whilst the death of the King George V may have disrupted the Fashion Group's coordinated showings in January 1936, the consequential coronation of George VI in May 1937 (after the intervening abdication crisis) offered an inimitable opportunity to promote London as a Fashion Centre.[107] In January 1937, as the Fashion Group held its first collaborative dress show, the *Daily Sketch*, in an article entitled 'London Steals a March on Paris', assured its British readers that because of this royal event the London 'dressmakers would be introduced not only to the smart well-dressed leaders of society and fashion in America and the Continent but also to hundreds who have never seen us or our Island before'.[108] New travel and communication technology and the heightened public interest caused by the infamous abdication of Edward VII certainly made this coronation the most viewed and followed royal event to date. Furthermore, for the Mayfair dressmakers, the Earl Marshal's decree that for the first time court dress rather than the traditional kirtle could be worn under the female guests' coronation robes ensured that this event was highly visible and also offered

Figure 2.3
Coronation of George VI, Royal Group, with ladies in court dress, London, 12 May 1937. *Source:* © National Portrait Gallery, London.

a platform for the demonstration of original fashion design[109] (figure 2.3). For its fashion pages, American newspapers took full advantage of the opportunity this created to turn the coronation into a source of glamorous spectacle. The *New York Times* included illustrations that depicted the peeresses as fashion mannequins more applicable to the cinema screen or the pages of *Vogue* than the aisles of Westminster Abbey.

The programme the Fashion Group produced for its first London-based dress show illustrates that this promotion took full advantage of the forthcoming coronation. Drawn in gold on a black background, its front cover had a crown in the top left corner and a sketch of a fashionable modern woman in a backless gown overlaid on a drawing of a peeress in traditional mantle and bonnet (figure 2.4). Inside, the description of the models demonstrates that the collection was dominated by afternoon, cocktail and

Figure 2.4
The programme for the first Fashion Group of Great Britain Dress Show for foreign
buyers, January 1937. *Source:* Reproduced courtesy of Adrian Woodhouse.

evening dress. *Women's Wear Daily* reported that the buyers who attended
this show were most interested in the 'clothes for grand occasions and coronation ceremonies' and appreciated 'anything with a coronation tie–in . . .
[particularly] evening gowns prepared for peeresses to wear under their
robes and wedding gowns for coronation season brides'.[110] This saw the
London couturiers' bridal wear quickly replace its Parisian counterparts in
many American publications. The coronation therefore not only brought
the London couturiers intense public interest and recognition but also provided the opportunity to demonstrate the diversity of their design capabil-
ity and show that as a fashion centre London could provide garments that
ranged from the practical to the spectacular.

Despite this recognition of London as a source of innovative and glamorous fashion, the Fashion Group's second joint show (a month after the coronation) saw the industry's important trade papers quickly reject London's presentation of 'soft' dressmaking. Although there were reports of good sales, *Women's Wear Daily* now claimed critics had questioned 'why London had to show dresses of this type, however lovely, when Americans only wanted to look at tweeds'.[111] *Draper's Record* also declared that the buyers came to Britain 'for things they can't get in New York or Paris, sportswear in tweed or leather, and a few dinner dresses and negligees . . . America expects from Britain garments, which are smart, exquisitely tailored, but have none of the eye-catching qualities of Parisian clothes'.[112] The coronation may have presented the Fashion Group with the opportunity to demonstrate that London could compete with Paris and produce extravagant, glamorous clothes applicable to the American market. However, the comments of industry trade journals offer clear indication that within the constructed idea of international fashion production there was an expectation that the London couturiers adhere to a specific design narrative. In particular it was the assumption of the American fashion industry that London should be promoted as the centre of elegant sportswear and most specifically the town and country suit.

Many of the press reports of the Fashion Group's July 1937 dress show correspond with the opinion of the industry's main trade journals and ignored the evening wear of designers such as Tinling and Motley and primarily focused on the daywear of Morton, Russell and Amies. This was invariably based on 'perfectly tailored', four-piece ensembles with colour-matched crepe blouse and tweed jacket, skirt and topcoat.[113] Press reports indicate a certain level of uniformity within these models; for example, the suits were all described as slim lined, with skirts cut to give freedom of movement, and fitted with single-breasted jackets with unexaggerated shoulders that finished at the hipbone. In spite of this, *Women's Wear Daily* declared that they were 'saved from monotony' by 'nice individual details'.[114] For instance, Motley was noted for its use of aspects from Highland costumes; Peter Russell for a distinctive flap treatment for his slim-fitting skirts; and Digby Morton for his combination of metal with tweed. It was therefore restrained design features rather than spectacular styling that caught the eye of fashion commentators. However, a number of the designers then used topcoats to incorporate an element of novelty. These counteracted the subtlety of the suits and appear to have been produced to generate as much interest as possible and attract the attention of the buyers and fashion press. Peter Russell, for example, presented an unusual flared coat, inspired by London's hansom cab drivers' jackets, which he christened 'The Cabby', while Hardy Amies at Lachasse had 'The Bulky', an exaggerated tweed coat, which hung straight and boxlike to the hip, with broad shoulders that spanned twenty inches across.

By July 1937, with the coronation over, it was both colour coordination and the prevalence of four-piece tailored outfits with conservative cut, subtle details and flamboyant coats which allowed a clear design theme to emerge in the London Fashion Group showings. In terms of colour, the designers not only presented brighter palettes, but ensured that aspects such as the blouses, jacket linings, saddle stitching on the seams, leather edges on pockets and belts were often colour matched to a prominent thread in the weave of each suit's fabric.[115] These multiple garments adhered to the concept of ensemble dressing based on colour harmony. This was a style of dress first articulated by Parisian couturiers, but turned into a mass-market merchandising concept by the American fashion industry.[116] So much so, that in the US by the 1930s, the ensemble wardrobe was 'a practical necessity for intelligent customer service and was generally adopted by all well-merchandised stores throughout the country'.[117] The Fashion Group's focus on colour-matched separates is therefore a clear indication that the Mayfair dressmakers' design process was guided by an informed awareness of the expectations and needs of the American market. The Fashion Group may have wanted to demonstrate that London could lead and control the direction of fashion; however, in order to construct a specific market position it needed a clear collaborative narrative. This came in the form of the colour-matched tailored ensemble.

By January 1938, the collaborative Fashion Group dress show was therefore predominated by suits, some in the sports category but the majority 'tweeds-for-town'. The typical presentation of this London show can be seen in Madge Garland's report on it for *Vogue*. As the new chairman of the British Fashion Group she presented a carefully selected narrative of London design, which disregarded everything except the couturiers' 'streamlined' suits. Through the medium of line drawing, the illustrations that accompanied this 'Preview', in its focus on structured jackets, plainness, stripes or checks and tailored panels accentuated the idea of simplicity, and thereby reinforced the narrative of restrained and elegant uniformity. Yet in these 'advance notes on the designer's main spring trends', Garland protected the couturiers' creative autonomy through her claim that 'the handling, the detail, the fine subtleties, are of course, as diverse and individual as the personalities of the designers themselves'.[118] In this careful balance of both conformity and individuality, reports such as Garland's are indicative of both the Fashion Group's selection process and their aim to produce mass 'fashion'.[119] This is a design form that values both standardisation and novelty, a paradox that allows consumers both to conform to the dress codes of their social group and to demonstrate individuality through what Gilles Lipovetsky describes as the key characteristic of fashion stock: 'marginal differentiation'.[120] Many scholars have pointed to this contradiction inherent within the complex codes of taste constructed around consumer goods within the capitalist system.[121] For example, the premise at the basis of Leora Auslander's consideration of taste professionals, who acted as intermediaries between consumers and distributors of goods, is that 'judgments of aesthetic value emerge from a complex interaction of desires for emulation, distinction and solidarity'.[122] In particular, Auslander notes the irony that in capitalist culture, which values and promotes individualism, taste is expected to comply with clear codes.[123] This idea was also fundamental to the sociologist Georg Simmel's influential thesis that argues that the key characteristic of fashion in mass society is this perpetual tension between conformity and individuality.[124] To ensure that the London dressmakers could act as tastemakers for the American market, the key driver behind the chosen models was a careful negotiation of this tension, a balance between design synchronisation (in the form of the town and country suit) and originality (in the subtle detailing).

The Fashion Group's shows used collaboration not to demonstrate the range of design available but to monitor design heterogeneity. The power this coordinated narrative held over the British couture industry is made evident by *Vogue*'s attitude towards Norman Hartnell, who never participated in the joint shows and focused on soft dressmaking rather than hard tailored couture. In 1937, when the Fashion Group's impulse towards collaboration and design synchronisation was at its height the magazine issued a rare and scathing review of his collection. Whilst it commended his competitors in the Fashion Group, it claimed his 'collection is something of a repetition. Hartnell continues his variations—on his own theme . . .

colours are in sharp and rather obvious contrasts . . . [and it included] many uninspired models'.[125] With the fashion industry intent on the pursuit of unifying trends, Hartnell may have been too big a name for British *Vogue* to ignore, yet his creative authority could be questioned. It is also telling that throughout 1939, when Hartnell's 'White Collection' for the Queen instigated a fashion for a 'Victorian' aesthetic, *Vogue* made no reference to his creative lead, and every mention of corsets, bustles and white lace as key trends in soft dressmaking were linked to French couturiers.

For a limited time, the coronation may have offered a unique opportunity for the promotion and sale of a broad range of English fashions, particularly its more creative cocktail, dinner and evening dress. After this event, however, to create 'a powerful magnet for overseas buyers', London couture was condensed into two main categories: 'matchless spectator sports suits and traditional tea gowns'.[126] This saw the Fashion Group present London as a complementary rather than autonomous fashion centre, part of a tripartite system of fashion with Paris and New York. Within this system of representation, national identity played a key role and provided each fashion centre with a specific design narrative. This can be seen in the shift in Victor Stiebel's promotional rhetoric when, in 1937, he visited America as a representative of the British branch of the Fashion Group. To promote the July showcase he set out a clear division between English and French couture and contradicted his previous statements, made three years earlier, about the internationalism of fashion design (see chapter 1). He now claimed that 'the male point of view is all-important in England . . . and the English consequently excel in classic tailor-mades, in tweeds and country clothes. In Paris, on the other hand, it is the feminine viewpoint, which matters'.[127] This gendered discourse constructed an imagined community of fashion with London the expert producers of 'hard' tailored sportswear in comparison to Paris' supremacy in 'soft' dressmaking.[128] This categorisation, in its appeal to the American market, was particularly astute. By the 1930s, as the fashion historian Rebecca Arnold has shown, sportswear was identified by the wider fashion industry as 'America's most distinctive form of dress', and London, the home of Savile Row, held a reputation as an authority in male tailoring.[129] Since the 1880s this had been appropriated into women's clothing, so that by the 1930s, the city's distinct 'power' in the production of female sportswear, in the form of the town and country suit, was 'well entrenched' in both Europe and America.

'If there is one thing that Paris designers allow to British designers it is the lead in sportswear and tweeds', intoned a journalist for the primarily male readership of *Referee Magazine* in 1936; 'this they say is because "we're a sporting nation" and now the strong movement towards tweedier styles in everyday dress (did anyone wear tweeds to town ten years ago?) is giving a big following to British fashion'.[130] The reference to the 'sporting nation' was consistently reiterated in press reports of the London couturiers. This narrative drew on a prevalent component of British interwar cultural propaganda, which presented the country not as imperialistic and aggressive but as competitive and fair. In addition, the idea of the 'sporting nation' was closely tied to the notional relationship between 'Englishness' and the countryside. In the projection of England, this constructed an 'anti-urban bias', whereby the country rather than the city was its representational essence.[131] During the 1930s, the conception of a sporting, rural nation was appropriated by many of Britain's design industries particularly for international exhibitions.[132] For example, sporting goods and the English countryside provided the main focus for the British pavilion at the Paris International Exposition of Art and Technology in Modern Life held between May and November 1937. This representation of England was one of 'fishing, tennis and weekend cottages . . . [which] took visitors far from Parisian urbanity into a country of sheep and cathedrals'.[133] The whimsy of the pavilion caused Kingsley Martin (the editor of the *New Statesman*) to famously claim that it was the depiction of 'a nice England, unlike any that had existed or could exist; England as seen by guests in a country house party where the servants were unobtrusively in the background, where all nature smiled and every luxury appeared as if by magic'.[134] When the Fashion Group was given responsibility for the British dress display at this exhibition the London dressmakers' field of design was separated into two 'typically English scenes': racing and the country house. This adhered to the Council for Art and Industry's stipulation to the Fashion Group contributors to 'concentrate on those things at which we know we are good—don't try to beat Paris at her own specialties, . . . [focus on clothes] for country life, sports, children, weekending and of course men'.[135] The Fashion Group's selection process for both the Paris exhibition and the couture showcase created a clear identity for London fashion. This narrative therefore drew on three key elements: not only the country's acknowledged pre-eminence in tailoring and its recognition as a 'sporting nation' but most importantly the lifestyle of its landed gentry.

The traditional dress culture of the aristocratic Englishwoman, who moved between her country estate and the London Season, ensured that particularly in America, British sportswear was seen through a 'prism of class, taste and status'.[136] However, this promotional narrative had to overcome a prominent cultural stereotype: that the archetypal Englishwoman dressed for comfort rather than luxury, and had no time for fashion. 'When compared to the Frenchwoman's innate dress sense', as one American journalist put it in 1932, it was necessary 'to teach the Englishwoman how to dress so as not to resemble a rare old piece of early Woolworth'.[137] In the same year, a British *Vogue* article, 'As They Wear It', provided a demonstration of the perceived difference in the dress culture of the French and English elites at the start of the decade. The article suggested its readers 'cast an eye' on the French Comtesse's Lanvin and Vionnet outfits, then 'take in Lady Wimborne's suit, with the neat and quite gaudy checks . . . the Countess of Oxford and Asquith, clad in her own style and superbly oblivious to revolutions in fashions'.[138] The images of the tailored daywear of the French comtesses in an urban setting were contrasted with their British counterparts photographed in the mud of the sporting and agricultural countryside. It made clear that the French, with their plain fabrics, tailored fitted waists, fur trims and high heels, had their couturiers for guidance, whilst 'the Britishers', with their practical footwear and androgynous poses, drew on the styles of the previous decade and were depicted as devoid of fashion sense.

The commercial drive to embrace the sportswear of the aristocratic country tradition could well have produced an aesthetic that was antimodern, and against the notion of fashion. However, as Edwina Ehrman has pointed out, under the direction of London couturiers, tailoring 'became more sensitive to fashion change'.[139] Digby Morton was central to this altered perspective. When he set up his eponymous business in 1933, an American syndicated press report announced that 'the old-plodding, tweed-matching, square-toed, sensible shoes image is being swept aside by the fashions of newer English Designers, rapidly making themselves felt as world leaders who are motivating fashion to think tailored instead of mannish'.[140] Morton's customers belonged mostly to the 'gay rich racing set', who wore his suits all day. His couture collections, which contained no dressmaking, were an innovation for London as they were restricted to town and country sportswear predominately in tweed, 'so fashionable that they could be worn with confidence at the Ritz'.[141] Morton's style of urban, sophisticated town and country wear is illustrated in his early adverts which demonstrated his tailoring was soft rather than masculine, given distinction by its fabric and the intricate construction of details such as a rosette or pleated front panel, with topcoats with their lapels matched to the suit or edged with fur. His mannequins were often presented as leisured inhabitants of the city, a daily walk in the park their sporting activity.

In order to construct an appropriate role model for contemporary fashion, as London couturiers began to specialise in these 'dressier tweeds', fashion magazines and newspaper columns began to alter the depiction of the Englishwoman's dress sense. Fashion illustrators in particular began to replace previous depictions of the English woman's penchant for shapeless hats and rugged tweeds with depictions of jaunty millinery and elegant town and country suits by designers such as Morton. The country tweeds of the landed gentry, originally intended for hunting and shooting parties, presented a plausible integrity and made English tweeds-for-town emblematic of a modern active lifestyle. By the time they became the mainstay of the Fashion Group's collaborative collection, the London couturiers' tweed suits may have drawn on the traditions of the landed gentry, which imbued them with connotations of taste and class, but they had replaced traditional rugged sportswear with softly tailored fashionable garments. Consequently, the promotional narrative that fashion magazines and the Fashion Group constructed around London sportswear supports the sociologist Herbert Blumer's contention that fashion did not 'stem from the prestige of the elite, rather it transcended and embraced this prestige'.[142]

★ ★ ★

In 1940, the American actress Mildred Shay commissioned an outfit from Hardy Amies and requested a garment that would be unmistakably British. The tweeds-for-town suit she received, which comprised a perfectly tailored single-breasted jacket with a straight, kick-pleated skirt, fulfilled this specification. The shape and cut of the suit conformed to the expectations of English tailoring, while the jacket lapel provided its novelty. Rather than

Figure 2.5a
The actress Mildred Shay in suit designed by Hardy Amies in 1940 alongside fellow
actors John Garfield, Geoffrey Steele and Geraldine Fitzgerald in the Hollywood
Canteen, July 1944. *Source:* Reproduced courtesy of Austin Mutti-Mewse.

discarding the selvage edge of the Linton tweed cloth, Amies had retained
it as a design feature (figures 2.5a and b). By including the selvage in the
lapel, the fact that the garment was 'made in England' was made explicit.[143]
Whilst Shay wore this suit in support of her English husband's country at
a time of conflict, its confident design represented the authority London
had gained as a transatlantic destination for the consumption of tailored
sportswear. This chapter has shown that from the mid-1930s the network
of fashion intermediaries and the abbreviated narrative of couture production cultivated by the Fashion Group of Great Britain had played a major
role within this confidence and ensured that London as a fashion centre
was defined as the international destination for tailored couture. For the
London dressmakers, this design consensus created unity but was also a
recurrent point of tension. By July 1938, press reports indicate a level of
uncertainty towards the boundaries being constructed around English couture, by designers such as Champcommunal, Hartnell, Russell and Motley,

Figure 2.5b
Detail of Mildred Shay's Amies suit. *Source:* Reproduced courtesy of Austin
Mutti-Mewse.

who were recorded as anxious to emphasise that their skill did not 'begin
and end' with the production of tweed suits.[144] This saw these designers
begin to distance themselves from the Fashion Group and refuse to participate in its collaborative showcase.

From 1936 until the outbreak of war, membership of the British branch
of the Fashion Group saw the London couturiers become part of a transatlantic network that validated their professional position and offers another
clear explanation for why, in London's recognition as a fashion centre, 1936
was the tipping point. Yet, as this consideration of the Fashion Group's
objectives and activity has demonstrated, whilst it created a supportive
network and promotional platform for the London couture industry, it
ultimately used this collaboration to construct a unified design narrative
that addressed the needs of the American market and thereby manipulated
the nature of the elite dressmakers' design process. The philosophy behind
the Fashion Group of Great Britain opened up a different way of viewing
the elite dressing of a select consumer group as it positioned fashion and

styling and in particular the London couturier as key to a national strategy for design. Yet, as Jonathan Woodham has pointed out in relation to the increased interest in the designer and design reform, design historians have often been misled by the amount of activity in the interwar period into a belief that there was a true sea change of attitude towards the designer in industry. In this context, whilst the Fashion Group may have positioned the couturiers as the key agents of change and innovation for the industrial marketplace, it was not really their creative design autonomy, but rather their compliance in the authentication of mass fashion that was invaluable. Original designers were needed to prove London a creative fashion centre; yet, ironically, the fashion industry needed to control uniqueness and individuality and designer collaboration and coordination were the most important elements in this process.

The couturiers' growing awareness and antipathy towards this manipulation of their practice was made apparent in July 1938, when they all refused to participate in any more of the Fashion Group's collaborative dress shows. Instead, the Group held a more exclusive 'party', at the Mirabel restaurant on Curzon Street, for which only ten houses (Busvine, Lachasse, Leathercraft, Digby Morton, Lydia Moss, Guy Olliver, Rahvis, Victor Stiebel, Rose Taylor and Teddy Tinling) provided one mannequin each to mingle amongst the guests dressed in evening wear from their latest collections, whilst the couturiers gave out invitations to their individual shows to suitable professionals. The rejection of the collaborative showcase was also a direct response to the Fashion Group's inclusion of Associate Membership for British wholesale and retail houses. Margaret Havinden may have proclaimed that this extension of the membership would now help to 'filter the success of English couturiers to a broad range of British manufacture'.[145] However, this was a step too far for many of the creative dressmakers and their withdrawal from the joint showcase was a rejection of the Group's design reform agenda. The ethos expressed in the Fashion Group's overriding aims had always had more in common with the commercial development of the mass market than its couturier-members would have been happy to admit. Participation in the collaborative export shows for foreign buyers and compliance with the needs of the distant American market had been a profitable form of marketing. However, the Fashion Group's aspiration, to use the creativity and prestige of the emergent couturiers for the benefit of the wider British fashion industry, contradicted the dressmakers' subjective reasons for joining the Group. In Britain, these practitioners had rejected the lucrative mass market in order to establish businesses that were based on hand rather than industrial production, on creative rather than purely commercial objectives. This privileged a form of non-economic capital based on creativity, exclusivity, social value and ultimately reputation. This cultural capital was hard fought for and needed careful protection. The acceptance of Associate Members, however, presupposed that the couturiers would share their designs, without remuneration, for reproduction by domestic mass-market providers. This was a development that would have undermined their creative autonomy, interfered with their fragile reputations and ultimately their future economic gain.

In 1938, the couturiers may have rejected the idea of collaboration, particularly as a way to raise the standards of design in the broader British fashion industry, and yet, during the Second World War, a number of them not only set up the Incorporated Society of London Fashion Designers but also played a major role within the government's Utility Scheme through the provision of design prototypes for the British fashion industry. Even though the London couturiers had collaborated within the Fashion Group of Great Britain in the 1930s, it can be argued that without the war further designer collectivism would never have happened. This is perhaps supported by the fact that the Incorporated Society was not created until over two years into the conflict. The next chapter is therefore concerned with an exploration of how the Society finally came together and how for the couturiers collaboration became more than merely a promotional activity. It will also show how the war allowed the aspirations of the Fashion Group to continue when they may otherwise have been rejected.

3

'BRISK ACTION ON THE MAYFAIR FRONT': THE WAR YEARS AND THE CREATION OF THE INCORPORATED SOCIETY OF LONDON FASHION DESIGNERS

The cover of the March 1941 edition of *Harper's Bazaar* featured a zoomorphic white RAF warplane that merged into a dove of peace (figure 3.1). In place of an olive branch, the dove carried two ribbons emblazoned with the names of Molyneux, Hartnell, Paquin, Victor Stiebel, Creed, Worth, Digby Morton, Lachasse and Peter Russell. This issue was dedicated to the fashion and fabric exhibition that was touring South America as part of the 'Britain Delivers the Goods' export campaign to this lucrative foreign market. The collection brought together the British textile industry and nine London-based couturiers to create the first fashion exhibition ever financed directly by the British government. With Britain at war, the auspicious symbolism of this patriotic cover suggests that the war had altered the national, economic and political significance of the London couturiers.

In 1942, the designers who participated in this exhibition went on to create the Incorporated Society of London Fashion Designers with its wartime aims to protect the London couture houses and ensure that the prestige of all levels of the British fashion and textile industry was maintained. The examination of the Fashion Group of Great Britain in the 1930s has shown the importance of collaboration within a vibrant commercial market. This chapter now moves to consider how the role of designer collaboration altered in response to a wartime economy when fashion became a seemingly irrelevant luxury. By 1938, the creative dressmakers may have begun to reject the objectives of the Fashion Group of Great Britain, yet war acted as the catalyst for the creation of an official couture trade association. What follows is an examination of the exact sequence of events that led to the creation of the Incorporated Society. This questions to what extent collaboration enabled the London couturiers to solidify their position, increase their national standing and sustain their businesses throughout the unstable period of total war. Couture represented an elite, class-based practice of clothing production; its maintenance at a time when luxury was condemned

Figure 3.1
Front cover, British *Harper's Bazaar*, March 1941. *Source:* Harper's Bazaar.

and production restricted to the needs of the war effort offers an interesting example of how the specific processes and narratives of design practice can change in relation to particular social and political agendas. An overriding concern is how these small-scale luxury goods businesses, throughout this period of egalitarianism and restraint, were maintained and how the Incorporated Society was formed in relation to its wartime context.

Within the historiography of London couture there is an understanding that 'during the war the government backed the [Incorporated] Society from the outset, recognising its export potential and the organisational advantage of working with a single group'.[1] To a certain extent this assertion may be true; however, as empirical analysis will show, governmental backing was not as immediate or sustained as this interpretation would suggest. For the first year of the war, English couture production was recognised only as a private and self-serving enterprise and the British government saw little reason to support its continuation. At the beginning of 1940, despite an appeal to the Department of Overseas Trade for funding, the British branch of the Fashion Group came to an abrupt end. Margaret Havinden, the Group's chairman, claimed that the British authorities perceived no apparent wartime role for either the Group or the couturiers and that with the onset of war, the government's only suggestion for the Fashion Group was that it should become a charitable 'offshoot of the British Council'.[2] This insinuated that the couturiers' only contribution to the war effort might be in terms of cultural propaganda rather than any intrinsic value to industry.

This dismissive attitude towards the designers began to change in the second half of 1940. June of that year saw France fall and, with the Nazi occupation of Paris, the international fashion industry severed from its principal creative source. By September, British *Vogue* announced that with Paris in 'eclipse' it was now 'London's opportunity to shine' and that it had 'a chance of taking the lion's share of the World's fashion trade'.[3] Whilst such a claim can be seen as jingoistic optimism, the Board of Trade's support for the 1941 South American showcase saw the idea of London as a fashion centre swiftly move from the editorials of fashion magazines into official government discourse. Despite both the unprecedented opportunity created by the removal of French competition and political support for export promotion, the London couturiers did not immediately band together to form the Incorporated Society. The continuation of rivalry and hesitance towards designer collaboration are made clear in a letter, from 1941, recounted in the autobiography of Edna Woolman Chase (the editor of American *Vogue*):

> On the heels of the [South American] exhibition came a wail from our harassed Harry [Yoxall, the business manager of British *Vogue*]: "I am trying to assist as a kind of mid-husband at the birth of an Incorporated Society of British Dress Designers but it is a pretty hard delivery, as all the limbs, so to speak, are kicking in different directions. But I feel that the couture boys and girls here will never get anywhere unless they form some kind of professional association and maintain as a permanent policy the temporary unity which was rather precariously achieved for the South American Collection. . . . I gave a cocktail party. . . . You know enough of the jealousy of the London fashion trade to realise what it means when I say that Hartnell, Stiebel, Digby Morton and Miss Campbell of Lachasse were fraternizing like buddies round the bar".[4]

The move towards wartime collaboration was therefore neither spontaneous nor smooth; however, a cohesive designer network became imperative to navigate the government's policies brought in to mobilise resources for the war effort.

Although the Incorporated Society drew on designers from within the Fashion Group, it included only six of its seventeen dress committee members. These were Stiebel, Russell, Morton and Amies, who had all participated in the collaborative showings to foreign buyers, and Hartnell and Champcommunal of Worth, who had not. The transfer of the British designers Edward Molyneux and Charles Creed from Paris, and the Italian Bianca Mosca, former designer at Schiaparelli (Paris) and Paquin (London), then increased the Society's number to nine. These were not the only couturiers who continued production throughout the war; Rahvis and Strassner, for example, also remained open but were not brought into this self-defined group. No documentation of the process of deciding membership for the Incorporated Society survives, so it is difficult to address how this network was formed or how those not involved felt about its inception. Yet the connections established by the Fashion Group in the 1930s clearly underpinned the collective process. Therefore, after a consideration of the couturiers' initial reaction to the war, this chapter focuses on specific examples of wartime collaboration and its formalisation within the Incorporated Society. This maps the transition of the design reform objectives of the Fashion Group in the 1930s into wartime to highlight aspects of continuation, consolidation and transformation within designer collaboration.

'FASHION MARCHES ON': THE ADAPTATION OF COUTURE PRODUCTION TO THE CONDITIONS OF WAR

To understand why the couturiers did not immediately group themselves into the Incorporated Society at the start of the war it is important to consider the changes that affected their business environment and design practice during the first two years of the conflict. With the declaration of war in September 1939, the British government immediately implemented policies to prepare for intensive mainland bombing. In London this resulted in air raid precautions and evacuation. These policies, alongside the bombing fears associated with the capital city and the immediate rationing of petrol, made it less attractive and more difficult for customers to come to the West End for the fittings required for made-to-measure clothing.[5] Between December 1939 and April 1940, Mass Observation (which from 1936 until the mid-'60s conducted social surveys) held a series of interviews with representatives from the British fashion industry. These evidence the war's instant and understandable effect on the couturiers' businesses and working lives.[6] Morton and Stiebel claimed that they had witnessed a noticeable fall in demand as their clients restricted visits to central London even in the early months of the war.[7] The December 1939 issue of *Vogue* verifies this claim and notes the designers' response to these changes, with many now 'taking the West End to the country . . . sending sketches and material swatches to their out-of-town clients and restricting fittings to a minimum'.[8] Under the heading 'Brisk Action on the Mayfair Front', it even highlighted a range of new business strategies that allowed clients to avoid fittings altogether; such as Morton's off-the-peg department that specialised in colour-coordinated jerseys and skirts and Madame Isobel's mail-order service where made-to-measure dresses were constructed with their fit based on a garment, which the client posted to London, from her existing wardrobe.

The last activity taken under the banner of the Fashion Group of Great Britain, a response to the drop in London clients, was a travelling mannequin parade with clothes by Stiebel and Morton, hats by Aage Thaarup, furs by Louis Wolff and cosmetics by Elizabeth Arden. In November 1939, this toured large hotels in Liverpool, Manchester, Cheltenham and Bristol.

The sixteen shows presented were reported to be particularly well attended by approximately 950 women, which the secretary of the Fashion Group informed Mass Observation ensured a 'greater recognition for these designers throughout England'.[9] The benefits from this showcase were not only promotional but also specifically commercial as the designers each took an unprecedented step and sent their best saleswomen and fitters to garner new customers and prepare orders. At a later date their staff then returned to undertake one fitting, before the garments were finished back in the London workrooms and forwarded to each client.[10] This was the first time London couture had been either displayed or fitted outside the capital in England. It demonstrates the extension of not only the Fashion Group's promotional strategies initiated for foreign buyers, but also the couturiers' production process to the wartime needs of its provincial clients.

The operations of many couture houses, alongside adjustments to their customers' changed requirements, were also disrupted and altered by the war duties taken on by a number of the designers. Unlike the First World War, the conscription of men between the ages of twenty and thirty-three was immediately implemented and the government also announced that all men between the ages of eighteen and forty-one not in 'reserved occupations' could also be called up.[11] With fashion design unprotected as an important wartime occupation, Digby Morton volunteered to become an air raid warden and Stiebel a river policeman, who was then moved to the Ministry of Supply's camouflage unit.[12] Hartnell joined the Home Guard.[13] Amies and Creed began fire brigade duties. The former, due to his fluency in French and German, was swiftly commissioned into the newly formed Special Operations Executive and was by the end of the war 'head of sabotage in Belgium'.[14] The latter, after his conscription was twice 'referred' because of his export work, was finally drafted into the Royal Artillery in 1943.[15] In terms of public relations, this engagement in the war effort ensured that the couturiers demonstrated not only their patriotism but also their machismo. Wartime press reports of their design activities, particularly in the case of the bachelors Amies and Stiebel, always utilised the designation 'private' or later 'captain', and were often accompanied by images of them in uniform (figure 3.2).

These wartime occupations did not stop their operation as designers. For example, Morton kept his house open throughout the duration of the war; however, financial difficulties saw Stiebel forced to liquidate his business and

Figure 3.2
Victor Stiebel at Jacqmar, press photograph, c. 1941. *Source:* Reproduced courtesy of
Adrian Woodhouse.

move his staff and operation to the textile house of Jacqmar.[16] Amies was unable to continue employment at Lachasse, but he took up an unprecedented opportunity to continue to work as a couturier under his own name in the London branch of Worth. The wartime environment also allowed Charles Creed to relocate from Paris and operate, without detriment to his prestige, from the made-to-measure department of the Knightsbridge store Fortnum and Mason. This move away from autonomous business activity allowed these couturiers to negotiate their restricted participation in the fashion industry and alleviate prohibitive production costs and staff shortages.[17] The engagement in war work bolstered the dressmakers' public image and also began a process of reciprocity, in which they worked with and received support from other dress houses and retailers.

War did not stop the production of couture or its consumption, as the dressmakers' clients continued to have the aspirations and funds to purchase new clothes. The conflict did instigate, however, a marked change of attitude towards both personal appearance and the style of fashionable dress. The Mass Observation interviews reveal the changed consumer attitudes confronted by fashion producers and retailers, as many industry representatives voiced their dismay at what they saw as the careless attitude to appearance that immediately developed.[18] For Stiebel, the change in dress was 'frightful' and he believed it was underpinned by a social attitude that meant women could 'forget all about fashion and go about just as they liked'.[19] In the first three months of war, he found the way women 'walked about Bond Street and Piccadilly with no hats and those disgusting slacks . . . [particularly] horrible'.[20] Madge Garland (the editor of British *Vogue*) described the 'dastardly' behaviour she witnessed develop in British women's fashion, which saw 'extreme carelessness and slackness add to the horror of sandbags and stripped windows'.[21] In her view this was a 'fatal attitude . . . [as] once you start letting yourself go, nothing is going to matter. It reflects on your mental attitude'. Yet both Stiebel and Garland professed a strong belief that these dress attitudes would primarily affect lower middle-class business and that the clientele of London's couture 'would never quite let themselves go', even if the type and quantity of clothing they consumed altered.[22]

The government's air raid precautions and curtailment of evening entertainments meant that the market for evening wear, a key component within the creative output of many of London's couturiers, 'evaporated almost overnight'.[23] The court-based activities of the social season were suspended for the duration of the war, and dress codes were immediately relaxed even at London's most exclusive and convention-bound hotels and restaurants.[24] Mary Joyce (the editor of *Women's Wear News*) informed Mass Observation that this led a 'number of high-end dressmakers' to send 'beautifully dressed mannequins' into restaurants to encourage the reinstatement of pre-war dress codes.[25] However, these new social attitudes were difficult to dispel. Donald Barber (secretary of the Retail Distributor's Association) considered the change ubiquitous and claimed that he had been in the Mayfair Hotel for two hours in the first week of November 1939 and had seen only 'one woman in evening dress'.[26] The new dress codes at restaurants in London hotels such as the Dorchester and Claridge's were set out in the December issue of British *Vogue*. In line with these stipulations the magazine encouraged its readers to 'Dress Down to Dress Up'.[27] This did not negate the role of fashion or couture production; rather, it promoted a new silhouette and featured images of 'demure' Parisian dinner dresses by Lelong and Alix, fitted to the throat with slim skirts. The styles featured in *Vogue* reflected the consumption patterns at Stiebel's dress house where his clients, as soon as war was declared, immediately rejected the frivolity and romanticism of 1930s evening wear. He reported that his 'ladies . . . [were] not buying evening dresses at all, except at a pinch ones made in wool with long sleeves, up to the neck and buttoned down the front'.[28] The austere, almost modest nature of the new styles of dinner dress, whilst practical and a reaction to an altered social arena, were also indicative of changes in social attitudes towards the consumption of luxury goods.

Whilst *Vogue* could quickly react to the changes in sartorial conventions, for many sectors of the fashion industry this new silhouette, in terms of production and supply, was particularly inopportune. War was declared as dressmakers and wholesalers prepared to present their new collections, and this changed aesthetic direction left many producers with useless stock. For the previous three seasons, both London and Paris couturiers had shown a convergence in style for their evening wear, and fashion magazines such as *Vogue* and *Harper's Bazaar* had promoted their decrees for flamboyant crinoline dresses with corseted waists. Many of the styles prepared for presentation across the industry corresponded with this ostentatious silhouette and were now incongruous at a time of war. As consumer taste moved towards more practical styles, not only couture but also 'all fashion stocks in the shops were completely dead as mutton'.[29]

In comparison to many other sectors of the British fashion industry the couturiers' production was on a small scale, and press reports of the September collections indicate that many postponed their shows by a week to replace models with practical, war-appropriate designs.[30] This left many with a considerable amount of their business collateral invested in models that had been designed and produced prior to the declaration of war. In December 1939, as a response, a number of the made-to-measure businesses, under the guidance of Edward Molyneux, held their first London-based collaborative wartime dress show. Entitled *Fashion Marches On*, it took the form of a charitable gala and was held at the Dorchester Hotel. The clothes presented, to an audience of 500 members of high society, demonstrated the designers' overriding aim to show the elaborate gowns discarded from many September collections. This first wartime instance of the couturiers working together was a blatant appeal to their clients to continue to dress in their pre-war manner and to support the London dress houses. It was the first collective showcase in which Hartnell and Worth, whose reputations rested on their production of elaborate evening wear, participated. Both had resisted inclusion in the Fashion Group showings to American buyers; however, the arrival of Molyneux and the sponsorship of evening wear saw them participate in a joint show.

The introductory text in this gala's programme, written by Lady Hart-Dyke (a producer of English raw silk with a commercial interest in luxury fashion) shows that the primary objective was to challenge the idea that the purchase of elaborate dress was frivolous and therefore unpatriotic.[31] Whilst Hart-Dyke acknowledged that consumers needed to economise for the 'wellbeing of the country', she made clear that this social attitude would destroy the fashion industry and argued that the support of the luxury trades was in fact a national duty:

> Don't be ashamed of fashion. Don't think it unnecessary because times may be hard . . . you must continue to buy the best to look your best. It means you daren't ration fashion (which is part of the heritage for which we are fighting) it means you must continue to live graciously, dress elegantly, and shop cheerfully. War isn't a challenge to fashion. War is a challenge to women to remain fashionable.[32]

This charitable gala therefore positioned the consumption of fashion within a specifically female articulation of the ideals of philanthropy, altruism and patriotism. In order to stabilize the nation's economy, this collaborative event encouraged the wealthy audience to remain active consumers and therefore to perform their patriotism through consumption.[33] This complicated the wartime desire to dismiss the purchase of luxury products as vain and hedonistic. Titles to the show segments, such as 'You Can't Ration Fashion', 'Look Your Part' and 'Out of Uniform into Our Evening Dress', were blatant propaganda to encourage the audience to view the perpetuation of a lavish dress culture as imperative to the continuation not only of couture but of English culture itself.

Nowhere was this ideological attack on restraint more blatant than in the pre-war styles of the evening dresses on display, which were mainly romantic confections with full skirts in chiffon, sequins and lace. The daywear shown by Hartnell and Paquin, which was dominated by silk and crepe dresses and fur trimmings on suits and coats, also ignored the war and followed pre-war conventions. The presentation of more practical woollen coats and dresses was left to the made-to-measure departments of Jaeger, Harrods, Aquascutum and Jacqmar. The only couturiers to present garments that noticeably responded to the war were Molyneux, who included dinner suits, and Morton and Stiebel who presented the new daywear they had designed for the Fashion Group's recent shows in Liverpool, Manchester, Cheltenham and Bristol.

For the presentations outside the capital, both Morton and Stiebel had been careful not to appear unpatriotic in the stimulation of demand for elaborate dress. The models they presented focused on tailored daywear with practical design features. Stiebel, for example, included cycling suits with functional culottes and built-in hoods and Morton designed a 'siren' trouser suit. The latter, an all-in-one design in heavy wool that could be worn over day or nightwear in preparation for an air raid, received a large amount of popular recognition as it was featured in Viyella's promotional campaign.[34] This textile company had previously ignored the English designers and used Schiaparelli for its prestige advertising.[35] With Schiaparelli, who had tried to relocate to London at the outbreak of war, subject to removal from Britain as an alien national, this commission was one of the first indications of the new opportunities for London designers to work in collaboration with the British textile industry.[36] In the Viyella advert Morton is declared a 'famous tailleur' who could prepare his clients to be confident citizens perpetually ready for an air raid. The image it presented was of an active woman, ready and alert, with gas mask and lamp. The advert claimed that the design of her impeccably tailored suit with 'lightning zip' was constructed so that it could be thrown on 'over night-things in an emergency'. The 'hidey hood to cover your head', if caught without proper grooming, allowed the wearer to stay 'beautifully warm' and therefore be practical without the negation of her femininity. As a solution to wartime needs, Morton's trouser suit, with its distinctive military buttons, was a clear example of the adaptability of couture tailoring to new social requirements. The Fashion Group provincial shows also saw the narrative that had been constructed in the late 1930s, of London as the centre for hard tailored couture, now bring further validation to this form of luxury production as it was adapted to a wartime need for practicality.

This was important as it was already noticeable to many of the couturiers, within three months of the declaration of hostilities, that their customers had taken up active participation in the war effort. By December 1939, the majority of Stiebel's clientele were already 'connected with some war work or other—ambulance driving, canteen, looking after evacuees, knitting for troops'.[37] This attitude was reflected in the pages of *Vogue*, which in November 1939 renamed its society column 'Our Lives in Wartime London', and changed its focus from reports of society women's usual round of leisure activities to their engagement in the war effort.[38] This column continued to note the link between specific designers and their customers, but now concentrated on the practicality of the design of their newly purchased clothing. The first of these columns, as just one example, described two of Molyneux's clients actively wearing his tailored daywear: Lady Baldwin as an ambulance driver and Lady Long as a nurse. It also noted Mrs Ronald Aird at work in the auxiliary fire service in a Peter Russell suit and Mrs Peter Thursby at an all-night canteen in her Women's Voluntary Service (WVS) uniform, which was designed by Digby Morton.[39]

The dress of the WVS was not a typical example of a mass-produced and regulated uniform. This was not simply because it was designed by a couturier, but because of the nature of the organisation itself. The social historian Arthur Marwick has described the majority of the membership of this Service as 'extremely upper-class'.[40] The Women's Voluntary Service was set up by the social philanthropist Stella Isaacs the Marchioness of Reading at the request of the government to aid in the implementation of its Air Raid Precautions Act of January 1938.[41] Its committees were created to oversee

and administer the work done by women in the country's many pre-existing
voluntary organisations, and its initial and most visible members were from
the higher levels of Britain's class system, with many drawn from within
Reading's own social circle. The uniform was non-compulsory as it was
costly and had to be purchased privately.[42] Every uniform was made (under
Morton's direction) in the Knightsbridge department store Harrods, which
later, as membership swiftly expanded, began to supply them to twenty
outlets around the country. The diary of Mrs Diana Brinton-Lee (a WVS
wartime volunteer) reveals how the lines of class definition were clearly
recognisable in the way the WVS uniform was worn. At her first attendance
at a WVS meeting in 1940, it documents her 'glancing round the room,
[at] shining sculptured heads, and elegant figures in [what she described
as] Savile Row tunics, which fell open to reveal ties pinned to the shirt
bosom with large regimental diamond brooches'.[43] This individualisation
went against the central property of any uniform, which operates 'above
all as a method of maintaining rigorous adherence to norms'.[44] It was this
conformity that ensured that the uniformed woman, whilst a particularly
prevalent image in magazines, newspapers and advertisements throughout
the war, was not universally liked. This attitude has been studied by the
historian Jenny Hartley, who has noted that female uniforms were placed
near the top of the *Daily Mail*'s poll of 'Wartime Grouches'. She also argues
that the ambivalence felt by many women—'on the one hand a desire to
join the war effort and participate in the people's war, and on the other hand
a resistance to being dictated to by the state—is exemplified perfectly in the
selection and wearing of the WVS uniform'.[45]

The subversive nature of the way this uniform could be worn was a fundamental part of the original concept and reason why Marchioness Reading
chose her couturier to design it (figure 3.3). She claimed that adaptability
was a crucial element of the uniform, a symbolic demonstration of the fact
that WVS members 'should do the same job in different ways, each of them
translating their personality into it'.[46] It could be argued that in 'personality' Reading was referring most specifically to her members' social position.
Morton designed this uniform, in 1939, as a version of his fashionable town
and country wear; with a well-cut woollen coat, jacket and skirt in that
season's distinctive colour palette of green and burgundy.[47] Charles Graves,
the historian of the WVS organisation, has documented how successfully
its wearers adapted this design to avoid sartorial conformity. He points to

Figure 3.3
Marchioness Reading and members of the Women's Voluntary Service, in Digby
Morton–designed WVS uniform, Olympia Rally, London, November 1941. *Source:*
© Reading Museum.

two specific instances where the fact that WVS members were wearing
uniform was overlooked. First, when King George VI asked Marchioness
Reading if her organisation was going to have uniforms and she was forced
to reply, 'Yes, Sir. I am wearing one" and second, when Winston Churchill
commented 'in disgust' on the sartorial 'lack of unity' in a WVS parade.[48]

To ensure both a high level of distinctiveness and fit, many of the
wealthier members of the WVS employed their own dressmakers to alter
the ready-made uniforms.[49] This practice, across a range of service uniforms, brought in new custom for made-to-measure businesses, and its
commercial importance in sustaining many workrooms is made apparent
in the account books of the house of Lachasse. One such example was the
Hon. Mrs Forbes-Adam of Skipton Hall, Yorkshire, who increased her
pre-war consumption of one new suit a year, to three in October 1939,

then returned in April 1940 and June 1942 to have her 'service uniform' remodelled and altered.[50] Wartime uniforms therefore offer an interesting example of the perpetuation of their wearers' desire for not only individuality but also class differentiation. This exposes certain psychological and social factors that ensured a continued demand for made-to-measure clothing. The manner in which the WVS uniform was adapted correlates with Peter McNeil's research into the contemporary representation of fashion in magazines and news reports, which refutes the idea that wartime mobilisation resulted in a democratization of clothing and concludes that 'class seems to have been ever visible in both service and civilian dress'.[51] For Digby Morton, the change in sartorial needs, particularly in the first year of the war, was to prove financially beneficial.[52] He claimed that to meet new demand his business increased by 25 per cent and was busier in the season the war broke out than in the same period in 1938.[53] The continuation of class distinction in dress, particularly for the upper-middle and upper class, therefore ensured that the move towards the consumption of practical daywear and uniforms was not detrimental to but supplemented couture production.

During the first year of war the need for new clothing brought in business for the London couturiers. However, towards the end of 1940 Britain's position within the war began to deteriorate, as the Blitz, the German Luftwaffe's long-feared bombing campaign, began. From 7 September 1940 London suffered fifty-seven consecutive nights of raids. Mayfair received heavy damage, with Bruton Street, Bond Street and Park Lane hit on the eleventh day of bombing.[54] Although wartime diaries show daily and commercial life in these streets to be 'carrying on as usual', the intensity of the bombing brought both physical and psychological restrictions to the continuation of couture production as working in London became more precarious.

The fashion industry was then put under further pressure by the government's decision to implement purchase taxation to curb demand and raise revenue. House of Commons debates, from August 1940, show the negative wartime attitude of many members of parliament towards luxury production. The tone of the debates is made clear by one MP's call for the Chancellor of the Exchequer not to be 'the least bit tender about taxing luxuries, if necessary, out of existence'.[55] The argument that revenue generation could contract if people stopped buying these products

was recognised, however, as this MP argued: 'if in a total war, we cannot use our labour more usefully than in luxury production, then we are
still not waging total war in the economic field and in the field of labour'.
There were, however, parliamentary calls for clothing to be exempt from
any future taxation, for as another MP claimed it would represent 'a very
poor reward to our women'.[56] Ministers opposed to taxation also argued
that it would be a tax on the poor, who would be 'obliged to consume and
purchase less, but [in comparison] if you place a tax on the rich, it does not
affect them at all . . . those who pay 100 guineas for a fur coat will willingly
pay 150 guineas for the same fur coat'.[57] Despite such opposition a purchase
tax was imposed on all consumer goods in October 1940, which saw the
cost of clothing rise by 69 per cent at the point of sale.[58]

Throughout the first year of the war the business objectives of many
of the London couturiers focused primarily on the British market. However, as the political climate grew increasingly antagonistic towards luxury
production, the end of 1940 saw the commercial viability of many of the
dress houses placed under pressure. With the introduction of this new tax,
Vogue rallied to support the couturiers' businesses. In December 1940, in
an unprecedented move, it produced a six-page feature that explained and
defended the high cost of a made-to-measure tailored outfit. The photographs by Lee Miller, of mannequins in perfectly tailored garments, hold-
ing scissors and posed with dressmaker's dummies, visually captured the
main message of the article. The focus shifted to the promotion and protection of the inherent craft skills needed to create the perfect fitted garment.
As the article pointed out:

> This is the thing London does best. . . . It is this combination of high quality,
> careful cut, hand work and skilled fitting which ensures the good line and long
> life of a suit. If the design is good there is no question of such a garment dating.
> Therefore, good tailoring is not expensive in the long run . . . all in all, it's this
> fanatically high standard that put London tailoring at the top and holds it there,
> to be the principal grounds of our fashion prestige, the principal impetus of our
> fashion exports.[59]

This proclamation reversed *Vogue*'s customary promotion of couture from
being a sign of fashionability and conspicuous consumption to a long-
term investment and indicator of frugality. In the suggestion that buying
these clothes was an investment not only in these specific businesses but in

the nation as a whole, it also pointed to the potential role the couturiers could play in the export agenda. This *Vogue* article was therefore not only a response to increased domestic taxation but also, in its claim that the couturiers should be viewed as a 'principal impetus' in Britain's export campaign, an acknowledgement of how the couturiers' business objectives needed to adapt in line with a new political agenda.

In June 1940, political economists had shifted their focus from mobilization and set out a new *White Paper* to increase 'dollar-earning exports' wherever they could be produced 'without detriment to war production'.[60] It was at this point that the need for formal collaboration to increase the export potential of British design, a pre-war aspiration of both the Fashion Group and many reform bodies in all fields of design, began to receive both industrial and governmental support. In the textile industry, the new export agenda led to the immediate establishment of centralised export groups.[61] Many of these groups were created from an array of existing trade associations; however, they brought cohesion and structure to this previously fragmented industry.[62] Although this new political stipulation also had immediate and important implications for the couturiers, they did not, as the next section of this chapter will demonstrate, immediately follow suit and rush to establish the Incorporated Society.

'BRITAIN DELIVERS THE GOODS': LONDON COUTURE, THE 'SHOP
WINDOW' FOR THE WARTIME EXPORT CAMPAIGN

As the export policy became fully operational, it was to have an impact on the way the couture industry presented itself and on the consolidation of a particular network that supported its continuation. Fashion magazines and newspaper reports shifted from a focus on practicality and a defence of luxury production to the economic role the designers could play in the export campaign.[63] An article in the February 1941 edition of *Harper's Bazaar* entitled 'Exports—From Zero to £500,000' exemplifies the altered narrative that now surrounded the London couture. It focused on the arrival of Edward Molyneux in London from Paris, 'an experienced and successful exporter', and claimed that his relocation represented an opportunity to 'transplant the economic viability of Paris onto Mayfair'.[64] This article, which drew on a letter Molyneux had sent to the Board of Trade, concentrated on the economic relevance of his two export collections of

1940.[65] In it Molyneux pointed to the case of only one American import house, which bought forty-four of his models. He estimated that the reproduction of these garments alone, in terms of model and textile sales for repeat reproduction, secured a net total of over $19,000. He also claimed that throughout North America there was 'the potential for about twenty other houses to order on this scale, with many smaller importers also taking between two to five models a season'.[66] *Harper's Bazaar* took these estimates to inform its readers that his business alone had helped to build up an export trade that 'provided England with three million American dollars . . . all placed at the disposal of the British Government'. In a carefully worded piece of propaganda it encouraged its readers to 'work out' what 'that meant in terms of ships, aircraft or ammunition'.

It was after the release of the export White Paper that the Department of Overseas Trade invited Molyneux to a meeting and asked him to bring together a number of couturiers to create the showcase for South America, to tour Buenos Aires, Rio de Janeiro, Montevideo and Sao Paulo, between March and May 1941.[67] The government now offered the couturiers an unprecedented level of support and immediately committed just over £5,000 to finance the promotion of this venture. This sum included payment for 5,000 copies of the exhibition's programme and its translation into three (unspecified) South American languages.[68] The sum also financed double-page magazine advertisements in *Art and Industry*, *International Textiles* and *Vogue*, all of which had a substantial circulation in South America. Some of the £5,000 was then used for the production and international distribution of over 2,000 copies of a special 'South American tour' edition of *Harper's Bazaar*.[69] Out of this budget a further £2,047 was allocated to pre-exhibition advertising in South America and a further £500 for entertainment. To ensure a locally astute post-exhibition publicity campaign, the Sao Paulo branch of the well-established Lintas advertising company was then hired, at the cost of £900.[70] In Britain, in order to boost morale, the Ministry of Information was given responsibility for the exhibition's internal promotion and an additional budget. Its Industrial Publicity Unit organised and paid over £700 to show the outgoing collection at a press reception at the Dorchester Hotel in London. A display was also financed in the Midlands and North Country alongside the annual press previews of new fabrics organised by the British Colour Council. To ensure the industrial relevance of the written elements of the exhibition's promotion,

Alison Settle and Margaret Havinden (who were both original members of the Fashion Group's board) were commissioned to write the programme and official press releases.

This coordinated and specific use of funds guaranteed a highly visible and controlled promotion of the South American showcase throughout national and international newspapers, magazines, newsreel features and radio broadcasts. In response to these initiatives, Board of Trade representatives claimed the press in South America had responded 'heroically to the event' and that publicity had also appeared 'very widely' in Canada and the Dominions.[71] The Ministry of Information also documented 507 carefully orchestrated references to the 'London Fashion Collection' in British newspaper reports. This ensured that the London couture industry and the nine designers who participated received a level of both national and international recognition unknown before the war.

This opportunity for free marketing was unprecedented for the dressmakers. Previous collaborative export shows, such as the aforementioned Queen Mary showcase of 1936 and the Fashion Group's presentations for American buyers, had in the main all been self-financed. Now, as part of the export drive, the couturiers saw the promotion of their collective showcase fully supported and financed by the British government. This level of expenditure on the promotion of these individual businesses would have been improbable without the circumstances of war. The government had never previously demonstrated an interest in financing the promotion of this luxury trade and, due to its endorsement of particular businesses at the expense of others, was in danger of accusations of industrial bias. The government support, however, was not given merely to ensure the continuation of these made-to-measure dress houses; the main political justification was to use the garments of these creative practitioners to act as a 'shop window' for the promotion of Britain's textile industry.[72] To a certain extent, this was prompted by the fear of repeating the loss of foreign markets experienced during World War I for what was Britain's third largest industry.[73] Sir Cecil Weir (executive member of the British Export Council) voiced this political agenda in an editorial in *Harper's Bazaar* and highlighted the 'double effect' the South American showcase had for 'increasing export opportunities for fashion clothes and for the materials from which they are made and bringing in currency for many things we need in fighting this war to a victorious conclusion'.[74]

Despite this visible support, Board of Trade staff registered a sense of political unease in the sponsorship of this form of luxury production. The government's initial proposal for South America was not only to hold a couture showcase but also 'to represent all the areas where British textiles could through quality and design operate at the higher end of the market'.[75] The showcase, as part of the government's 'Britain Delivers the Goods' export campaign in South America, was also intended to include interior decoration and a full range of mass-manufactured womenswear.[76] Board of Trade communications show that these sections never materialised because of the 'magnitude of the war effort', which made it impossible for many mass-market producers 'to devote more than a small proportion of their resources to export'.[77] In terms of governmental propaganda, the restriction of the tour to only couture production was seen as politically delicate and in need of careful navigation. This is evidenced in a letter sent, at the request of the Board of Trade, by Lord Derby (patron of the British Colour Council, Cotton Board and the future Incorporated Society) to national and international press agencies, which took care to dispel the idea that the tour was an inappropriate 'frivolity in the midst of war'. It positioned the couturiers firmly in the broader export campaign with Derby's stipulation that, 'just as the famous dress houses of Paris were in fact the "shop window" for the display of the French silks, wools, and laces, so will these displays of the latest London dress models serve the same purpose for our British textiles on the other side of the Atlantic'. The tour, in its 'bold bid to retain supremacy as arbiters of world fashions', was presented as a promotion of not the nine couturiers but rather the British textile industry. [78]

Export performance was important to fund the war effort; however, the governmental endorsement of elite fashion also fulfilled a broader political agenda. It not only generated money for the Exchequer, by promoting the country's fashion and textile industry, but also operated as a highly visual component of national projection, which is why Hartnell described it as an 'essay in the art of export-cum-propaganda'.[79] By 1941 the government was under constant pressure to convince its transatlantic suppliers that Britain could pay for all of its imports. This was dictated by the neutral stance maintained by America towards the war, which left Britain unable to rely on automatic assistance. A transatlantic propaganda campaign was instigated that promoted an image of Britain as a 'sturdy ally with only temporary economic troubles'.[80] In line with this political agenda, the unreserved promotion of creative made-to-measure dress should be viewed as an example of the national projection of prestige. A flamboyant and luxurious couture display was a particularly appropriate way to demonstrate that business was carrying on as usual and that Britain could literally 'deliver the goods'. For the government the couturier's role was therefore multifaceted: their practice was utilized to boost morale on the home front, increase export by acting as a 'shop window' for British textiles, demonstrate the continued creativity of British production and prove that Britain was still a capable manufacturing nation.

To fulfil the role of 'shop window' the couturiers had to produce all their models for South America in British fabrics. This was facilitated by the support of an array of textile manufacturers who agreed to produce materials to the couturiers' design specifications and donate them without charge.[81] This unparalleled level of cooperation was made possible by the infrastructure offered by the newly formed textile export groups, which offered a clearly defined network through which the production and supply of fabrics could be coordinated.[82] The British Colour Council operated as the fulcrum within this arrangement. For four months its members undertook all the negotiations and worked with the separate textile and couture houses to coordinate the design of the models.[83] The Colour Council not only secured the supply of fabric but also convinced the Export Groups for the cotton, wool, rayon, lace, silk, hosiery and hat industries to provide just over £3,500 to pay the designers for their workroom costs. It also persuaded the Leather, Footwear and Allied Industries Export Group to loan all the accessories.[84] Robert Wilson (the Colour Council's director) pointed out to the Board of Trade that in this way, the government and the couturiers were 'finally able to benefit from the good will we have built up with the textile industry over a number of years'.[85]

For the production of the South American models, the cooperation and financial commitments of an array of textile manufacturers was as exceptional as the government's funding of their promotion. Since the Colour Council was set up, in 1930, it had been one of Wilson's primary convictions that in terms of both prestige and design innovation 'British textiles need the input of the London couturiers to create a solid export market and gain a lead over the competition'.[86] The collaboration for the South American showcase clearly fulfilled this pre-war aspiration towards design reform. Throughout the 1930s, despite the Council's best efforts, there was only a limited level of cooperation between British couturiers and textile manufactures. Many designers' use of British fabrics had often been curtailed by the textile producers financially prohibitive demands that 'if they wanted exclusively designed pieces they had to pay up front and take a minimum of fifty yards'.[87] Apart from British tweeds, the couturiers had primarily used fabric from the continent for their collections. The importation of dress fabric had doubled in the two years that preceded war, and dressmakers, at all levels of the market, had increasingly brought their fabric from France.[88] These consumption patterns led to both political and industrial debate, which concluded that the popularity of these imports was due to the 'fashion content' of the fabric's design.[89] This was constantly repeated at the Board of Trade and was also a key element in the initial debates that began in 1942 and led, two years later, to the establishment of the state-supported Council of Industrial Design. These debates noted that in comparison to many foreign fabrics the designs used by a majority of British textiles manufacturers were 'uncreative' and 'cautious' as they often relied on the reproduction of already successful French designs.[90] This lack of innovation is highlighted in the personal diary of Raymond Streat (the chairman of the Cotton Board) where he noted that the cotton manufacturers in particular were characterised by 'their ability to turn out efficient but possibly hum-drum designs'.[91]

British cotton fabrics, due to their style, texture and low cost, had previously held little interest for the London couturiers, as they were considered inappropriate for their clients and detrimental to their reputations.[92] However, the cotton industry put up the largest amount of money for the 'Britain Delivers the Goods' couture showcase.[93] This was not only because cotton was considered particularly suitable for South America's hot climate but also because this industry's development was a vital element in the British export agenda. The weakness in the design of British cotton fabric, which was often aimed at the lower end of the market, had caused anxious debate at the Board of Trade.[94] The war, which placed an embargo on foreign textiles and increased the pressure to improve the quality and competitiveness of British goods, created the opportunity for the production of more original and high-quality cotton fabrics. In September 1940, the government financed the opening of the Cotton Board's Colour, Design and Style Centre in Manchester with a mission to actively improve design standards within the industry. The South American campaign offered the first chance for this new venture to demonstrate that the British cotton industry could respond to the government's design reform and export agenda, meet the needs of high-level fashion and thereby offer a competitive substitute for fabrics previously produced in America or on the continent.

The collaboration between the Cotton Board and the couturiers was widely disseminated in *Queen Cotton*, a British Council film produced to coincide with the tour.[95] This film began with a didactic consideration of the cotton industry's technology and skilled production techniques before it concluded with a flamboyant mannequin parade of the couturiers' models. This array of elaborate and often impractical dresses and coats was filmed in the Colour, Design and Style Centre's exhibition room in front of a small audience of fur-clad women and their male escorts. *Queen Cotton*, like many other British Council films, practically 'cut the war out altogether', not only as it made no direct reference to it, but also in the elitist presentation and aesthetic of the models on display.[96] Yet the film's commentary, the fabrics used, and the styles presented are a particularly pertinent example of the changes instigated by the wartime economy. The film's narration constantly drew the viewers' attention to the design of the textiles rather than the clothes. It focused on the 'multiple fashion-uses of cotton' for both 'simple, inexpensive dresses' and 'elaborate gowns that fulfil the finest ambitions of the designer's art'.[97] Many of the fabrics, produced to the couturiers' aesthetic specifications, were particularly distinctive and responded to Raymond Streat's design brief to 'encourage the bold and the brave rather than give endorsement to the ordinary'.[98] Throughout *Queen Cotton* the commentary made specific reference to this collaborative design process and pointed out that all the fabrics were 'the results of London's leading designers, working with the Lancashire mills . . . who have excelled in exploring the infinite possibilities of cotton fabric'.[99] This extended the definition of the couturier's role of 'shop window' from merely a source of promotion to align with the narrative, constantly endorsed by the British Fashion Group and Colour Council throughout the 1930s, that their creativity should play an important component within industrial design reform.

The styles displayed in *Queen Cotton* illustrate the couturiers' efforts to extend their design repertoire and produce clothes and fabric outside the typical boundary of English dress culture. This is made clear by the dress, probably by Bianca Mosca, shown in figures 3.4a and b, with its cutaway

Figure 3.4a
Day dress designed in cotton specifically for the South American market. Still from
Queen Cotton (British Council Films, 1941). *Source:* British Council Films.

back, large bow and printed and appliquéd fabric. This model is indicative
of the strategy to envisage the needs of South American women and therefore extend the couturiers' design range. Figure 3.5, a full-length dress by
Worth, also highlights the speculative nature of many of the models. In its
appropriation of the styles associated with the American Civil War of the
1860s, it gave a clear nod to *Gone with the Wind*, the most popular film of
1940.[100] This was a sign that Madam Champcommunal (Worth's designer)
anticipated that this film's spectacular costumes would have an influence
on international fashion. A notable design feature, in both of these models, was the set of the sleeves, which created an exaggerated raised shoul-
der line. This construction technique was evident in many of the models
and operated as a clearly defined stipulation for future fashion lines. This
design synchronisation was a visual representation of a narrative that
underpinned the tour's promotional material. The primary objective was
to emphasize London's ability to replace Paris and operate as the arbiter
of fashion, not only for tailored garments but also for dressmaking, the

Figure 3.4b
Back view of day dress, 1941. Still from *Queen Cotton* (British Council Films, 1941).
Source: British Council Films.

'soft' element of couture production. This goal was substantiated in British *Vogue*'s editorial on the South American showcase, in its hopeful claim
that 'they used to dress in Paris, now the women of South America can
choose from the London fashion collections specially designed for them'.[101]
This collection saw the couturiers finally work with the textile industry
and construct a creative industrial network. The importance of the British
Colour Council in the realization of this collaborative and unified design
process should not be ignored as it illustrates how the conditions of war had
finally led to a fulfilment of the Council's and Fashion Group's long-held
objectives.

In order to understand the true nature of the Incorporated Society it
is now important to explore the specific events that led to its formation.
This section will therefore argue that the couturiers were in fact given little
choice and that it was the result of a specific political policy that finally
forced them into this formal collaboration. The recognition of this is
important to understand not only why the Society came into being but

Figure 3.5
Madame Champcommunal of Worth (London) design for garden frock of printed
cotton. Still from *Queen Cotton* (British Council Films, 1941). *Source:* British
Council Films.

also how it came to operate in the post-war period. In March 1941, Sir
Cecil Weir's introduction to the South American showcase in the special
edition of *Harper's Bazaar* declared that this bid to promote London as the
world's fashion centre was not viewed by the government as an isolated and
'splendid example of effective collaboration between dress designers and
fabric manufacturers . . . [but pointed] the way for other exhibitions of
a similar character'.[102] Despite this exceptional governmental support, the
South American tour was not, as might be expected, the automatic impetus
behind the formal construction of the Incorporated Society, although it did
define its membership. It was the reasons behind the cancellation of the next
collaborative venture, an ill-fated exhibition prepared for North America
that finally, after more than two years of war, secured the establishment of
this official couture trade group. Consideration of this thwarted exhibition
can therefore offer a more accurate understanding of the principal objectives behind the creation of the Incorporated Society.

In July 1941, the Ministry of Information began to release details of a New York showcase. Newspapers quickly began to produce features on the preparations being undertaken in the workrooms of Russell, Hartnell, Morton, Mosca (who had recently left Paquin) and Worth.[103] When Amies and Stiebel also became involved, the *Sunday Referee* commended their release from army duties in its article, 'Fashion "Aces" Get Leave—To Design for U.S.' and highlighted the continued support being offered to the couturiers by the government and textile industry.[104] It pointed out that once again the production of the models would be funded by the wool, cotton and rayon textile export groups, which contributed £9,000, a three-fold increase over their sponsorship of the South American collection. *Women's Wear Daily* also reported that the Board of Trade would continue to support this 'collaboration of the fabric industry with dress designers' through the supply of raw material and the finance of both the production of original fabrics and a robust publicity campaign.[105] Yet the designers' participation was not as forthcoming or cohesive as the first export showcase. The houses of Molyneux and Paquin chose not to become involved, and those that did decided to show only half their models in the group presentation and follow up with separate exhibitions of their full collections in New York. To a certain extent this was due to the commercial objectives of those couturiers with established trade links in the North American market, yet it also demonstrates continued unease about participation in joint exhibitions.

In September 1941, after all the models for the New York showings had been completed and were prepared for shipment, the Board of Trade suddenly cancelled the showcase. Reports across a range of national newspapers were brief and the explanation for this boycott particularly vague. They merely reiterated a Ministry of Information press release that noted that 'the designers and textile groups concerned had agreed that a trade promotion effort into the North American market [would be] untimely'.[106] It could be suggested that the cancellation was because of the competition London designers posed to their American counterparts. In New York in particular, the occupation of Paris in June 1940 had again raised questions about the American fashion industry's reliance on French inspiration and guidance. In July the influential *Tobé Fashion Report* immediately pointed out that manufacturers and retailers across the country needed to 'build up authority for American designers as . . . the real future of American fashion business lies in the creation of American fashion authority'.[107] In response, by September 1940, the *New York Times* had proclaimed the 'beginning of an American couture'.[108] By the time of the proposed showcase of London couture, over a year later, the American fashion industry had already made a concerted effort to promote its own designers and to stake New York's claim to design authority. Through fashion shows, press weeks, advertising credits and design awards, American designers gained a 'celebrity status' not known before the occupation of Paris.[109]

The designs the London couturiers submitted for the second collaborative export showcase provide clear evidence that the sensitivity of American fashion producers had not been taken into account. The garments made in cotton for this tour saw the London couturiers extend their range beyond tailoring, their traditional market stronghold, and included many boldly printed dresses.[110] Amies, in particular, produced a range of idiosyncratic dress designs. These featured low-slung belts, sharply defined waists and wide, loose Magyar armholes to emphasise the hips (figure 3.6). In retrospect he pointed out that this speculative and exaggerated styling was not an example of 'good designing [as it was] difficult for anyone to wear, and far too different from the current fashion'.[111] Such dresses clearly challenged the protectionism evident in the American industry as their design laid claim to the couturiers' ability to create and direct fashion. The promotion was therefore antagonistic to the American fashion industry's own aspiration to develop New York's design status.

Yet this was not enough to cause the cancellation of the tour. The governmental decision for this was taken not by ministers at the Board of Trade but by those at the Foreign Office in line with broader political objectives focused on securing American aid. When the White Paper which set out a political agenda to increase export was released in June 1940, the Treasury had hoped to meet import requirements from gold reserves and exports, but by the beginning of 1941 it was clear that this was not feasible.[112] Britain therefore began a series of delicate negotiations with America, to encourage more lenient trade terms, which any external propaganda had to be careful not to jeopardize. So, whilst the Board of Trade made preparations for a large-scale transatlantic promotional campaign for a selection of luxury fashion businesses, unease began to develop at the Foreign Office. The first indication that 'to hold a fashion show in New York in November might be harmful to national interests' was included in a letter Anthony Eden (the Foreign Secretary) wrote, in August 1941, to Sir Robert Campbell at

Figure 3.6
Hardy Amies dress of black and white batik cotton, 1941. *Source:* Image courtesy of Manchester Art Gallery.

the British Embassy in Washington. This asked for his opinion on the viability of the Board's proposed couture showcase.[113] Eden drew on a letter he
had received from Raymond Streat and informed Campbell that the main
purpose of the tour was for 'reasons of prestige' and 'to sell models and fabrics'. He also highlighted the two areas that he believed could be problematic: first that the exhibition would consist of only 'four or five designers
and four business executives' and second that 'considerable publicity would
be essential to success'. With this concerted publicity campaign due to start
in October, Campbell pointed out that America was 'a seller's market for
such goods as the United Kingdom can export [which left] little need for
exceptional expenditure on promotion and publicity'. He recommended
that 'on the contrary selling and marketing expenses should be cut to the
minimum to offset higher prices' and also pointed out that 'we [the British]
cannot develop new lines without running into criticism'. After consultation with other officials in Washington, Campbell then went further and
stipulated that they were all 'unanimous in advising that a Fashion Show on
lines proposed should be abandoned'.[114] He explained the reasons for this in
his assertion that the dress shows

> would not, I fear, be acceptable in state of public feeling here, and might be
> assailed with some acrimony. It not only gives opportunities to isolationists for
> attacks but might also give rise to unfavourable criticism from friendly elements
> on grounds of British wasteful expenditure on luxury production and addiction
> to 'business as usual', at a time when American industries and consumers are
> being exhorted to restrict production and consumption of civilian supplies in
> order to step up production essential for Britain and national defence.[115]

The previous export drive into South America had led to a 'heightened
competition between the United States and Britain and had drawn pro-
tests from manufacturers in America'.[116] The main government priority was
now to secure the Lend-Lease Agreement to provide American credit for
the British war effort. The New York showcase of London couture was
cancelled in response to the American negotiators' demands that for this
finance, 'Britain agree not to export goods received through or replaced by
this Agreement', whether or not these materials were American imports.[117]
This placated American exporters, 'who struggled to see why they should
be deprived of materials if British competitors could then use them to
gain an advantage in overseas markets'.[118] The promotion of the couture

showcase, due to the competition it posed to the American fashion industry and its reliance on fabrics produced with imported raw materials, was
therefore not only politically insensitive but also a contravention of this
new proviso in the Agreement.

Lend-Lease, which was finally agreed in March 1941, gave Britain a
guaranteed financial support system, which reduced the political urgency
of revenue generation. Its introduction relaxed the need for export and
allowed the British government a much greater degree of specialisation on
war mobilization than would otherwise have been possible.[119] With this
financial assistance secured, the government immediately turned its attention to protecting British resources. With the pressures of revenue generation removed, government microeconomics began to implement controls
to restrict supply, curb inflation and decrease consumption. A political
campaign of central planning to enforce these priorities was swift: this
implemented rationing to curtail consumer demand, industrial quotas and
the concentration of production in civilian industries into large units,
and both the central allocation of scarce resources and manpower budgets
to allocate labour.[120] This had a direct impact not only on luxury production but on all areas of manufacture. In terms of the clothing industry this
saw the immediate introduction of the Civilian Clothing (Restriction)
Order. This limited the amount and type of material and trimmings that
manufacturers, dressmakers and tailors could procure and use. The Clothes
Rationing Coupon Scheme based on a simple points principle followed
in June 1941, with members of the public each allotted sixty-six coupons
annually. Every type of clothing was given a specific coupon value that had
to be surrendered at the point of purchase. This meant, for example, that a
dress, regardless of quality or price, needed eleven coupons.[121]

These policies, whilst restrictive, were not immediately detrimental to
the couturiers' businesses. Digby Morton told Mass Observation that when
rationing initially came in he was able to maintain a 'good steady business'
and that by not being allowed to purchase a range of goods, customers
'were opting for a better class of things'.[122] Many of his clients were also
able to save their coupons for quality items as they had large wardrobes
of pre-war clothing in comparison to less-wealthy consumers. Morton's
claim is supported by the social historian Alexander Calder's examination
of government surveys, which demonstrate that those with the money to
buy couture had increased their wardrobes during the war, 'possibly as their

pre-war garments were of better quality, lasted longer, and could be more easily patched'.[123] However, running a fashion business was now a completely different prospect. Within three months of the Lend-Lease Agreement being signed, Morton now allocated a disproportionate amount of time to 'writing letters to governmental departments' and had to 'fight like hell to get anything'.[124] His workroom staff had been cut by a third to twenty-five, and his business had reduced to the production of 'approximately eight suits a week'. *Women's Wear Daily* quickly reported that even Hartnell and Molyneux, London's largest and most prestigious couture houses, were struggling. It pointed out that Hartnell now employed around one quarter of his pre-war staff and operated on approximately half the number of the previous year.[125] Molyneux was also reported to be 'just ticking along [and only working] on orders for plain un-extravagant garments with a limited staff'.[126] The Lachasse customer account books for the spring of 1942 show that one of the main occupations of the London couture workrooms was now the 'reconfection' of quality dresses and coats from elaborate pre-war styles into more appropriate wartime clothing.

This depletion of the couture industry was a direct response to the full implementation of the Lend-Lease Agreement. This not only put an end to the New York export show, but most importantly, it indirectly led to the enforced withdrawal of the couturiers' workforce and the 'concentration' of the whole clothing industry. The need for export revenue was replaced with demand for recruits to factories and the Women's Auxiliary Services, and the fashion industry at all levels was suddenly faced with the enforced loss of its female staff. The move to concentrate the industry saw the government retain only those clothing manufacturers which used the most efficient mass-production methods and enforced the closure or merger of small firms in order to create larger factories and production runs. By June 1942, these measures had cut the British fashion industry by nearly three quarters.[127] To retain a requisite workforce and supply of raw materials, firms had to be designated under an Essential Works Order. This could be obtained only if at least 80 per cent of output was for export, military or essential civilian production, a stipulation that couture producers could not meet.[128] Essential civilian clothing now had to conform not only to the coupon system but also to Utility Regulations that controlled their production, distribution and cost. The Utility Scheme was introduced in order to control quality and design within all manufactured products so that the needs of the civilian population were met with the minimum of labour, material and power. For the clothing industry it prescribed the fabric yardage of each garment and aspects such as the number of buttons, pockets, seams and flaps allowed in their construction.[129]

Creative fashion and luxury production were clearly no longer needed within a fully mobilized economy. Even in August 1941, when the New York showcase was yet to be abandoned, the Department of Overseas Trade found it difficult to get the Ministry of Labour to agree to allow ten couture firms to keep a nucleus of staff.[130] Strassner aside, the dress houses that the Department asked to be preserved had all cooperated on the South American tour: Creed (at Fortnum and Mason), Hartnell, Morton, Paquin, Molyneux, Stiebel, Russell, Lachasse and Worth (which alongside Champcommunal as its head designer also housed the businesses of Amies and Mosca). Only six months earlier an unprecedented level of support had been offered to the couture for the tour; now, however, the Cabinet viewed this request as politically 'sensitive' and was concerned that in acceding it might be accused of 'bias toward luxury trades and encouraging the expanding black-market'.[131]

On 10 November 1941, two months after the cancellation of the New York showcase and as the government's policy towards full mobilisation took effect, Harry Yoxall, the business manager of *Vogue*, drew up the constitution of the Incorporated Society; on 6 January 1942 it was finally established as an official and permanent body. The fact that the objectives of the Society were set out not by the couturier-members themselves but by an employee of *Vogue* should not be ignored. As with key members of the Fashion Group in the 1930s, such as Alison Settle and Madge Garland, who were both editors of this magazine, Yoxall was fully versed in the needs of the promotional culture of modern consumerism, as his work was primarily involved with advertising and marketing and the exertion of control over the fashion industry. When the Society's aims ('objects a–r', set out in the appendix on pages 235–236) are considered in this light, it is clear that they were written not to address the specific needs of the couturiers and the wartime economy but with an eye on the future needs of the broader international fashion industry. The Society was given eighteen objectives, the majority of which (objects g–r) were generic and adhered to the Incorporated Society Act of 1908. These primarily ensured the legality of the association's financial transactions so that in terms of public liability its identity was separate and distinct from its members. The first six objectives (objects a–f) met the legal dictates of the Act, which specified that this form of Society needed a precise set of rules that were open to public scrutiny. It can be argued that it is in these first six objectives that many of the Fashion Group's pre-war aspirations to regulate design and control demand for consumer goods in the broader fashion industry became enshrined within the Society's constitution. For example, this can be seen in its aims '(a) to maintain and develop the reputation of London as a creative centre of fashion', '(b) to collaborate with groups of fabric and other manufacturers, and with companies, firms and individuals, with a view to increasing the prestige of British fashions . . . in home and overseas markets' and '(f) to organise or hold exhibitions of British fashions'.[132]

It should be recognised that an incorporated society was a collective form where the ultimate aims were to protect its members' professional standing and eliminate bogus practitioners. This new body sat in the historical traditions of other professional associations primarily formed in Britain between 1880 and 1925, such as the Incorporated Society of Musicians, the Incorporated Institute of British Decorators and Interior Designers, the Incorporated Society of British Advertisers or the Incorporated Association of Architects and Surveyors. Geoffrey Millerson's work into the history of these 'qualifying associations' has shown that their ultimate goal was to divide 'the "professionals" from the rest . . . in search of prestige'.[133] The formation of this Incorporated Society set out the boundaries of which businesses produced couture and therefore which were worthy of this professional identity. It gave a specific structure to the London couture industry and qualified its members as genuine couturiers, whilst the dressmakers that sat outside its boundaries were discredited. Yet unlike other such qualifying bodies, the repeated references to 'British fashions' rather than 'London couture', in the first six aims of this new Society, indicate a broader mission clearly formulated to benefit clothing producers and retailers outside its membership. The decision to make it an incorporated society for 'fashion designers' rather than for 'couturiers', whilst indicative of the nationalism and egalitarianism of the war years—as couture was a foreign and elitist form of clothing production—should also be seen as representative of the broader aims of the Society's constitution. Rather than merely provide protection for this form of luxury production and the couturiers' individual businesses it was constructed as part of a network of prestige and design reform for the wider British fashion industry.

Whilst the fact that this new association was created for members of the London couture industry was not made apparent in its name, and in its aims it appeared to address the commercial needs of the broader fashion sector, it can be argued that the decision to become an incorporated society, rather than a trade union, export group or chamber of commerce, operated as a vehicle to separate its members from the interests of trade. For as Millerson makes clear, this particular form of professional body 'has comparatively little in common with trade unions, in some ways, they resemble the medieval craft guilds . . . as trade unions represent their members for the purpose of negotiating remuneration and working conditions thus [they are] concerned with economic status'.[134] A key benefit of an incorporated society was that as a not-for-profit body it sat between the state and the private sector and its identity had civic overtones as a social and professional endeavour rather than a collective created merely for economic gain.

For the couturiers, membership in an incorporated society rather than an export group (the form adopted by the textile industry) was a way to avoid status ambiguity and define and demarcate their occupation as a specific, and therefore nationally relevant, profession. Having explored the political situation and the impact this was now having on the couturiers' businesses, it can be suggested that of all the aims set out in the Society's constitution, it is perhaps 'object d'—'[to represent] their views to government and trade bodies and the press'—that offers the clearest explanation for why the designer-members finally agreed to this formal collaboration. Within the war economy the impetus towards collaboration and assistance of the wider British textile and fashion industry should therefore be recognised as a clear result of business protectionism brought about by wartime mobilisation and the concentration of the industry. This challenges the understanding that 'during the war the government backed the Society from the outset' as this clearly misrepresents the construction of the Society.[135] The institutional history of London couture and the formation of the Incorporated Society can instead be understood as a reaction to very inconsistent state intervention and the drastic restrictions on export, labour and materials. This move towards formal collaboration was in fact a reaction not to governmental support but more precisely to the impact of its removal.

FROM CHAMPIONS OF EXPORT TO 'FAIR SHARE' PROTAGONISTS
IN THE 'PEOPLE'S WAR'

For the couturiers the creation of the Incorporated Society was not a choice but a necessity, a strategy to ensure that their businesses survived the conflict. The stipulations of the Lend-Lease Agreement saw the couturiers' relationship with not only the government but also the textile industry unravel. The Cotton Board, for example, had envisioned that the New York show would mark its entry into the dollar market; however, the garments produced for this were in fabrics that could not leave the country (as the raw material was imported from America) or be sold in Britain (as they were produced for 'export only'). The only role the clothes could now perform was in a catwalk display in the Colour, Design and Style Centre's exhibition hall when it officially opened in January 1942. This, as *Textile Weekly* pointed out, saw the models presented as 'a shop window to illustrate the possibility of using cotton as a fashion fabric in a really big way in happier times to come'.[136] Minutes of the Incorporated Society's meetings show that its designer-members were ambivalent towards participation in this presentation as it held little commercial incentive; they cooperated 'as a gesture of good will', but only when the Cotton Board agreed to pay them for their work.[137] This 'good will' did not extend, however, to a similar request by the Wool Export Group to present the models in an 'educative' show to British wholesalers in Bradford.[138] This proposal was rejected and the official reason given was that 'the models were not suitable for the home market'.[139]

This accusation was similarly applicable to the cotton models; however, this rebuff corresponded to a loophole in the Lend-Lease Agreement, as in January 1942, after much negotiation, the Department of Overseas Trade released a list of traditional (and therefore acceptable to Lend-Lease) British exports: these included some apparel, in addition to raw wool, woollen goods and linen. This meant that the wholesale industry could still produce woollen garments for export. The Wool Group's domestic presentation of the New York models was therefore antagonistic towards the couturier's own commercial objectives. More importantly, the Bradford show interfered with some of the couturiers' current negotiations with specific wholesale companies to act as contracted design consultants.[140] Many of the designers, in particular, Russell and Morton, now had design contracts with the wholesale industry. For instance, by 1944, Russell was reported as working 'in factories as much as in Mayfair, evolving the perfect basic patterns to fit every figure type for the mass market'.[141] With the need to retain the cooperation of the Wool Export Group (which gave £1,000 to enable the designers to finance the creation of the Incorporated Society), the designers were persuaded by their vice presidents and chairman to show their models in February 1942.[142] In return the Wool Export Group paid the couturiers £30 for each model along with a pool of coupons for accessories. The models remained the property of the designers so that after the show they could be 'adapted and sold to their clients'.[143] Later that month, the woollen models were then displayed in New York.

After this, rather than the more adventurous designs in cotton and rayon, the presentation of London couture in America was limited to traditional woollen day and dinner wear. Sandra Buckland's analysis of American newspaper adverts shows that, from this point in the war onwards, this type of London suit began to receive an increased level of promotion in the transatlantic market.[144] This ensured that the recognition of English couture as essentially tailored, wool-based garments then became more firmly entrenched in the minds of American consumers. This put an end to the aspiration to present London to the American market as the world's creative fashion centre and wartime replacement for Paris. Instead, it allowed the continuation of the narrative (promoted by the Fashion Group of Great Britain in the 1930s) that London was merely a complementary fashion centre to Paris and that it should still be viewed as the destination for 'hard' tailored couture.

The couturiers had no choice, within the changed economic environment, other than to agree to any requests from the government. The next request came from Sir Thomas Barlow (the director of Civilian Clothing), who asked the Society to design a range of outfits that adhered to the Utility Regulations, 'as inspiration to the making-up industry'.[145] For the government the couturiers' participation was not only a service to the nation's manufacturers but more importantly a propaganda exercise to boost acceptance of the Utility Scheme. From its inception, the Utility guidelines had met with resistance from manufacturers and consumers. This was heightened by a public relations faux pas by Hugh Dalton (minister of Economic Warfare), when in an interview with the *BBC News*, a month before the scheme became law, he referred to Utility dress as 'standard' clothing.

This was then often reiterated in the news reports that surrounded the scheme and instigated much debate in government circles about the right way to promote these regulations.[146] The couturier-designed models were therefore proposed as a counter to claims that the standardisation inherent in the Utility restrictions made it impossible to create well-designed or desirable clothes.[147] All of the couturiers (with the exception of Molyneux) were wary about a scheme that would, without full remuneration, give a competitive edge to the wholesale trade. Mrs Mortimer (the director of Worth) highlighted the attitude of the designers to the scheme when she claimed that the proposition was 'potentially dangerous to their business . . . [and could] prove to be the thin edge of the wedge for the wholesale makers-up to exploit the "haute couture", and . . . might ruin the name of Worth'.[148]

It took careful negotiation by the Society's non-designer members to convince them that it would be 'desirable . . . to identify themselves with this National effort'.[149] In light of the deterioration of the role of luxury production within the export campaign all the designers (except Hartnell, who had a well-publicised contract with the mass-market producers Berkertex to produce Utility models) finally agreed that 'they had no choice' but to demonstrate that they were 'very keen to do everything possible to help in the national emergency . . . and were ready and willing to collaborate to the full'[150] (figure 3.7). The couturiers chose to participate because it gave them a viable role within the concentration policy, enabling them to show the government that they could offer practical style guidance to manufacturers who had lost their designers and key workers. This engagement with the government therefore portrayed the couturiers' practice as important and beneficial to the whole nation, not just private commerce. Another incentive to participation was the anticipated release of the L-85 Regulations in America, which were set to restrict transatlantic clothing production along similar lines to the British Utility scheme. Introduced on 8 March 1942, these American regulations placed restrictions on evening jackets, skirts and dresses, blouses, culottes or skirts, straight coats, fitted coats, jackets and slacks. They prohibited dolman, balloon, leg-of-mutton, bias-cut sleeves, all-around pleated skirts, wide belts, aprons and tunics and dictated the maximum length of jackets, skirts and dresses. The London couturier participation in the British government's Utility Scheme therefore had a commercial incentive for the designers as it helped to convince

Figure 3.7
Utility designs. Left: suit by wholesale company Dereta; right: suit by Norman
Hartnell for Berkertex. *Source:* © Imperial War Museum.

American retailers that they had developed a specific expertise that would
be relevant to their newly restricted market.

Thomas Barlow initially only asked the designers to produce sketches
for the scheme; however, the couturiers claimed these would be 'misleading and practically useless' as the mass-market producers would need to see
exactly how they looked in material form.[151] They therefore agreed to produce thirty-four models that included blouses, skirts, jackets and dresses.
The Treasury then purchased these at thirty guineas each and pattern templates were made cheaply available to the industry. To ensure that participation in the scheme did not damage the couturiers' prestige, the Society

requested that the models were made outside their own establishments, in the workrooms of specific wholesalers. Barlow presented the 'Couturier Scheme' (as it was known in the Board of Trade's correspondence) to the designers as a chance for them to act as design reformers, who would create the 'opportunity for the Government to produce garments of such taste and quality as had never before been available to the masses'.[152] This idea was promulgated in the first public relation's exercise undertaken by the designers for the Scheme when, in order to understand how clothing was mass produced, they all attended a demonstration of the production capacity of the Brook Manufacturing Company in Northampton. In documenting the event, local reporters were quick to ask these 'famous designers' their reasons for participation in the Utility Scheme. In response, Bianca Mosca claimed that she and her fellow couturiers were 'going to educate women to dress with simplicity and charm, without expense and with real taste and in a year's time the "average woman" will be a transformed being'.[153] When it presented the scheme to the wholesale trade, the Board of Trade was careful, however, to avoid accusations of enforced design reform and issued an announcement that stated it 'in no way wanted to adopt the role of fashion dictator'.[154] *The Times* utilised the Board's press release and reassured the trade that the scheme was concerned only with making economies in material and labour resources and had 'no intention of interfering with the "styling" of utility clothes by any manufacturer, provided that he produces clothes which conform to the specifications and are satisfactory in fitting and durability'.[155]

In the seemingly altruistic offer of guidance to mass-manufacture, participation in the Utility Scheme cast the newly formed Incorporated Society as a body of official taste professionals. Within much of the design historical documentation of the Utility Scheme, it is this ethical dimension within the design process that has received recognition. In particular, the manner in which many designers seized on the rationalizing agenda of the Utility Scheme as an opportunity to instil an appreciation of 'good design' in the general population.[156] Unlike many designers working in other fields such as furniture and ceramics, this agenda did not underpin the couturiers' decision to participate.[157] Despite Mosca's suggestion of a desire towards design reform the main reason for the designers' compliance with the government was to secure protection for their workforce in line with the concentration of the industry.[158] In November 1939, *Vogue* had declared the war an opportunity 'for all the great merchants of Britain to look to the prophets in their own country for the models that they have heretofore purchased elsewhere'.[159] However, the minutes of the designer's meetings (whilst noticeably self-censored) allow us to understand that this was not a business objective for many of the couturiers. Their production of made-to-measure clothing was founded on social elitism. The couturiers did not see themselves as altruistic proselytisers for the reform of British industrial fashion design and had no urge to inspire their wholesale competitors.

This first attempt at design collaboration between the mass-market manufacturers chosen to produce the prototypes and the couturiers was to prove problematic. The Board of Trade, in interviews with both the designers and the participating wholesalers, found that both parties were swift to criticise each other's design or production methods. The couturiers did note, however, that Molyneux's working relationship was 'smooth and efficient', Stiebel's coat was done with 'excellent co-operation' and Creed's suit and coat was produced through a 'satisfactory collaboration'.[160] However, they also pointed out that Mosca had 'considerable concern' about the cut of both coat and suit and a new maker had to be found, and whilst Russell's suit achieved a 'very good cut' by the first maker, the second (by an unconnected factory) was not as successful. Similarly, Champcommunal was pleased with her suit, but found the maker-up not as 'style conscious as desirable', and Amies 'struggled to get makers who could find a sense of balance in their production'. Whilst Morton found his suit 'satisfactory', 'members of the fashion trade' informed the Board that the suit, as produced, would not be 'suitable for mass production'. It was the couturiers' move away from tailored suits and their design for dresses, however, that caused the most 'hostility from the trade'. The Board of Trade informed the Incorporated Society that it was more than 'a little disappointed' in them. Some designs, particularly those by Molyneux and Creed, were criticised for the cut and details, which were both considered 'more intricate than the trade desired'. The dresses by Champcommunal and Russell were also criticised for needing more yardage than the restrictions and coupons allowed—an accusation denied by Russell, who stated that his dress 'was cut from the yardage and was extremely simple to make'.[161]

The production of the utility prototypes placed the couturiers outside their field of expertise and proved a test to their skill as they were exposed to considerably different agendas and working practices. This led the Board of Trade (in its assessment of the Couturier Scheme's production process) to conclude that the venture 'had not proved that a well-established name ensured expert cut and production'.[162] The Board was also aware of the dangers inherent in the use of the Mayfair designers, which could result in a paradoxical effect and encourage desire for new clothes. The couturiers' participation was intended not to stimulate but to stabilise the market; the government was therefore wary of any undue promotion, as it had no desire to prompt unnecessary consumption. To counteract this effect, models were sold without distinguishable labels, although retailers were allowed to use window displays and advertisements 'to draw attention to the Mayfair designs'.[163] The caution taken to introduce the couturiers' models to the press is made clear by the mannequin parade the Board of Trade organised in September 1942. This carefully controlled publicity exercise was not a dress show in the ordinary sense. Much of the glamour and spectacle of a typical fashion display was removed by the government's decision to present the clothes on young women in its employ without accessories or make-up. It is also clear that the Board of Trade used the display as an opportunity to promote a fashion for bare legs, this responded to the current restrictions on the supply of women's stockings, which were made from materials now reserved for war production. The fact that this was a trade show was also made apparent as the couturiers' original prototypes were shown alongside their industrial copies. This ensured that the Board made consumers clearly aware that the models available to them would be mass-manufactured adaptations. The press images demonstrated few distinguishable differences between the original models and the ones adjusted for mass production (figure 3.8). The similarity of the couture and mass-produced models could easily have lain open the couturiers' design skills to question and had a negative impact on their prestige and claim to creativity. This was counteracted by the reportage in trade magazines such as *Draper's Record* and *Women's Wear Daily*, which were quick to note that the elimination of 'design detail to make production simpler' had stripped certain garments of their 'character and main interest'.[164] At the same time the Board's donation of the couturiers' models to the Victoria and Albert Museum was a clever manoeuvre that ensured the original prototypes were immediately recognised as historically significant and the couturiers' contribution an 'important landmark' in the Utility Scheme.[165]

Figure 3.8
Board of Trade fashion show to launch the couturier designs for the Utility Scheme, London, 22 September 1942. First and third from left: Original models by the Incorporated Society of London Fashion Designers; second and fourth from left: wholesale models produced from the design templates. *Source:* Topfoto.

For the Board of Trade the symbolic success achieved by the Couturier Scheme proved to be more important than the practical impact on British manufacture. The sale of the templates achieved only 'moderate success', with only 1,200 sold.[166] Tom Heron (the director of Cresta Silks, who oversaw the Couturier Scheme) was able to praise the venture, however, as it challenged trade opposition to the Utility guidelines. He also offered the government an informed account of the main factors that led to the trade's mediocre response. This ranged from reasons such as the 'timing of the scheme', which was introduced at a point when manufacturers were 'more interested in price control than in styling' and when they were wary of a 'hidden agenda for further governmental controls' to manufacturers' dislike of 'long runs in a limited number of styles' and their disappointment at 'the simplicity of the models having expected something more sensational'.

The most important element behind the manufacturers' rejection of the Couturier Scheme was that the 'trade resented the implication that it was necessary to go outside itself for designing talent'.[167] Contemporary press reports support this last aspect of Heron's summation, for whilst theoretically the scheme appeared unproblematic many garment manufacturers were reported to be 'as mad as hornets with it in practice'.[168] *Women's Wear Daily* pointed out that many wholesalers dismissed the scheme as 'much ado about nothing' and questioned what the couturiers could offer that the concentrated industry, 'which now constituted the best mass manufacturers in the country', could not. Heron reported that, ironically, this industrial antagonism was in fact beneficial as the Couturier Scheme raised design standards, not through the prototypes created but by its encouragement of 'many of the industry's leading firms to prove that they could do better than the couturiers'.[169]

The designer's participation within the Utility Scheme may have been principally symbolic, and any impact on the mass market limited.[170] However, it did position couture production within the collectivist strictures of the Peoples' War (a populist view that class divisions and individual objectives were forgotten as the whole nation pulled together to defeat the common enemy).[171] For the Board of Trade, the most important aspect of the Couturier Scheme was that it acted as a morale-boosting demonstration of the government's commitment to the concept of 'fair share'. The Couturier Scheme can therefore be seen as a central component within the political message that the war had seen the nation pull together, what historian Geoff Ely describes as the government's 'narrative of popular democratic accomplishment'.[172] The Board of Trade, by allowing every British woman access to couturier-designed outfits, had apparently made the unattainable clothing and taste of the elite available for all. The Incorporated Society's elitist form of fashion production was therefore made compatible with what Sonya Rose, in her study of the contradictory articulations of citizenship that emerged during the conflict, has called the 'egalitarian morality' of the official discourse of Britain during World War II.[173]

Despite the restrained approach taken in the official mediation of the Couturier Scheme, *Vogue* chose to present the models in a more glamorous and exclusive manner. Its coverage, of the Utility prototypes, featured fully accessorised mannequins and a distinct emphasis on surface, polish and pose, and retained much of the couture clothing's pre-war sensibility of aspiration. This representation was very different to the government dress parade and challenges the popular understanding that surrounds the Utility scheme: that class divisions were removed. In fashion magazines such as *Vogue* the products of the London couture (despite propaganda and the popular belief that claimed social distinctions were suspended during the war) continued to remain a signifier of class and status. This aligns with Sonya Rose's contention that 'if the [wartime] nation was one people, it was certainly a people who saw themselves differentiated by social class'.[174] *Vogue*'s presentation of the Couturier Scheme also corresponds with Martin Francis' analysis of the photographer Cecil Beaton's wartime work, which highlights the 'elaborate confection of continuity and change that characterized British culture between 1939 and 1945'. He argues:

> For all its collectivist fervour, the People's War imaginary contained space for the production and articulation of alternative aesthetic codes and, by association, for the promotion of anti-collective and anti-populist social values and cultural sensibilities. Beaton did not stand alone in this respect, and similar political and cultural desiderata can be retrieved from a medley of contemporary sites.[175]

Features in fashion magazines operated as such a site, where the plutocratic system implicit in made-to-measure dress can be seen to have retained a reassuring presence. This reveals a complex layering within the collectivist wartime rhetoric; for example, in February 1943, *Vogue* chose a new softly tailored, collarless dress by Amies for a feature that purported to help women adapt to a 'new whirlwind beauty routine'.[176] Whilst the text was a response to wartime needs, its accompanying photograph made no reference to the war and presented the model, in her made-to-measure dress, leaving for work with a leopard skin fur coat casually draped over her arm. Amies' clothes were also used in a *Harper's Bazaar* feature in November 1943 in which the models were depicted, as though in a continuation of life before war, on 'an expedition to Constance Spry's to choose posies'. Such examples, taken from many, demonstrate that the production of elite, made-to-measure clothes for a class-based society continued to have considerable purchase in the symbolic economy of the war.

The continuation of consumer interest in luxury production and the trappings of elite dress culture is also made clear by *Ship with Wings*, the first feature film collaboratively costumed by the Incorporated Society (figure 3.9).

Figure 3.9
Film still of one of the costumes designed by the London couturiers for *Ship with Wings*, directed by Sergei Nolbandov (Ealing Studios, 1942). *Source:* Mary Evans.

Where later wartime films concentrated on collective heroism, this example of stiff-upper-lip propaganda from Ealing Studios was based on personal redemption. The film went on general release in cinemas across Britain at the same time as the government presented the Couturier Scheme to the public.[177] Yet it had gone into production eighteen months earlier and was conceived as part of the export drive. The first forty minutes were set pre-war, primarily in nightclubs and the drawing rooms of the officer classes, which allowed full scope for the couturiers to present glamorous, desirable day and evening wear. By the time of its release the attitude to luxury production had completely altered and it was therefore attacked by a number of critics and intellectuals for its 'lack of realism'.[178] Despite this, *Ship with Wings* received an overwhelmingly positive reception from both the public and the popular press. In a Mass Observation survey it garnered the highest approval rate of any British wartime film, at 80 per cent.[179] In terms of popular reception this positioned it alongside the costume melodramas of the Gainsborough Studio, which the film historian Pam Cook, in a challenge to the official discourse of egalitarianism and self-restraint, has interpreted as a wartime yearning for hierarchy and expressivity. The success of the first film with costumes collaboratively designed by the London couturiers offers a clear indication of the continued appeal of an elite culture of dress amidst the destruction and egalitarianism of war.

★   ★   ★

In May 1944, after nearly five years of war, when the American trade journal *Women's Wear Daily* examined the position of the London dressmakers, it was able to report that there were

> [n]o casualties among the establishments that had been well-known in the American market prior to 1939, although many now operate on so small a scale as to be practically non-existent, but the threads of business are there to be picked up. . . . [S]mall collections, six-month delay on orders, shared premises, constantly diminishing staffs and the practically non-existence of the seasonal element characterize the private dressmaking trade in London today. . . . The Incorporated Society of London Fashion Designers is still an active body and has done a lot during the war to smooth out wartime regulations for its members. The society has been instrumental in working up closer collaboration between fabric manufacturers, which will bear fruit in better times.[180]

In comparison to their position in 1939, the war had depleted the operation and production capacity of the individual couture businesses. Yet, rather than disappear into obscurity, these small craft-based fashion houses survived the devastation with an increased level of power and agency. During the war collaboration amongst the separate couture businesses became a prerequisite to survival rather than a choice. To sustain their businesses a small number of London's couturiers used collaborative activity and created the Incorporated Society, to not only navigate the microeconomics of war mobilisation but also to bring the narrative that surrounded their practice into line with the ideology of the 'People's War'. This saw the representation of their design practice, particularly in the national press, move from the pre-war celebration of privilege and creativity to one of national importance and civic virtue. In 1944, when the Ministry of Information photographed Molyneux in his dress house, pre-war glamour and elegance had been replaced with an austere business space; the couturier presented as a professional focused on export and business (figure 3.10). In comparison, the Ministry's images from Hartnell presented a different vision, which addressed an anti-collectivist yearning for pre-war sensibilities, with his designs for evening wear symbolically displayed in the miraculously preserved fragility of his mirrored and chandeliered salon staircase (figure 3.11). The representation of both couturiers had a specific agency within the narratives of the People's War.

Throughout the sustained period of national emergency, it could be expected that luxury fashion would have become ultimately irrelevant as the Incorporated Society's field of production sat in contradiction to the fundamental concept of the People's War. However, a complex and extraordinary network of support saw the couturiers emerge in 1945 not as anachronistic elitists but as proponents of Britain's export campaign and the government's morale-boosting political narrative of 'fair share'. The war was therefore a seminal moment for English couture. It created an extraordinary combination of circumstances that allowed the previously impossible objectives of agencies of design reform, such as the Fashion Group and British Colour Council, to be realised. Despite their diminished workforce and output, the members of the Incorporated Society of London Fashion Designers and their elitist form of fashion production emerged from the People's War in a strengthened position in the eyes not only of the British

Figure 3.10
Ministry of Information photograph of Captain Molyneux seated in his London salon
(1944). *Source:* © Imperial War Museum.

Figure 3.11
Ministry of Information photograph of two mannequins posing for the camera on a staircase at the fashion house of designer Norman Hartnell (1944). *Source:* Imperial War Museum D23068.

public, but also, most importantly, of those of government officials and the textile industry.

Ultimately, this chapter has shown that after the British government received the financial support of the Lend-Lease Agreement in 1941, the need for exports, and therefore couture production, was removed, and as a direct response, to protect its members' businesses within a fully mobilized economy, the Incorporated Society of London Fashion Designers was formed. For the couturiers the Society's main aim was to create an identity that would convince the government to protect their field of

luxury production. The stated aims contained within the Society's constitution were impossible to achieve in the war-time economy, so it is difficult to assess how fully its designer-members believed in these objectives
or whether they were written merely as a justification and to fulfil the legal
requirements for the formation of an incorporated society. After the war,
however, these aims (many of which had been formulated by the Fashion
Group in the 1930s) took on a political edge of some urgency. It is in the
immediate post-war period that this study can now analyse how the Incorporated Society actually operated and to what extent its members were able
to meet the aims that had been set for them.

LONDON CAN MAKE IT: THE POST-WAR RECONSTRUCTION OF A FASHION CENTRE

> It must be admitted that the factors that made Paris the centre of international social life are changed almost beyond recognition, today, therefore we must believe reluctantly but inevitably that it may be some time before the Paris couture will again share in the fashion leadership of the world. Yes we said share, and that's just what we meant for we think that after the war, . . . fashions will emanate from more than one centre. Certainly, America will be one. Certainly, London will be another. The English designers were just beginning to come into their own at the beginning of this war. The return of Molyneux to London has certainly helped them still more, and if he stays there he will be the nucleus for a London couture, since everyone in the fashion world will go to London for his collection.[1]

In October 1944, when the Parisian couturiers presented their first post-liberation collections, the New York Fashion Group held an important luncheon to debate the future structure of the international fashion industry. At this point, as Mildred Smolze, a representative of the influential *Tobé Fashion Reports*, made clear, there were doubts over whether 'the French capital could ever recapture its crown and reign once more as the undisputed fashion queen of the world'. Her encouragement for the American Group's members to take every effort to ensure that New York did not 'lose the fashion leadership it has established in the past few years' captured a protectionist attitude towards the post-war reconstruction of the industry. Throughout the war American ready-to-wear designers, due to concerted industrial and promotional support, had increased their public recognition, and proved to manufacturers and retailers that they could provide them with style guidance without the creative influence of Paris couturiers.[2] At the same time, the creation of the Incorporated Society of London Fashion Designers under the chairmanship of Edward Molyneux had given structure to the British couture industry and offered a clear European alternative to Paris. Whilst Smolze voiced her support for the re-establishment of

Paris as an important fashion centre, this was immediately tempered by her assertion that this would be 'some way off' and she asked her audience to divorce themselves from their 'nostalgia for the pre-war situation and look at the cold hard facts' of the economic and cultural position of war-torn Europe.[3] The view of the Tobé organisation was that in the future there would be three main fashion centres, New York, London and Paris, each with its own identifiable strengths that would have equal claim to creativity and design authority. As the war drew to a close, although their businesses had been seriously reduced by the conflict, the couturiers were faced with a clear opportunity to position London as the most important European fashion centre for the American market.

In Britain, the members of the Incorporated Society also found themselves in a fortunate position as the need for export revenue and therefore creative design once again became a political priority. British design reform was given state sponsorship through the creation, in 1944, of the Council of Industrial Design (CoID), which had a remit 'to promote by all practicable means the improvement of design in the products of British industry'.[4] When he agreed to the funding structure of this new Council, Hugh Dalton (the president of the Board of Trade) made specific reference to the problem that had fuelled much of the work of the Fashion Group of Great Britain and Council for Art and Industry in the 1930s: the import of American cotton dresses. He informed the War Cabinet Reconstruction Committee that the post-war prospects of Britain's export trade were dependent not only on industrial efficiency and marketing but also on their design:

> Unless we can be ahead of the other fellows in the efficiency (and if possible the novelty) of our designs for machine-made goods, we shall be competing on a price basis pure and simple; and there we may well be at a disadvantage. . . . Something like an industrial revolution has taken place in the United States in the last fifteen years—a revolution of industrial design. It has made many of our exports old-fashioned and less acceptable. . . . On design alone we were threatened pre-war, even in our home dress trade by American importation . . . and after the war things may well be worse, because of the large progress made in other countries (particularly America), while our need to export will be even greater than it was.[5]

The focus of the CoID may have been on machine-made products; however, this did not negate the role luxury goods could play in design reform.

In the immediate post-war period textiles still formed the largest single category of British exports.[6] The couturiers' participation in the 1941 South American tour had qualified their position as 'shop window' for this particular industry. It had also ensured that their ability to promote the prestige and 'eye appeal' of British-made goods abroad had been recognised within government circles.[7] This acknowledgement is illustrated in a letter sent to Dalton in February 1944 from Lord Woolton (who had chaired the Council of Industry and Art's aforementioned Dress Subcommittee's report on the British fashion industry in the late 1930s). In it, the newly appointed Minister for Reconstruction informed the Board of Trade that the future Council of Industrial Design should

> [b]e concerned with doing all it could to establish London as a centre for women's fashion after the war. If after the fighting is over, Europe is slow in settling down and returning Paris to its position within the dress trade, I believe there will be a great opportunity for making London into such a centre. . . . [During the war] you have established close contacts with the British designers: I should have thought on the whole, they would welcome the establishment of studios for the development of London's prestige.[8]

Dalton's response was positive and assured the Minister that the new Council would make every effort to 'back the couture, . . . [and not] let slip the opportunity of making London a centre of fashion after the war'.[9] A fashion centre was an important trade stimulus that focused attention not only on the garments produced by elite couturiers but also on the ability of the products of British manufacturers to compete in world markets. In light of this correspondence, which saw the pre-war aspirations of the Fashion Group of Great Britain enter the political agenda of the country's main institution of design reform, it appears that the couturiers' ability to promote London as a fashion centre had become an economic concept with political potency.

As World War II drew to an end the London couturiers were therefore positioned within a favourable industrial and political climate in both America and Britain. The abrupt termination of the Lend-Lease Agreement in August 1945 meant that exports, once again, moved to the top of the government's agenda. The British designers were up against stiff competition from Paris, however, particularly as France immediately set out to re-establish its own position and devoted 36 per cent of its first post-liberation foreign policy budget to cultural propaganda.[10] In comparison, having won the war and faced with what were seen as more pressing economic problems, the British government felt little need to finance this type of 'soft' policy. The country had emerged from the conflict a bankrupt, debtor nation; it had sold its foreign investments, sacrificed its export trade and lost its shipping and international insurance industry.[11] The war may have ended with the surrender of Germany to the Allies in May 1945, but restrictions, rationing and austerity not only continued but also increased. With the safety net of Lend-Lease money removed, the main economic problem for Britain was how to generate the revenue needed to pay for the imports indispensable to national recovery.[12] The government's reaction was to restrict imports, to control the movement of funds out of sterling and to embark on an export drive. The main concern, as the economist Sir Alec Cairncross points out, was not the balance of payments deficit but the drain of gold and dollars from the country's reserves. This meant that 'in a world of inconvertible currencies' it was not exports per se that were important but their destination: 'if payments were made in sterling, Britain was no further on in finding the means to settle accounts with the United States, her principal supplier . . . it was only too easy to end up with a large export surplus to countries making payment in "soft" currencies and a deficit in "hard" currencies'.[13] Paddy Maguire's work on post-war export demonstrates that for many British manufacturers it was particularly difficult, 'far more so than in markets elsewhere in the world', to expand exports to the highly productive and competitive North American market.[14] The couturier's collaborative shows for American buyers in the 1930s and the 'Britain Delivers the Goods' showcase during the war had fortuitously already demonstrated to the Board of Trade the role luxury clothing could play in the promotion of British fashion and textiles to the crucial dollar markets. This was duly recognised in a governmental policy change in November 1946, which was implemented specifically to allow the makers of high-level non-utility clothing to increase their export capacity. For these producers the new regulations extended their fabric and coupon allocations, lifted the policy of a ceiling price on their profits and granted import licences (if two thirds were used for export) for high-grade foreign fabric.[15]

The London couturiers were therefore positioned within a particularly positive environment, and yet, to a certain extent, the race to become the world's most important fashion centre was ended in February 1947 by the launch of Christian Dior's seminal 'New Look' collection, which re-established the creative power of Paris. This suggests that the London couturiers had 'let slip the opportunity' they were presented with at the end of the war. This chapter will therefore consider the immediate post-war years, with a specific focus on 1946 and 1947, when expectations for the ability of the newly formed Incorporated Society to position London as the most important world fashion centre were at their highest. To explore the construction of the post-war identity of the Incorporated Society it will focus on specific examples of mediation undertaken in the national arena, in the form of the couturiers' export shows and their participation in specific films and the *Britain Can Make It* exhibition. This allows a consideration of not only how the Society operated but also the extent to which it achieved the objectives set out in its constitution. The external identity of London couture will then be considered in direct relation to Paris to demonstrate the impact Dior's New Look had on London's identity as a fashion centre.

THE CONTINUATION OF POST-WAR COLLABORATION, PROTECTIONISM AND THE CONSTRUCTION OF POWER

The formation of the Incorporated Society, which did not happen until over two years into the war, was the result of specific wartime conditions, not a choice but a necessity for the London couturiers. It is therefore understandable that the minutes of the designers' meetings throughout the first year of peace show that the couturiers were reticent about collaboration and the continuation of the Society, and its dissolution was regularly discussed. To understand the exact nature of the Incorporated Society it is therefore pertinent to explore the factors behind the post-war continuation of this official form of designer collaboration. The couturier's ambivalence towards the Society should be seen in terms of the microeconomics of their day-to-day business. The onset of peace positioned them within a seller's market, driven by a pent-up demand for consumer goods of all kinds. 'Business', as Hardy Amies discovered when he returned on leave from the army in 1945, 'was so good that the workrooms were jammed to capacity'.[16] The increased level of demand for made-to-measure dress, despite the continuation of rationing and coupons, is demonstrated in the Lachasse customer accounts for this period. A typical example that illustrates the swift increase in individual consumption is Countess Gurowska's account. In 1942 it records an expenditure of £40 at the house, when the client initially (alongside many other customers) purchased only hats, and had her suits altered and shortened. Gurowska's yearly expenditure at this dress house then increased to £158 in 1946, when she began to order new clothes; then to £233 in 1947.[17] A similar increase in demand was reported at all the separate dress houses.[18] This brought about a return to competitive business objectives. In October 1946, however, despite the resignation of Molyneux, who returned to Paris, the members voted unanimously to continue to operate within the Incorporated Society's framework.[19] To understand this decision, it must be viewed in the context of the continued instability of supply and demand, which had a serious impact on both the production and consumption of couture.

In terms of economic policy, the war and the immediate post-war years can be seen as a single period, since many controls not only continued but also increased after May 1945. To control inflation, for example, the government implemented one expedient after another: high taxation to take up surplus purchasing power and to balance government expenditure, wage freezes and limitation on dividends, propaganda for increased personal savings and encouragement of the banks to impose restrictions on credit. Such measures, and in particular the deflation of buying power by Purchase Tax at the rate of 22 per cent on each quarter's sales, had serious effects on the whole of the British apparel industry.[20] These political policies made clothes significantly more expensive, and although the couturiers found ready demand in the domestic market, the purchasing power of their clients remained highly unstable. Similarly, the couturiers' ability to sustain production continued to be compromised by other government regulations such as import duties, rationing and the coupon system, the limited and controlled availability of materials and a shortage of new and trained workers.[21] Such factors prolonged the members' reliance on the protective framework provided by a specific couture association.

Wartime shortages and controls brought the couturiers into unprecedented contact with government departments such as the Board of Trade and the Ministry of Supply. This brought the negotiating function of business association to the fore. The economic research of Leonard Tivey and Ernest Wohlegemuth demonstrates that, in the twentieth century, as governments became more important within the economic and social sphere, trade associations grew and increased their influence.[22] This was because they operated as interest groups and fulfilled a political and industrial need for voluntary business organisations that could represent, to successive governments, their members' commercial interests and collective views. Both during and after the war, this 'marked trend' in business organisation became a 'permanent and indispensable feature of modern industrial organisation', which made it necessary for almost every trade to work 'hand-in-glove' with government departments.[23] For the couturiers (who all produced the same type of product and were similarly affected by political policy) membership of the Incorporated Society therefore gave their businesses professional definition and a mouthpiece to present their specific interests to the government.

The structure of the INCSOC also allowed the couturiers to collectively deal with matters of common concern, such as recruitment and labour protection. For example, the designers were able to share the costs and time commitments of a recruitment campaign to 'promote the job prospects in their workrooms', which in 1946 was considered 'the most pressing and important piece of work which the members could perform'.[24] This saw the couturiers all agree to participate in joint lectures and dress parades at 'nearly all of the country's trade and elementary schools'.[25] In addition, to protect their investments in the training of new recruits, the members also agreed to a 'gentleman's understanding' that ensured 'no bribery of staff from each other'.[26] Throughout the life of the Society, this particular rule, as Michael Talboys (a design assistant at Hartnell in the 1950s) pointed out, 'left a strict code of conduct and it worked all the way through, even if you were a junior girl in a workroom, you were virtually owned by that house you worked for'.[27] This continued even when houses closed down as the Society's members quickly employed each other's redundant staff.[28] The INCSOC therefore offered a level of business protection and created the space for collective bargaining between both the government and its separate members. The continuation of this collaborative framework was therefore, as with many trade associations of the period, 'a matter of plain logic and straightforward economic interest'.[29]

For the government, the most important contribution the Incorporated Society offered was to increase exports. It must therefore be recognised that the identity of the Society was constructed as an export group and that in the later part of the 1940s collaboration was always focused on this economic agenda. Yet, whilst the couturiers' engagement within the British export campaign may appear self-explanatory, the minutes of the Incorporated Society meetings evidence that this was also undertaken under duress. The Society's designer-members initially considered the development of exports 'a sacrifice' in terms of their 'time and labour', as the home market was large and growing, their resources were limited, and there remained the distinct possibility that this 'distraction' could leave them at a disadvantage when a competitive buyers' market returned.[30] September 1945 saw William Haigh (the Society's wool industry vice president) forced to cajole the couturiers into an appreciation of the macroeconomics of their position. He recommended that they 'look beyond the current situation' and see the Society's engagement in the export campaign as 'a case of working in the national interest for the future . . . a long-term policy dictated by the economic conditions of the world today, for unless Britain did attain sufficient exports the home trade for any type of luxury good would eventually become non-existent'.[31] Haigh's argument may have been persuasive; however, it was more probable that the couturier's active engagement with the export campaign was prompted by the access it now gave them to luxury foreign fabrics. A focus on the conservation of raw materials and revenue generation saw four fifths of the country's textiles remain under government allocation and luxury fabrics produced for 'export only'.[32] The Board of Trade's policy change (to guarantee import licences for high-grade foreign fabric if two thirds were used for export) meant that the only way the couturiers could gain legal access to any high-quality fabric for their British clients was to use the one third of foreign material allowed within the new import/export regulations.

The couturiers may have agreed to participate in the export campaign under the banner of the Incorporated Society, yet, despite requests from the Board of Trade, foreign buyers and the fashion press to replicate the joint collections of the pre-war Fashion Group, they steadfastly refused to participate in a centralised showcase at a large hotel.[33] Instead, coordinated over four days from January 1946 onwards, with timings that did not clash and restricted specifically to foreign buyers and the press, the Society presented 'export only' collections from each of its members' individual dress houses. It is telling that although several of the couturiers also 'considered it desirable' to coordinate the home collections, to bring 'further focus of attention to the Society's members', this idea was vetoed.[34] Collaboration was not undertaken to promote competitors' businesses in the home market but was aimed solely at the export market. The Society's twice-yearly export shows, rather than a mutually supportive network of competitors, was an example of business preservation and an appeal for support from the government and textile industry.

For six months of the year, at the expense of their home market, all the members of the Incorporated Society turned their workrooms over to export production. In so doing, the designers received not only orders from foreign buyers but also a boost to their reputations. Press reports once again positioned them as important 'ambassadors' for the export campaign: 'their success', in the words of *Woman's Journal*, was also 'the nation's success'.[35] This continued the wartime narrative that the Incorporated Society was not an example of individual commercialism but an altruistic component of the British economy. The type of imagery disseminated by the couturiers supported this view. Figure 4.1, the press release image of the dress rehearsal of Stiebel's first export collection of 'Non-Austerity Fashion for Foreign Buyers', demonstrates this by its inclusion of the workroom staff as its audience. Their worried expressions and clear personal investment in the collection counteracted the lavishness of the model on display. This was an image sensitive to political austerity where, to use the historian Sheryl Kroen's words, 'one sees the continued insistence upon the importance of the worker and the dignity of labour in the post-war social order'.[36] The couture dress no longer represented an elite frivolity, but instead, the livelihoods of not only this female audience but also the nation as a whole. This type of image ensured that couture production was promoted and recognised not as an individual capitalist venture but as a social commitment to the nation's economic agenda.

The reports of the first export collection also supported this narrative; for example, *Women's Wear Daily* informed its transatlantic readers that in the presentation of 'the fruits of their versatile minds to potential buyers from all over the world . . . London's celebrated haute couturiers have made a magnificent effort to assist the country in her year of need'.[37] British *Vogue* went further and presented them as the lone saviours of the British fashion industry, in its declaration that it was 'largely due to the members of the Society that we owe the fact that London, while fighting for her very existence, has kept its high place in the fashion world'[38]—an assertion that was surely galling not only to those couturiers who were not members but also to the rest of the 'concentrated' fashion industry who had also sustained

Figure 4.1
'Non-Austerity Fashion for Foreign Buyers': Dress rehearsal for Victor Stiebel's first
Export Collection, watched by Jacqmar's workroom employees, January 1946. *Source:*
Reproduced courtesy of Adrian Woodhouse.

production throughout the war and been culled to the most efficient and
productive manufacturers. The couturier's commitment to export therefore continued the wartime understanding that the production of elite
made-to-measure clothing was beneficial to the nation, which in turn
elevated the industrial and social standing of the Incorporated Society's
members. The narrative constructed by such reports demonstrates how the
Society operated as a vehicle of exclusion; those who were members were
the professionals who had saved the industry, whilst those who were not
held little power or agency.

Cooperation with direct business rivals clearly had its advantages as it
brought a greater measure of stability to couture production, a far more
attractive option than unfettered competition. It also ensured a level of
control over the identity of the London couture industry as promotion

became a joint venture. For example, to inaugurate the start of the January 1946 collections and take control of its publicity, the Society organised a press conference at Norman Hartnell's dress house and for three weeks rented a room at Claridge's hotel to entertain buyers and supply members of the press with promotional material. Yet commercial rivalry was not eradicated. It can therefore be concluded that for its members, the Incorporated Society had a strictly limited and defined purpose; as a trade association it gave each member professional recognition; as an interest group it made the views of its members known to the government; and as an export group it extended the couturiers' market and encouraged support from the government and textile industry.

The January 1946 export collections recorded the attendance of approximately sixty foreign buyers, from America, Scandinavia, Belgium, Denmark, Norway, Turkey, Iraq, Egypt, Australia, Canada, Bermuda and China.[39] Sales were reported as 'healthy', except to the all-important American dollar market.[40] In April, Hardy Amies used a two-week tour of a number of large American department stores to determine why. From this research he produced an optimistic report for his fellow couturiers on the nascent capacity of the American market.[41] He found that sales to the American market had been slow in January because 'buyers had restricted budgets and were instructed "to examine the market"; to go slow until they found out just what sort of clothes we were producing' and 'what they want is our tailored suits'.[42] Amies saw three key factors that he claimed would give London couturiers an advantageous market position. First, he found that American consumers were currently 'British minded'. This commercial expediency was also acknowledged in the British Council's 1945 report, *The Case for Cultural Publicity*, which found transatlantic attitudes to Britain were 'at an all-time high . . . [and the country whilst] possessing only limited means in the political and economic fields of living up to its newly acquired reputation . . . [was] enjoying enormous prestige and popularity, due to the nation's conduct during the war'.[43] Amies' second observation was that American protectionism had dissipated, and that 'the campaign that certain sections of the fashion press, stores and garment manufacturers waged during the war against buying in Europe, is definitely admitted to be a complete failure. . . . Yet there remains a very slight anti-French feeling which together with the slightly higher price of Paris models, swings the market into London's favour'.[44] The lukewarm response to the Paris collections of 1946, expressed in some sections of the American daily press, provides evidence of this anti-French attitude. For instance, in March, the *New York Times* (which played a crucial role in the promotion of American designers throughout the war) even questioned the prestige of French couture and claimed that its high cost had deterred 'smart' Parisians, so it was bought by vulgar 'black market' clients and was now 'branded as a sign of bad taste'.[45] This newspaper also provided a damning estimation that for the American consumer the French couturiers were 'too flamboyant, presented little that was new and showed no design unity or leading trends'.[46] Amies' third point, in support of London models, was that they were seen as 'more in tune with American taste'.[47] The 'flamboyance' of Parisian models meant they were 'of course a wonderful source of inspiration', but in comparison to their British counterparts, they had to be adapted rather than sold as originals. The couturier found that the scarcity of high-quality clothes meant that certain American retailers were currently able to sell his original models at a profit rather than use them as prototypes for cheaper in-house copies.[48] This claim is verified in a Marshall Field of Chicago advert for an imported tweed dress and jacket outfit by Amies, which shows this 'original' retailed at $700, nearly double its original cost price.[49] Amies' report on the market potential of London couture in America could therefore conclude that its unique selling point was its 'reputation for designs that were restrained and wearable'.[50]

In many British and American newspaper and magazine reports there was an accusation that whilst under occupation the French capital had lost its ability to produce clothing appropriate for the American market. By way of illustration, the idea that French designers had 'lost touch with reality through wartime isolation' dominated both the text and images of an article Alison Settle wrote for *Picture Post* under the heading 'London: Can It Become a World Fashion Centre?'[51] Clothing from the Paris house of Alix, with elaborate mutton-chop sleeves, abundant use of fabric and exaggerated millinery, was chosen to illustrate French 'lavishness out of keeping with the spirit of the day'. In contrast, the dinner dresses and coats of the 'London style designers' were described as 'anxious to eliminate the dressy Christmas-tree-with-everything-on-it type of dress and to foster the classical lines of fine tailoring'. In comparison to a French mannequin who was positioned at leisure in front of a gilt mirror, her London counterpart was shown in a demure position, in an almost funereal setting. The photographs of the British mannequins were also careful to present the clothes as a product, either in the process of fitting or with the mannequin handling export fabrics. In the London designers' rejection of ornament and exaggeration there was a clear message: British clothes were not for conspicuous consumption but were practical, patriotic (as they did not waste materials) and in moral alignment with the straitened world situation. Settle also described the London couturiers not as 'fashion' but 'style' designers, a subtle shift, which positioned the concept of 'style' within a discourse of universality, simplicity and functionality. In 1946, Settle therefore used the notion of style to indicate the appropriate, restrained and authentic taste of British dress design in comparison to the extravagant constructed fashions presented in Paris. This narrative was also taken up in American press reports, where the Incorporated Society's models were often congratulated for their ability to modify the 'exaggerated silhouette' of the Paris collections for 'more practical and easy wear'.[52] With the L-85 regulations (America's war time scheme to restrict the materials and styles used in clothing production) still in operation, fashion journalists, producers and promoters could therefore claim that in comparison to Paris, both London and New York had evolved austerity styles that adhered to similar cultural and social objectives.[53]

There was now a 'London school of fashion as distinct from a Paris school', Amies informed the listeners of the *BBC Home Service* in June 1946, and 'the two centres barely conflict, because the sort of things we make best are based on our tailoring, whereas, the sort of things Paris makes best are based on their dressmaking'.[54] In October the American department store B. Altman supported this assertion when they opened their prestige fashion show with every one of the twelve suits produced for Amies' second collection.[55] These tailored garments constituted a third of the couture models the store had bought in Europe. The second part of the show, from a range of Parisian couturiers, contained just five suits alongside sixteen day and evening dresses.[56] In this instance, London and Paris were presented as equal but also very different fashion centres. The narrative that had evolved in the Fashion Group of Great Britain in the 1930s, of London as the centre of hard, tailored and practical couture and Paris of soft, novel, feminine dressmaking gave the English couturiers a commercial advantage. Due to the continuation of restrictions American and British dress cultures were presented as comparable. Tailored styles and a rejection of exaggeration gave many of the London couturiers not only the moral high ground but also an appropriate aesthetic for the American market.[57] With America a seller's market for restrained tailored clothing, it was an opportune time, despite the economic situation and the restrictions placed on production, for the members of the Incorporated Society to become a key component of the British export agenda and make London an important fashion centre for transatlantic buyers.

A QUESTION OF TASTE AND FASHION FANTASY: DESIGN FOR
RESTRAINT AND FUTURE PROSPERITY

London's identity as a fashion centre for hard couture may have been particularly appropriate for the immediate post-war period, yet in 1946, just as it had in the 1930s, it led to disagreement amongst the designer-members of the Incorporated Society. Edward Molyneux, for instance, supported this narrative and believed that the Society's main aspiration should be to 'develop the prestige of London's Tailor-mades and Sports-clothes in wool, cotton and rayon . . . [as it] would never supersede Paris in dressmaking; the "soft" end of couture production'.[58] The most vehement opponent to this identity was, unsurprisingly, Norman Hartnell, who argued that before the war American buyers always took a 'big percentage of his day and evening dresses [and would] continue to do so'.[59] In the first joint export collection, the separate design agendas of the Society's members was not synchronised to support the singular narrative of London as the fashion centre of hard couture. A series of simple tailored suits of brilliantly coloured tweed and a range of sports dresses constituted Molyneux's collection. The dresses and blouses were all in crepe and printed in textile designs by the couturier that featured traditional English sporting images of horse-riders and golfers.[60] The garments' construction was kept simple, whilst the buttons in the shape of hearts, horses' heads and even poached eggs allowed a reserved element of novelty. The collection focused on 'impeccable cut and fastidious attention to detail', whilst the fabric's prints made the clothes immediately recognisable as English and the buttons made them 'amusing'.[61] In comparison to Molyneux's 'restrained' collection Hartnell's was reported to be 'dramatic, even theatrical'.[62] He included a handful of suits, but the majority of his collection reinstated his pre-war dressmaking and focused on evening wear, which featured wasp waists, exaggerated crinolines, lavish beadwork, sequins and velvet evening coats trimmed with cock feathers.[63]

As he prepared to reopen his expansive Paris-based dress salon, Molyneux's London collection could adhere to a contained vision of English clothing production. In comparison, Hartnell's projection of a national design identity created a wider definition for the creative scope of his couture house. The idea of London as the centre of 'hard' couture, propagated most specifically by Molyneux, Creed, Amies and Morton, fitted with a particular vision of British dress culture in the aftermath of war. However, Hartnell's international recognition as dressmaker to the female members of the royal family gave credibility to more spectacular dressmaking. The styles and names of Hartnell's models, such as 'Cinderella', a sequin-covered crinoline, and 'Brazilia', a lavishly embroidered crepe dress, which had a floor-length cloak with epaulets covered in beads, 'some as big as the Crown Jewels', pointed to a reinstatement of extravagance and opulent display. At a time of austerity, Hartnell's 'Cinderella' proclaimed that London couture 'would go to the Ball', and, as he immediately undertook a tour of South American department stores, his 'Brazilia' presented a glamorous challenge to Parisian dressmaking in that particular export market.

In 1946, the Incorporated Society's January export shows may have rejected the idea of a coordinated presentation of only practical suits and knitwear; however, the presentation of the separate collections was carefully sequenced to give an overall narrative structure. The 'key-note' of the first day of showings at Morton and Molyneux were 'eminently wearable', 'tailored' and 'British'.[64] The collections then became steadily more 'soft' and flamboyant so that on the fourth and final day they focused on the elaborate crinoline evening gowns at Hartnell and Worth. There may not have been agreement on the type of clothes the designers should present to the foreign buyers, but a sense of design unity was created through the development of a new, softer and rounded silhouette. Accordingly, all the designers removed the sharp slim-line silhouette of the war years. Suits by Stiebel and Hartnell, for example, had similar rounded lapels, and focused on curves rather than angularity (figure 4.2). To create a rounded figure, Amies padded the hips of coats and jackets with horsehair; Russell used innovative pleating; and Champcommunal at Worth introduced laced-up corsets to ensure the emphasis on the waist. Whilst no export data survives on the sale of these clothes, press reports suggest that the attendant

Figure 4.2
Victor Stiebel suit for London Couture Export Collections, January 1946. *Source:*
Reproduced courtesy of Adrian Woodhouse.

buyers and journalists appreciated this coherent approach to a new, more feminine fashion silhouette, which in turn brought verification to London's ability to generate new and internationally relevant fashions.[65]

The juxtaposition of the elaborate dressmaking practices of Hartnell and Worth with the tailored aesthetic of Amies, Morton, Creed and Molyneux shows there was clearly space in the export collections for both opulence and restraint within the narrative that surrounded the Incorporated Society. The films *A Question of Taste* and *Fashion Fantasy*, which were both produced in 1946 and respectively featured Amies and Hartnell, demonstrate that this dichotomy also had a place within the London couturiers' mediation in Britain.[66] At a time of austerity and political egalitarianism, these films offer a fascinating site to explore the conjunction between the restrictions placed on post-war consumer culture and the desire for luxury fashion. They shed light on the representational position of the London couture industry in Britain and allow a consideration of how this form of design adapted to the political discourse and socialist manifesto of the new Labour government. It also demonstrates the interconnected nature of the different levels of the fashion market with couturiers presented as tastemakers for all levels of the mass market.

A Question of Taste was produced by the Scottish Committee of the Council of Industrial Design (CoID) and the Pathé Documentary Unit and used Hardy Amies as an authoritative and didactic tastemaker. This film was essentially instructional and not made for general release but for distribution in British secondary schools. It sat firmly within the Council of Industrial Design's agenda to modify and control consumption. The film paradoxically uses a dress designer to encourage young women of 'modest means' to reject fashion and 'the variety of clothes', which the commentary claimed were 'considerable, even in these days of shortage!'[67] The press release for *A Question of Taste* states that it was created to give 'correct pointers' to the female 'school leaver' who 'when free to exercise her right to choose what she is to wear, all too often, throws authority to the winds, as she is inclined to select garments that are unsuitable, or uneconomical'.[68] In a continuation of the role the couturiers had adopted for the Utility Scheme (where they provided paternalistic guidance, so that consumers could achieve style through restraint) the Council used Amies to provide these authoritative 'pointers'.

Figure 4.3a
Still from *A Question of Taste*, featuring Hardy Amies as the presenter (Scottish
Committee of the Council of Industrial Design and Pathé Documentary Unit, 1946).
Source: Design Council Archive Brighton.

   The film follows 'Brenda' in her choice of an 'off-the-peg wardrobe for
work and play'. Amies, as a 'leading fashion house expert who has devoted
years to matters of dress', both features in the film and delivers the scripted
commentary to reveal that the 'real secret to being well-dressed . . . is just a
question of taste'[69] (figures 4.3a–c). In line with the nationally altruistic discourse that accompanied the Incorporated Society's export shows he states
that whilst 'my colleagues and I do not specialise in dress for the young, we
are anxious to do all we can to help'. To improve the aesthetic judgements
of young female consumers, Amies then instructs the film's audience to
'try to acquire a sense of taste', through the choice of a 'few simple things'
that 'fit'. And warns 'Brenda' and all young women not 'to fall for something because it is glamorous or the latest fashion'. This advice, and idea
of taste as representative of control and restraint, highlights the moralistic
and paternalistic outlook of the CoID, which advocated a consumerism

Figure 4.3b
Still from *A Question of Taste*, recommendation for a 'wardrobe of taste'. *Source:*
Design Council Archive Brighton.

of protection, control and guidance rather than one of individual choice.
This attitude aligned with the political ideology of the new Labour government, which, as Mathew Hilton shows, 'supported the productive, rational,
Utility-scheme purchasing consumer, but shied away from advocating the
rights of the people to novelty, fashion and mass-market comfort'.[70]

One of the most interesting moments in the film's commentary, in terms
of the couturiers' position within the discourse of post-war consumption,
is when Amies discusses Brenda's choice of coat, and asserts that 'of course
personally I think it would look better still if it was just a fraction longer,
but there again I don't want you to go chasing after the latest fashions'.
The rest of the film negates his role as a fashion designer and adheres to
a design reform agenda wary of the stimulation of consumer desires. In
this context, the comment on the coat can appear subversive, whilst for
the 'school leaver' it can appear patronising. Yet it points to the contradictions that surrounded the British mediation of the London couturiers

Figure 4.3c
Still from *A Question of Taste*, featuring 'Brenda' being guided to choose a correct wardrobe of taste. *Source:* Design Council Archive Brighton.

in the 1940s. Within the politics of consumption, where there was a commitment to price control and the 'fair shares' of commodities, there was a moral distinction between luxury and necessity and between fashion and utility.[71] This was applicable, however, only to the British consumer. The secret to national recovery was economic efficiency based on a combination of restrained domestic consumption and increased production for export. Amies' fashion-conscious sensibility was important to ensure that British products could seduce foreign consumers and thereby increase export quotas. His personal opinion on fashion and the abstinence from fashionable consumption of the 'school leavers' should therefore be seen as mutually compatible components with the country's economic reconstruction.

A similar impetus can be seen to underpin Norman Hartnell's contribution to the film *Fashion Fantasy*, which focuses on a de-mobilised Wren (a member of the Women's Royal Navy Service) who falls asleep and dreams of becoming a fashion mannequin.[72] After the Wren's preparation

at a modelling school, the film moves to Hartnell's salon where she partic-
ipates in a short presentation of his January export collection (figure 4.4
a–d). Here, as the commentator points out, 'hunters of non-utility glamour
arrive in style to see all the lovely things you can't buy, only look at'.[73] The
design of the clothes may have promoted the continuation of an elaborate
dress culture, but this was only for foreign consumption. Instead of a provocation to a viewing public whose lives were shaped by austerity and shortages, this display of elaborate couture was made acceptable not only by its
role within the export agenda but also by its supposed inaccessibility to all
British women irrespective of class or wealth. *Fashion Fantasy* may also have
operated in a similar manner to escapist films of this period, which Richard
Dyer points out provided 'a much-needed utopian fantasy in opposition
to everyday deprivations'.[74] Hartnell's contribution to the film provided a
panacea for the female consumer that offered reassurance that the restriction of material goods was universal throughout the nation, whilst it also
fulfilled a psychological need for luxury, spectacle and escape. If the film's
display of exclusive fashion invited its British viewer to imagine herself
as a consumer, it was apparently as a consumer who accepted 'continued
austerity in order to ensure the healthy recovery of the economy'.[75] This
fitted with the British government's ideology, which held up abstinence
from consumption as the path to future prosperity for all.[76] Public compliance with this political philosophy was not uncomplicated or universally
accepted, however. This is demonstrated in Ina Zweiniger-Bargielowska's
study of rationing, controls and consumption in the period 1939–1955,
which effectively destabilises the myth of a blitz-spirited country, where
individual grievance disappeared and austerity measures were altruistically
embraced for the good of the nation.[77] Her comprehensive summary of
the effects on the British consumer of the system of controls introduced by
the government shows that the idea of universal sacrifice was more complex and that 'grumbling' and dissatisfaction were widespread, especially
amongst women who bore the brunt of the persistent shortages.[78] This may
have been a period of austerity, when restrictions were tolerated, but it was
overshadowed by the anticipation of future affluence.[79]

Fashion Fantasy, whilst aligned with the propaganda for consumer abstinence, clearly addressed the female viewers' constrained desire for material
goods and expectation for future prosperity. 'Perhaps the dream will come
true one day', the last line of this film's commentary, spoken by the narrator

Figure 4.4a
Wren falls asleep and dreams of employment as a Hartnell mannequin in *Fashion Fantasy* (Condor Film Productions, 1946). *Source:* British Film Institute.

Figure 4.4b
Wren dreams of getting accepted at a modelling agency. *Source:* British Film Institute.

Figure 4.4c
Wren models Hartnell's export collection inside his Bruton Street dress house. *Source:* British Film Institute.

Figure 4.4d
Wren models Hartnell's export collection inside his Bruton Street dress house. *Source:* British Film Institute.

as the Wren wakes up, opens the film to this interpretation.[80] This ending suggests that, for an audience who continued to live within the economic restraints of post-war Britain, whilst couture production sat outside the experience of everyday egalitarian consumption, it could exist without antagonism, as propaganda for the fulfilment of hope for future material plenitude. In this context, the utilisation of Hartnell's export collection was a pertinent choice for the film, as throughout the war this couturier had produced an eponymous, well-promoted range of utility garments for the mass-market producer Berkertex. It was therefore a credible prospect that in the future his designs would once again be available not only for the royal family and the wealthiest members of society but also for consumers at all market levels. In 1946, films such as *A Question of Taste* and *Fashion Fantasy* gave the London couturiers a level of agency within the consumer practices and aspirations of many British women. Both also demonstrate the inherent contradictions within the domestic identity of the Incorporated Society, which allowed freedom for both the articulation of egalitarian restraint and anti-collective consumer sensibilities.[81]

The appeal to future affluence and the London couturier's dichotomy as restrained tastemakers and producers of glamorous luxury was also made apparent at the main design event of 1946: the *Britain Can Make It* (BCMI) exhibition. This was conceived not as a trade show in the traditional sense but, as the organisers of the exhibition made clear in its *Notes for Guidance to Selectors*, 'as a vehicle for the education of manufacturers and the public in the aesthetics of "good design" . . . [and] first and foremost a prestige show . . . to let the world know that British industry is busy recreating goods of taste and modern design'.[82] In contravention of the Board of Trade's direction that 'no "precious" stuff' be included at this event, and that it all be '*manufactured* goods—not handmade', the made-to-measure dressmakers contributed one fifth of the exhibition's fashion display.[83] This event at the Victoria and Albert Museum in London, organised by the newly established Council of Industrial Design, forms a dominant part of the documentation of British design in the immediate post-war period.[84] Yet the role of fashion, which occupied one quarter of its floor space, has not been acknowledged.[85] To a certain extent this can be explained by the glamorous and commercial nature of the female fashion display, which points to an ambiguous relationship between the protagonists of design reform and this gendered design practice.

Figure 4.5
Revolving couture carousel display at the *Britain Can Make It* exhibition, Victoria and Albert Museum, September 1946. *Source:* Design Council Archive Brighton.

The couture display, which consisted primarily of evening wear, was presented on a revolving, fabric-draped carousel, accessorized with feathered peacocks, bouquets of flowers and rococo stands. This, as figure 4.5 illustrates, was a particularly abundant, mise-en-scène of visual fancy that conformed to a traditional concept of the material culture of femininity. This aesthetic was singled out for condemnation by Raymond Mortimer (editor of the centre-left political magazine *New Statesman and Nation*), who proclaimed that 'the large revolving affair looks as if it had escaped from a Hollywood "musical": not only is it clumsy in its effort to be rococo, but it stifles the clothes it is supposed to display'.[86] James Garner (the chief designer of BCMI) may have claimed that a lot of the exhibition's 'décor— was all Barnum and Bailey . . . [and] made him a name for being a rather airy-fairy designer'.[87] Yet the main impression of the displays and settings is that overall they were 'often imaginative and witty, and widely praised . . . structured in a logical and informative manner . . . from the organisational experience and techniques developed in wartime propaganda'.[88] The overall design of BCMI was therefore defined in masculine terms, and the theatrical, feminine aesthetic language of the couture display stood in stark contrast.[89] In comparison, the womenswear section, with its couture carousel and the wholesale model houses' 'Hyde Park' and 'Palladian Terrace' sets, was made incongruous by its adoption of the more traditional techniques of shop window display.[90] This turn to feminine commercial culture sat in contradiction to the aspirations of the British design reform movement.[91] The design historian Penny Sparke, in her work on the sexual politics of taste, has highlighted the fact that since the nineteenth century, design discourse had developed a 'condemnation of feminine culture', with the 'most vociferous attacks directed at the role of fashion, novelty and display'. She has shown that the CoID's concept of 'good design' (which informed the design and selection process for BCMI) drew on the ideological framework of Modernism, which was constructed through a language of masculinity. Sparke explores how the 'British design reform movement, excluded feminine taste from its self-definition through the formulation of a hierarchical, binary system of terms and concepts: thus "private" was contrasted with, and valued less than, "public"; "fashionableness" with "universal values"; "surface ornamentation" with "minimal form"'.[92] In terms of production, this criticism was aimed at what were seen as the unscrupulous profit motives of manufacturers and retailers who supposedly used these elements, in both design and promotion, to stimulate false desire in the passive female consumer. The womenswear section's use of the visual culture of the feminised shopping experience was therefore a clear contradiction of the design sensibilities of the exhibition's organisers, an illustration that women's clothing (and by extension the idea of London as a fashion centre) sat outside the aesthetic and ideological 'comfort zone' of the proselytisers of design reform.

There is nothing, however, within the CoID's, Board of Trade's or INC-SOC's documentation of the event to suggest that the organisers found the inclusion of couture problematic. In fact, the members of the Society were given full control over what garments they provided and, despite the assertion that this was not a trade show, were promised that their models, which were available for immediate sale, would 'not be exhibited anonymously'.[93]

Unlike the justification for the support of the designers' businesses espoused by the government and within the daily press, the exhibition's catalogue, which documents only the name of the fabric manufacturer for five of the twenty-eight couture garments, suggests that the exhibition's organisers also felt little need to fulfil the Incorporated Society's usual political and industrial disclaimer of 'shop window' for the textile trade.[94]

In light of this neutrality it is therefore insightful, in terms of the operation of the Incorporated Society and the networks of support that developed around it, to address its inclusion in relation to the two main politically sensitive problems design historians have shown were encountered by the Exhibition's organisers: first, the encouragement of and inability to fulfil consumer demand and, second, the accusation of industrial bias in the selection process. The first problem, caused by the lack of product availability, arose as many of the overall exhibits were prototypes or for export only. This led to the unfortunate re-christening of the exhibition, by some sectors of the press hostile to the government, as 'Britain Can't Have It'.[95] The audience at the exhibition may have been primarily 'artisan working class', yet in terms of consumer provocation, both social surveys and press reports suggest that there was little negative criticism of the inclusion of unattainable made-to-measure and exclusive ready-to-wear dress.[96] In fact, after the furnished rooms, Mass Observation recorded the women's dress section as the exhibition's second most popular category.[97] This favourable public attitude can perhaps be explained by a review of the Incorporated Society's January export shows in *Reynold's News and Sunday Citizen*. In the article, 'Clothes Go Abroad but Ideas Stay Home', this egalitarian, cooperative party-owned publication argued that the post-war inaccessibility of couture was 'actually less irritating' than it sounded. For the home-dressmaker, there were 'some good ideas to be had in these new collections and even in pre-war days less than one Englishwoman in a thousand could afford to get her clothes from Hartnell, Molyneux and the other big dress designers'.[98] The hand-made production process and the price of couture positioned it well above the expectations of the exhibition's audience, which meant that it provided 'ideas' and entertainment value rather than a trigger for consumer dissatisfaction. The high price of their crafted products positioned them above the fashion trade, and this justification is important to understand what membership of the Incorporated Society brought to these dressmakers. It demonstrates how the support and promotion of the

Incorporated Society took on neutrality because the designers' work could be viewed as a form of cultural rather than commercial production. So, for example, in 1946 Cecil McGivern (the BBC's director general) granted a dispensation to the members of the Incorporated Society which excluded them from its policy to stop inadvertent advertising because the couturiers were not seen as 'advertisers in the accepted sense of the word'.[99] This meant that they became the only fashion designers automatically credited if their work featured on British television.

The second problem encountered by the exhibition's organisers (something that continued to haunt the CoID) was industry antagonism caused by their selection process. The 67 per cent rejection rate of items submitted to the selection panel by 3,385 separate firms was primarily caused by the excluded producers' equation of 'good design' with their best sellers rather than the aesthetic ideals of the CoID.[100] This disjuncture between the ideological opinions of the advocates of design reform and the commercial knowledge of particular producers led to accusations of industrial bias.[101] To offer a fair representation of London's high-fashion businesses the selection panel included garments from both the ten couturiers in the Incorporated Society and four non-members (the couture houses of Jacqueline Vienne, Lachasse, Strassner and Rahvis). It then contained ready-made garments, many by members of the recently formed London Model House Group, which represented the interests of what was known as the 'wholesale couture' and included companies such as Susan Small and Frederick Stark.[102] These businesses were swiftly establishing West End showrooms with similar décor to the couture houses where they held exclusive presentations of their new collections at the same time as the couturiers. Whilst their designs were not original and primarily adapted models, their output in comparison to mass manufacture was relatively small and individualistic; their products were entirely non-utility; and their standards of craftsmanship and quality were high. Although clothes were not made-to-measure, they were cut and made individually on the stand and no bulk orders or long production runs were taken. Their distribution, through the model departments of high-class stores and through small specialist shops, was also highly selective and guaranteed a level of exclusivity as each manufacturer generally confined their models to a specific outlet in any particular town or city.[103] The members of the London Model House Group also had the capital to devote to expensive advertising campaigns in magazines such as

Vogue and *Harper's Bazaar*, which made many of these businesses household names. The 'wholesale couture' therefore presented a new level of competition to the 'bespoke couture'.

The minutes of the Incorporated Society's meetings show that its members were uneasy about showing their designs next to the 'wholesale couture'. The BCMI organisers therefore constructed a discernible difference between the products that were made-to-measure and those that were off-the-peg. This construction of industrial hierarchy is made clear not only by their separation within the exhibition's dress display, but also in the promotional images used in the Council's publication *Design 46: A Survey of British Industrial Design as Displayed in the Britain Can Make It Exhibition*. Here a simple representational strategy was used to ensure industrial distinction and hierarchy, whereby the different types of fashion production were presented in either an interior or exterior setting. The fashion section of the publication, created under the direction of Audrey Withers (editor of British *Vogue*), therefore adhered to conventions upheld by high-fashion magazines, where it was customary for couture to be presented in illustration or photographed in formal studio settings, while outdoor, reportage-style photography was usually reserved for ready-to-wear products. This conferred greater exclusivity to the former, as the artificial confines of the studio bore little relation to everyday life. In comparison, the outdoors seemingly brought the ready-to-wear clothing closer to reality, 'albeit', as the fashion historian Rebecca Arnold has pointed out, a reality 'seen through the prism of photographers' and fashion editors' idealisations of real lifestyles'.[104]

In figures 4.6a–c, the couture mannequins adopt static poses of haughty grandeur and elegance, in front of either blank studio sets or ones that suggest an opera house or art gallery. These are not the claustrophobic spaces of the *femme d'intérieur* (although they draw on the cultural understanding of her leisured lifestyle and respectability). Rather, they are the spaces of fashionable society's elite recreation and display.[105] In contrast, the wholesale mannequins are represented at an empty fun fair or on an anonymous street, which suggests a slightly different type of woman, one who is not only socially mobile and open to the everyday urban experience but also closer to the lower middle-class consumer (figures 4.7a–c). The more sculptural quality of the couture evening and daywear seen in the angular shape of Hartnell's single-shouldered black velvet evening dress with jutting

Figure 4.6a
Norman Hartnell single shouldered evening dress of black velvet and faille, from the
images of the Incorporated Society's evening clothes featured in *Design 46. Source:*
Design Council Archive Brighton.

Figure 4.6b
Images of the Incorporated Society's evening clothes: a one-shouldered, jewelled white slipper satin evening dress by Norman Hartnell, a black lace over biscuit-coloured net evening dress by Angle Delanghe and a slim, white crepe evening dress with jet embroidered bodice by Victor Stiebel, featured in *Design 46. Source:* Design Council Archive Brighton.

Figure 4.6c
Images of the Incorporated Society's day clothes: a wrap-over light-weight tweed
dress by Hardy Amies, a highwayman's coat by Charles Creed and a tweed greatcoat
with spade-shaped pockets and three buckle belt by Bianca Mosca, featured in *Design
46*. *Source:* Design Council Archive Brighton.

Figure 4.7a
Images of wholesale model house clothes; a softly tailored tweed dress from Frederick
Starke, a town suit by Rensor and a Regency silhouette three-quarter jacket suit by
Brenner Sports, featured in *Design 46*. *Source:* Design Council Archive Brighton.

Figure 4.7b
Images of wholesale model house day clothes: green barathea suit, with plastic
buttons, by Matita, featured in *Design 46*. *Source:* Design Council Archive Brighton.

Figure 4.7c
Images of wholesale model house day clothes: ensemble of worsted suit and topcoat
by Marcus, featured in *Design 46. Source:* Design Council Archive Brighton.

skirt; the turned-up, pointed collar of Creed's suit; and the sharpness of Thaarup's millinery is suggestive of a higher level of creative design. The wholesale model houses' clothes are less dramatic; angularity is removed; and the silhouette, from the turbans to the rounded lapels and the less detailed construction, is softer and therefore less aesthetically defined. The separation of both the photographic space and the clothing styles therefore conferred different ideas of leisure, class and respectability and alleviated the misgivings expressed by the couturiers about presenting their models alongside those of the high-level ready-to-wear industry.[106]

In this way, the BCMI organisers constructed an apparently unchallenged design hierarchy for British fashion. However, although there appears to have been an unproblematic industrial consensus, antagonism caused by the CoID's selection process (which included only fourteen couture and thirty-six high-end wholesale model houses) is made apparent by the actions taken by the Guild of British Creative Designers. This trade association represented twenty-two ready-to-wear houses, and saw all but three of its members excluded from *Britain Can Make It*.[107] This prompted the Guild's large-scale *Parade of Fashion* held nearby at the Royal Albert Hall shortly after the exhibition opened.[108] This presentation received a large amount of public attention, as the clothes were presented on Cochran's showgirls and it was broadcast by the BBC and filmed by Pathé under the (misleading) heading *Mayfair Modes: Albert Hall Fashion Shows Couture Ball, Guild of British Designers*. In an obvious challenge to the 'official' representatives of creative British fashion, the showcase was then taken on the maiden voyage of the *Queen Elizabeth* to Canada under the heading 'The British Ambassadors of Fashion'.[109]

The Guild, to draw attention away from the official exhibits, also orchestrated a form of guerrilla intervention, when it sent the Goldwyn Girls (an American dance troupe), dressed in a selection of its models, to pose for the press in front of the couture display (figure 4.8). The cultural understanding of showgirl identity, as Andrea Stuart has shown, 'is that of the sexual predator as well as that of the corrupted innocent, an emblem of European wickedness as well as Broadway glitz . . . a cipher on to which her audiences have projected profound social anxieties'.[110] The Guild's use of showgirls was therefore subversive as it linked their clothing to sexual display and unrestrained consumption. Antonia Lant has fully explored the precarious status of female glamour that developed in Britain throughout the war,

Figure 4.8
Press publicity photographs of Goldwyn Girls in garments by the Guild of British
Creative Designers in front of the *Britain Can Make It* couture display. *Source:* Design
Council Archive Brighton.

where 'female sexuality was threatening to wartime security, as well as the climate of austerity'.[111] The Guild's use of the showgirl as fashion manne-quin therefore contradicted the politics of post-war British consumption, where rationing, the utility scheme and propaganda for restraint contin-ued to politicize female glamour. An example which demonstrates a more acceptable form of mediation can be seen in figure 4.9, which shows the actress Valerie Hobson on the couture carousel inspecting a rose-printed evening gown by Norman Hartnell. Hobson, as one of her obituaries points out, 'exuded breeding and class' and 'had a certain upper-crust aloofness' and therefore an appropriate persona for the embodiment of the London couturiers' work. As the lead actress of David Lean's recently released film *Great Expectations*, in which she played the alluring Estella, Hobson could easily have brought a level of cinematic glamour to the exhibition; instead, the official press photograph, staged and released by the Council of Indus-trial Design, presented her in heavy topcoat and head scarf—a more accept-able image of British femininity.

The BBC may have officially reported the Guild of British Creative Designers' omission from the Council's exhibition as a consequence of the limited floor space within the Victoria and Albert Museum.[112] However, when comparisons are made of the clothes contained in the Guild's *Parade of Fashion* and those accepted for display at the *Britain Can Make It* exhibi-tion, the role of the organisers' aesthetic judgement is made apparent. This selection criteria is illustrated in Audrey Withers' text in *Design 46* where she pointed out:

> The couture and the wholesale field have this year made their first collections completely free from austerity restrictions. The result, in the couture collec-tions and in those designed by the best wholesale firms, has been wholly admi-rable, but progressively less so the further one goes down the scale of fashion production. It is the old trouble of confusing liberty with licence, one only hopes one is seeing the first fling of reactions for it would be a sad thing if, after four years of war clothes that have at least been clean and uncluttered (enabling English women to live down their deserved-pre-war-reputation for being all bits and pieces) our manufacturers were unable to replace the discipline of offi-cial restrictions with the discipline of taste. . . . All in all, London's new season models are for the most part exceptionally wearable and becoming, adjectives most gratefully used by women to describe clothes which look as if they had been designed with them in mind, and not merely as showpieces for display by showgirls.[113]

Figure 4.9
Council of Industrial Design publicity photograph of the actress Valerie Hobson on
the BCMI Couture Carousel inspecting Hartnell's white satin evening dress patterned
in 'white rose of York' design. *Source:* Design Council Archive Brighton.

Withers' comments, written before the exhibition opened, appear aimed at the Guild of British Creative Designers, whose rebellious use of glamorous mannequins was matched by the design of many of its clothes. The outfits presented at the Albert Hall saw many of the Guild's members turn to overstated ornamentation rather than 'clean and uncluttered' design, with large bows on pockets, feathers, pannier skirts and enlarged shoulders with exaggerated epaulets and fringing (figure 4.10). These design styles appear to fulfil Withers' worst fears for the lack of restraint brought about by a relaxation of restrictions. With the British post-war social and political order imagined around an austere, self-abnegating consumer, the Guild's promotion of mass-market luxury and feminine transformation clearly threatened the official ideology that now surrounded fashion production and promotion.

The hand-made process of couture production was to a certain extent an anachronism and sat precariously within the CoID's doctrine of 'good

Figure 4.10
Designs by Guild of British Creative Fashion Designers, *Parade of Fashion*, October 1946. *Source:* Pathé.

design', which was based on the ideals of Modernism, aimed to produce timeless (therefore not subject to fashionable change), standard-quality products, through mass production, at the best price, for the benefit of a universal consumer. This objective, however, was part of a long concern for rational design that prioritized integrity over commercial expediency, and in this way the high quality and small scale of couture production fitted the design reform agenda. The aesthetic of the couture's carousel display at BCMI may have sat uneasily within the CoID exhibition, yet in comparison to the work of the Guild of British Fashion Designers, this was a gentrified and officially sanctioned presentation of feminine consumer culture. The style of the models and their target market exemplified class-based English good taste, which in turn legitimised fashion production for a design reform establishment often adverse to its stimulation of conspicuous and supposedly irrational consumption. Throughout 1946, despite made-to-measure dress sitting precariously within the Council's definition of 'good' industrial practice, the members of the Incorporated Society of London Fashion Designers were therefore (as they had been in the pre-war Fashion Group of Great Britain) repositioned as a legitimate body of expert tastemakers. This, for both the Council of Industrial Design and the Board of Trade, rendered their inclusion within a state-funded event immune to accusations of industrial favouritism. The construction of hierarchy it created ensured that the Incorporated Society as a professional organisation operated as a vehicle of exclusion and power.

LAND OF HOPE AND GLORY: THE DIOR EFFECT IN A COUNTRY
OF NO PRIVILEGES

By the end of 1946 the members of the Incorporated Society held an enviable commercial position. However, in February 1947, just as Britain entered a period of greater austerity, the newly established couture house of Christian Dior presented its seminal first collection. Re-christened the 'New Look' by the fashion press, its voluptuous and exaggerated silhouette, with highly defined waist and bust and excessively long, full skirt, was quickly adopted and promoted as the new style for day and evening wear, particularly in the all-important and receptive American market. In terms of exports to the American market, Dior's New Look was released at a particularly astute moment as four months earlier Congress had removed the L-85 clothing restrictions. With America set to become a buyer's rather than a seller's market, the flamboyancy of the ninety-seven garments in this collection, which used an unprecedented amount of luxury fabric, fulfilled a pent-up consumer desire for a new, more unrestrained style. The response of the international press, fashion industry and public to Dior's collection reasserted Paris' position as the world's fashion centre and altered the discourse that surrounded couture production.[114] This section will explore how the reconstruction of London's couture industry and its national identity as a fashion centre were closely aligned with both Britain's economic and political situation and the effects that Dior and the New Look had on the international fashion industry.

Victor Stiebel, in the press release for his January 1947 collection, may have recognised the need for this new silhouette in his assertion that 'the essentially geometric shape of the early '40s has been broken down and is giving way to curves and femininity . . . the breath of fresh air, which stirred development in the dress trade in '46 will become a minor hurricane of experiment in '47'.[115] However, the members of the Incorporated Society, constrained by government regulations, a shortage of high-grade fabric and increased austerity, were not positioned well to fulfil these expectations of novel innovation. The start of 1947 saw Britain's economic recovery come to an abrupt halt when production and export were interrupted by a fuel crisis and one of the coldest winters on record.[116] The resultant dollar shortage saw austerity measures increase and the couturiers found business operation more difficult. The government even informed the Society's members that they would no longer receive their previous allocation of luxury export fabrics, a threat prevented only by a large amount of lobbying from the textile export groups. In the end, the July collections were made possible only by this 'good-will of the textile industry' and a 'coupon float' for accessories from the government.[117] 'In bomb-damaged London', where the fashion journalist Bettina Ballard claimed one was constantly 'reminded that this was a land of no privileges . . . a country where rationing was accepted by all classes, where integrity, and fair play were in full force', there was little space, particularly in the production of daywear, for overt showmanship. Dior's New Look, with its excessive use of fabric, was a direct assault on clothing regulations and undermined political propaganda for consumer restraint.

The British government considered the new silhouette an act of 'irre-
sponsibility on the part of France' and sought to distance itself and the
public from what it saw as 'immoral French behaviour'.[118] The Board of
Trade therefore issued a request for the nation's fashion industry to 'boycott
the Paris styles' and reassert the British virtues of frugality and restraint.[119]
The government also called a meeting of the press where it asked its members not to publicise or support the longer skirt.[120] In response, Anne Scott
James (editor of *Harper's Bazaar*) sent a letter to *The Times*, to question the
economic viability of this political intervention:

> Fashion is to the clothing trade what design is to the textile, pottery, leather
> and other trades. Happily, the government is showing a sincere faith in the
> importance of design. Now it must begin to believe in fashion, too. . . . But if
> they [the London fashion producers] are expected to lag years behind design-
> ers in America, France, Italy and other countries, they have no hope at all.
> Sir Stafford Cripps [the Chancellor of the Exchequer] cannot halt the world
> march of fashion. He has the choice of encouraging our manufacturers to keep
> up with fashion or of forcing England to trail behind, an isolated pocket of
> dowdiness.[121]

By August 1947, the press and fashion industry had ignored the Board's
requests, and fashion reports of the Incorporated Society's collections were
overshadowed by commentary on the 'battle of the long skirt'.[122] In particular, much was made of Hartnell's rejection of the 'frivolity' of the longer
skirt versus Stiebel's embrace of the fashion as 'inevitable'.[123] So much so,
that in a radio broadcast for the *BBC Home Service* in October 1947, Stiebel
was forced to defend his collection's skirt length as he claimed he had been
'accused of introducing a fashion which is uneconomic, impractical, unat-
tractive and worst of all, unpatriotic'.[124] The initial government intervention, therefore, had not stopped the influence of the New Look, and by
the end of 1947, as initial political and public outrage dissipated, it became
undeniably popular and its effects began not only to overshadow but also to
direct the newspaper coverage of the Incorporated Society.[125]

In 1946, London couture's restrained aesthetic of subtly tailored suits
and elegant evening wear had an advantage in an American market still
guided by austerity and controls. However, after the launch of the New
Look, with the L-85 regulations removed and Britain subject to further
austerity, a marked difference in attitudes to dress design emerged amongst

London, Paris and North America. In 1947, for instance, when the Canadian fashion co-coordinator of Eaton's department store wore a dinner dress in the new shape and longer length, she 'had difficulty gaining admittance at London hotels and restaurants', as their dress codes encouraged frugality; she countered that the English women admitted wore 'floor-length tatty old velvets and brocades in mid-summer'.[126] In Britain, restraint, except within the boundaries of export production, was the expectation, and social and political attitudes presented a deterrent to most forms of ostentatious display. 'The loud-voiced blasé hostess of enormous [pre-war] cocktail parties', as Amies pointed out in an interview at the end of the year, had 'given place to the quiet chatelaine giving her whole charm and attention to the small intimate parties which are the most her rations will allow'.[127] At a time when any form of conspicuous consumption or demonstration of social inequality was to be avoided and the members of high society's ability and inclination to put itself on display disappeared, London's ability to present an authentic platform for fashion, as it had in the 1930s, was severely restricted.

Fortunately, in November 1947, the city was offered an inimitable opportunity for extravagant pageantry by the royal wedding of Princess Elizabeth. The marriage of the twenty-one-year-old future monarch offered incomparable scope for a flamboyant promotion of British fashion, just as the coronation of her father had ten years earlier. Now, however, the country found itself in a very different economic position. The Palace therefore took a decision that the wedding would be a projection of austerity: there would be no state ball; instead of full pageantry, the procession would be small with no public stands along the route or near the abbey; even the attendant troops would wear battle rather than regimental dress. Guests were limited to fewer than a hundred and requested to wear morning dress with daytime-length skirts, with only the royal party allowed full-length gowns. In line with government policy for all British brides, the princess would also forgo her trousseau. In response to this decision, Digby Morton wrote a signed letter to *The Recorder* newspaper. The couturier had just taken the position of British Merchandise Manager at the Chicago department store Carson Pirie and found his 'trousseau display of London couture' immediately substituted by a group of French models. He therefore questioned whether the King had been badly advised:

Sir—when I read of the decision to eliminate a royal trousseau for Princess Elizabeth because of the economic conditions of this country I feel sure that no consideration can have been given to the fact that a unique and wonderful opportunity to stimulate one section of our much-needed export trade is being deliberately thrown away. . . . I can only imagine that those who recommended a policy of planning the Royal wedding on austerity lines can have no conception of the intense interest which anything concerned with Princess Elizabeth's wardrobe has not only for the women, but also for the executives of the stores throughout the States and Canada. . . . I would like to suggest that each designer [of the Incorporated Society] should contribute one model to form a royal trousseau of ten ensembles. The publicity value overseas of every material and style included in this small collection would far outweigh the amount of material used and labour expended and even the most socialist critic must admit that we need to take advantage of every asset we have to increase our national income. What European country today would not prize such an opportunity of attracting world attention—is it not too late for this matter to be reconsidered?[128]

However rational in terms of export promotion this suggestion may have appeared, this public challenge to the validity of the king's decision was controversial. Many sectors of the British press responded to Morton's request as a display not of national altruism but of self-serving commerciality. For example, *Fabric and Fashions*, which as an export publication could have been expected to support Morton's view, claimed that the couturier had allowed his own commercial agenda and 'transatlantic ideas to influence his better judgment'. It issued a strong rebuke, that the heiress to the British throne was

not the all-British mannequin that Mr. Digby Morton apparently visualizes . . . it is the Royal family and no one else who should and do decide what is appropriate for an occasion of this kind. It is their wish, obviously, to share as far as possible the austerity and rationing, which govern the lives of their people. . . . The world including the American republic—has more to learn from a demonstration of that spirit than from copying a few gowns the royal bride might otherwise have permitted herself. . . . [The royal family] symbolise Great Britain to the world, and to the world Great Britain is a country committed to seeking economic salvation in self-denial. It is a country where brides do not have a trousseau, but where all have a share of deprivations, including the heiress to the throne.[129]

This criticism drew on a depiction of Britain developed within wartime propaganda, which positioned the country as the 'world's morally responsible political player'.[130] This national identity was clearly at odds with any form of undemocratic display. The wedding gave Hartnell a prestigious commission, as he produced the bride's dress, the eight bridesmaids' dresses and the going away outfit (figure 4.11). However, at a time when London's ability to present an authentic platform for high fashion was severely restricted, the decision to hold what the press dubbed an 'austerity wedding' was in promotional terms an inimitable lost opportunity.[131]

Prior to the event, the Board of Trade may have been unable to use the wedding to promote British industry, yet immediately afterwards, to secure 'solid trading benefits from this admirable, if somewhat rarefied

Figure 4.11
Wedding of Princess Elizabeth and Philip Duke of Edinburgh, with bride and bridesmaids' dresses designed by Norman Hartnell, 20 November 1947. *Source:* © National Portrait Gallery, London.

piece of solid "prestige advertising"', Harold Wilson (the Board's president) wrote to the Palace to request permission to use both the original wedding and bridesmaid dresses for the 'unexampled climax' of Hartnell's future New York show and a number of replicas for exhibit in American department stores. Wilson supported the request by pointing out that one of the main 'difficulties' for British fashion design in the American market was 'the absence of "great names" of international standing . . . the French, have almost a monopoly of these names . . . yet as a result of the wedding, Mr. Hartnell has certainly achieved more widespread recognition than ever before as a designer of the first rank, and the clothes worn by Her Royal Highness have given rise to a new interest in British fashion design generally'.[132] This letter to the Palace demonstrates that by November 1947 the Board of Trade was fully aware of the positive impact Parisian couturiers such as Dior were having on French export levels, which in turn encouraged the British government to reassess its attitude towards its small-scale couture industry. When the Palace rejected Wilson's proposals, and insisted the original dress remain in Britain to 'give the people, particularly those in the "textile" areas, a rather special favour', the Board of Trade agreed to finance a twice-yearly reception to launch the couturiers' export collections.[133] This sponsorship was a specific response to trade figures released by the Chambre Syndicale, which claimed that by the end of 1947 both the number of foreign applications to gain access to the Paris dress shows and the export of French textiles to dollar markets had 'increased almost three times since the first Dior collection was shown'.[134]

The economic success of Dior's new couture house, as the fashion historian Margaret Maynard demonstrates, not only became 'locked into the trade wars' of a number of 'post-war economies', but also brought about a fundamental change in both the design practice of the French couturiers and the reportage of the fashion press.[135] Each season, there was now an expectation that couturiers would present a flamboyant new 'line' and newsworthy vision of future fashion. The new 'staffs of the mass media', as the business manager of *Vogue* pointed out, focused on 'the more extreme models, on the principle that news means sensation', and many Parisian couturiers quickly 'learned that they must produce extravaganzas to obtain publicity'.[136] So, while Dior created controversy through the reintroduction of a corseted waist and excessive skirt, other French couturiers began to design impractical models such as the much-reported tubular skirt of

January 1948, 'so slim that at Paquin's the model girls could just step down from the displaying platform . . . [whilst the] restricted 'hem-span' at Jacques Fath's made the mannequins teeter on the runways'.[137]

In 1947, with London couture constrained by social, political and economic austerity, its collections, particularly in comparison to those in Paris, lacked novelty and glamour. The restrained aesthetic of the London couture shows therefore led a number of the newer British journalists to question not only the validity but also the competency of the Incorporated Society's members. The young fashion correspondent Patricia Lennard, for instance, in her summation of the January collections in February 1947, made a direct assault and claimed to 'feel cheated . . . [as] British fashion seems forever to hover on the fringe of something really lovely, but never quite makes it. . . . It is about time the British fashion industry, particularly the end which calls itself creative, stopped patting itself on the back at organised shows and fashion balls and realised there is very little that is creative in British fashion'.[138] The exaggerated models presented by Parisian newcomers such as Dior and Fath led fashion journalists to expect couture houses to include 'novelty models', which would give them something interesting to write about.

American buyers also fuelled the expectation for sensation rather than restraint. Faced with a shift to a buyers' market, they now needed new fashions to avoid market saturation and also eye-catching models for either publicity purposes or inspiration for modified versions by mass manufacturers. French couture houses were able to do this because their collections were bigger than those presented in London. For example, after the success of the New Look, Dior moved to the presentation of around 200 models per collection; around a quarter of these models did not sell, because they either were unsatisfactory to the buyers or were created merely for publicity.[139] In comparison, Hardy Amies, who operated one of the Incorporated Society's most successful businesses, only ever presented a collection of approximately 60 garments. These were evenly distributed between suits, day dresses and evening, cocktail, dinner and party dresses, with 'perhaps two little numbers which may be just to give the whole thing a fillip, or merely for publicity'.[140] By the 1950s, even mid-scale Parisian couture houses presented twice this number of models.[141] One of the main reasons for this difference was the financial support offered to Parisian couturiers by the French textile industry.

The infrastructure and business paradigm of Maison Dior is the most pertinent example of this supportive network. Tomoko Okawa's analysis of this company's records shows that it 'marked a total departure from the way French couture had been run in the past'.[142] This new couture business was based on unprecedented finance: it was capitalised with an initial investment of old F5 million (about $48,000), and opened with three workrooms and eighty-five members of staff.[143] By 1954, it had five buildings, twenty-eight workrooms, and 1,000 employees; it was a multinational corporation doing business on five continents, with eight overseas branches and sixteen associated companies; and by the time of his death in 1958, Dior's products represented half of France's haute couture exports.[144] This was made possible because it was financed by Comptoire de l'Industrie Cotonniere (CIC), a vertically integrated textile business operated by the French cotton magnate Marcel Boussac. From its inception, the Maison Dior had three interrelated objectives: to sell cotton textiles; to expand into the international market as a ready-to-wear company with wholesale offices in New York, London and Caracas; and to develop licensing agreements.

Christian Dior was the company's chief designer, whose bonuses were based on the number of licences he signed with mass-market manufacturers to produce lines under his brand name. To achieve these objectives the company needed Dior to be a household name and acknowledged fashion dictator. The publicity generated by spectacular models was therefore a particularly important component within this business model. Dior and newcomers such as Fath, who followed this business model, made considerable impact on the traditional approach of couture: it was no longer produced in order to sell models to inspire foreign reproduction and ready-to-wear but primarily to provide the prestige and branded identity for a range of licensed products.[145] Company records reveal that despite worldwide acclaim Maison Dior did not show a profit until 1950 when its licensing arrangements became fully operational. London couturiers, in comparison, did not have the financial support to design for publicity or make a loss from their collections. They needed to ensure their designs were relevant and wearable so that the majority would sell to both clients and buyers. The sizes of the London collections were also contained by the couturiers' lack of financial backing from the British textile industry. Except for Jacqmar, which housed Victor Stiebel's operation, no records survive of any other British textile company or manufacturer that invested directly in a London couture business. The Incorporated Society may have received financial support from the textile industry; however, its records show that this was nominal. The contributions in October 1946 from the International Wool Secretariat, National Wool Textile Corporation, the Cotton Board and the British Rayon Federation were £300 each—not even half the amount they contributed to the aforementioned South American tour ten years earlier.[146]

The lack of a substantial investment from the textile industry saw the Society's export collections make only limited attempts to fulfil the role of 'shop window' for its manufacturers. In fact, one of the most notable aspects of the London couture collections was their use of French fabric.[147] For example, in the spring/summer collections of 1947 only French rayon was used in all the dresses and blouses[148] The Incorporated Society's unpatriotic use of imported material can to a certain extent be explained by the government policy that allowed one third of imported high-grade fabric to be used for domestic production, while its quality British material was for export only. Yet the reliance on foreign fabric was also because the couturiers claimed that British textile manufactures could not supply products of a similar quality and quantity. Stiebel, in defence of his prevalent use of imported fabric in July 1947, told reporters that although he required twenty tweeds for his collection he was able to secure only five from British producers, 'of which two had been known to the American trade for a year'.[149] The scarcity of high-grade British textiles resulted from three specific government policies: import restrictions, export quotas and purchase tax. First, treasury restrictions on the amount of raw material imported into Britain reduced production capacity, particularly in the silk and cotton industry. Second, the government took the decision to set export targets in weight, rather than quality or suitability to demand. While the export market was reported to be interested in 'light fabrics, that adhered to the stipulations of the "new look", British textile production was therefore focused on 'heavy woollens, or solid rayons'.[150] Third, for textile manufacturers the high level of purchase tax imposed on non-utility fabrics until 1955 discouraged the production and retail of high-quality materials for export because 'if they were not suitable for any particular market there was little opportunity of sales in the home market because of the high price'.[151] Appropriate couture fabrics were therefore difficult to come by. When the dress designers did find British fabric in the right weight and quality, they claimed that it was often difficult to meet demand because fabric merchants 'failed to redeem their undertaking to reserve certain quantities of fabric'.[152] With British textile manufacture focused on bulk production of mid-range fabrics for export and utility fabrics for the domestic market, cooperation between the textile industry and the London couturiers was severely restricted. The role of 'shop window' for the textile industry, one of the key objectives set out in the Society's constitution, was therefore inhibited and proved an unattainable goal.

Due to the size of the Parisian couture collections there was more scope for the generation of ideas and changes in each season's styles. French models were often used not for direct sale but as guidance for the mass-market wholesale trade, the home dressmaker and, after 1948, the paper pattern industry, from which the couturiers received substantial royalties. This dissemination of the designs throughout different levels of the fashion market was beneficial for the sale of fabric; subsidies from the French textile industry ensured that the Parisian couturiers were financially compensated when new models generated mass-market demand for specific materials. In comparison, the London couturiers were given little financial incentive to generate textile sales, and due to problems with supply often used foreign fabric. In terms of the Incorporated Society's export collection the focus was primarily on the sale of models to retailers with exclusive made-to-measure dressmaking departments rather than inspiration for adaptation by mass-market manufacturers. It was therefore notable that the main American buyers present at the London collections were sent by department stores rather than mass manufacturers, often for products that were ready for immediate sale without adaptation. With only limited support from the textile industry the London couturiers had to ensure that they could sell the majority of their models, and this in turn controlled the type of garments they produced and their design identity within the export market.

In February 1948, the front cover of *Everybody's* (the weekly tabloid magazine that was widely syndicated in the United States) featured a suit by Hardy Amies under the heading 'Goodbye Uniformity' (figure 4.12). The model with long pleated skirt and tailored jacket was chosen to signal an end to austerity and restraint. At this point, the long economic period of uncertainty, which started in 1945 with the termination of the Lend-Lease aid agreement was seen to be coming to an end due to the much-anticipated first payments of American Marshall Aid (the European Recovery Program).[153]

Figure 4.12
Hardy Amies suit, 'Goodbye Uniformity', *Everybody's* magazine, February 1948.

By July the access this aid gave to raw materials had increased the capacity of the British textile industry, so that the couturiers' ability to source British and in particular high-level woollen fabric had increased. In September the confidence evident in the declaration that 'Tweed Returns' by *Fashion and Fabrics Overseas* (the British export magazine), which was accompanied by an image of a mannequin in a tailored Victor Stiebel outfit with one foot on a map of the London underground, was a specific response to Britain's increased production capacity brought about by Marshall Aid and a clear acknowledgement of the London couturiers' specific design strength and market position (figure I.1).

In both January and July 1948, tweed town and country suits with long pleated skirts were the most notable feature in the members of the Incorporated Society's export collections where they made up two thirds of all their models.[154] These garments are a clear indication of the recognition that, as a fashion centre, London was the source of quality bespoke clothing rather than inspiration for mass-market fashion. The classic 'tailor-made' was an expensive garment to produce, as it needed five people to complete the order: a tailor, his assistant, a skirt fitter, and a second fitter. The fit had to be exact and needed adjustment; this took time and skill. Pleating, in particular, was an expensive process that at this point was difficult to reproduce at a mass-market level. This not only raised the price of London clothes but also made sure that they were demonstrably luxury products. The role of the London couturier was to create exclusive clothes that whilst fashionable and sure to generate sales, sold primarily for their luxury craft production rather than for their adaptation by the mass market. This identity and market position for London couture had been clearly defined during a period of austerity and economic instability. In the 1940s, whilst Dior may have pointed the way forward for the economic viability of couture production, the members of the Incorporated Society were in no position to follow this business paradigm. They therefore continued to operate as bespoke, exclusive producers, and by 1948 as Britain began to emerge from austerity their business model and design identity was set.

★ ★ ★

The London fashion scene should from now on be looked on by fashion experts, stylists, buyers, coordinators and those simply following fashions as

a complementary market to Paris. The London designers have no intention of
competing with Paris. What they know how to do and make is as different in
mood as the American approach is from the French. . . . The British are second
to none in tailoring, and their reputation as a complementary source is growing
annually. The demand for clothes in which the British specialize is growing
annually in the United States.[155]

When the war ended London may have been presented with the opportunity to become the most important European fashion centre; however,
during the process of reconstruction, its couturiers reacted to a specific
social, political and economic environment, which shaped not only the
type of models they designed but also their professional identity. In January 1949, the *New York Herald Tribune* could therefore point out that London had forged a clear space, as a complementary fashion centre to Paris,
and buyers went there not for eye-catching designs to generate trends in
mass fashion but for exclusivity and restraint.

To understand the true nature of the Incorporated Society this chapter
has recognised that it was formed at a time when the mechanisms of state
occupied the most dominant position within its network of operation. The
consideration of the Society's activity in the late 1940s has demonstrated
not only the role the national egalitarian atmosphere that surrounded this
form of luxury production played in establishing a hierarchical position
that moulded its identity, but also the impact of the French couture industry and the need for its members to differentiate themselves from the close
competition of the high quality of the 'wholesale couture' being created by
members of the London Model House Group.

In 1946, the London couturiers' ability to create restrained, wearable
models had catered fully to America's regulated clothing market, but
within the space of a year as US legislation was removed and a buyer's
market evolved, these styles had been eclipsed by the spectacular fashions
shown by Parisian couturiers such as Dior. The success of Dior's business
model set up a new expectation for couture production, yet the members
of the Incorporated Society lacked the support offered to their Parisian
counterparts. Whilst industry insiders such as Cecil Beaton may retrospec-
tively have derided the Incorporated Society's designs of the late 1940s as
an exemplar of 'stick-in-the-mud dowdiness', the models they produced

were a commercially informed response to their specific market and business infrastructure.[156]

The end of the 1940s saw the clothes of the London couturiers distinguished from their Parisian counterparts by a discourse of national identity. London was a closed world of restraint, simplicity, social adherence to norms and a high level of gentility; Paris, since the launch of Dior's New Look, the source of more experimental and creative fashions and of inspiration for mass fashion at an international level. Nowhere is the construction of this narrative more clearly demonstrated than in two films commissioned by the International Wool Secretariat and Associated British Pathé in 1950: *She Walks in Beauty: An Evening of Fashion at the Savoy Hotel* and *Paris City of Fashion*. Whilst the same director created both films, they adhered to the specific national identity that had developed for each fashion centre. The Paris models were filmed in the 'city of fashion' at a range of iconic locations: the Moulin Rouge, the Champs Elysees, the Palace of Versailles. As two mannequins pose in front of shots of the Eiffel Tower (figure 4.13), the voiceover proclaims: 'her name caresses the lips with the lightness of Champagne—Paree . . . there is more glamorous elegance to the square foot in the Champs Elysees to a square mile anywhere else on earth'. The narrator refers to the 'trends' Paris creates and 'the full power of her magic', while the clothes are described as 'artful', 'absolutely fabulous' and 'ultra-sophisticated'; they 'inspire rhapsodies' and 'dreams for the future'.

In comparison, the presentation of London took the form of a mannequin parade at the Savoy Hotel in front of a small 'distinguished audience . . . stars, celebrities and Britain's top fashion designers' (figure 4.14a–c). London is presented as exclusive and for a select few, while the Paris models are presented to crowds of spectators and the city 'invites the whole world to join in her fashion parade'. The London couturiers' Savoy show is a working environment that started and ended with evening and dinner dresses, while each mannequin is introduced by her first name, the designer of the model they wore specified, as well as the type of fabric used. The models are described by the same narrator as a demonstration of 'grace' and 'elegance'; they are 'designed to look charming at any time of the day' and the couturiers' creativity is merely a reaction to the fabric, which 'enabled the designer to execute his idea'. During this 'non-stop parade of high fashion and fabrics' the audience examine their programmes, while the camera goes

Figure 4.13
Still from *Paris City of Fashion* (director: Terry Ashwood; Associated British Pathé,
1951). *Source:* Pathé.

behind the scenes to explain that 'the whole secret of the unruffled elegance
out-front is calm organisation and a well-planned schedule'. The London
couturiers present a trade show; this is a job of work and these clothes are
for sale, whilst the Paris mannequins are shown as inhabitants of the city,
modelling for fashion photographers and attending a cocktail party which
links them to the world of high fashion and the fantasy of the fashion magazine. Paris is presented as the city of art and its designers as artists; London
as the city of business and the members of the Incorporated Society the
tradesmen of couture.

   This chapter has considered a specific moment when wartime patriotism was subsumed into post-war reconstruction in order to construct a
nationally acceptable identity for London's couture industry. The narrative
this created was shaped by the continuation of austerity and the restrictions
placed on the production and consumption of luxury goods. Yet it was also

Figure 4.14a–c
Still from *She Walks in Beauty* (director: Terry Ashwood; Associated British Pathé, 1951). *Source:* Pathé.

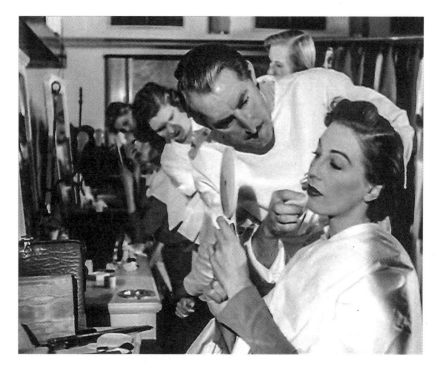

Figure 4.14a–c (continued)

a time of optimism for the future represented by the installation of a Labour government with a policy of full employment and a comprehensive welfare state that offered a utopian vision of future plenitude for all. Within the socialist, egalitarian agenda of the government, which promoted controlled consumption, the expensive clothes produced for the elite could easily have held an uncertain position. This, however, was alleviated by the couturiers' restrained design aesthetic and participation in the country's export campaign, which constructed a narrative of national ownership whereby the creativity of the Incorporated Society was presented as beneficial to the nation. Consequently, as the differences in the Pathé films produced for the Chambre Syndicale and the Incorporated Society show, the narrative that evolved had a clear downside, as it both restricted the international identity of the London couturiers and undermined their creative reputation in comparison to Paris.

Through the difficult process of collaboration the Society's members had therefore achieved one of the main aims set out in its *Articles of Association* in 1942: 'to maintain and develop the reputation of London as a creative centre of fashion'.[157] London may not have supplanted Paris as the principal source of inspiration for the international fashion industry, yet it had survived the war and an intense period of austerity to become an established complementary fashion centre. It had a clear national identity, and although this did not compete with Paris, the skill and craftsmanship of London's couturiers was internationally recognised.

CONCLUSION: THE 'TOP TEN'—THE MOST EXCLUSIVE
PROFESSIONAL BODY IN BRITAIN

In June 1949, as the rationing of British clothing ended, the successful romantic comedy *Maytime in Mayfair*, directed by Herbert Wilcox, was released. Set in the world of London's elite fashion houses, the film follows the fortunes of a 'man-about-town' (Michael Wilding) who inherits a couture house, becomes romantically involved with its manager (Anna Neagle) and overcomes personal and business competition from a rival establishment. Based in glamorous and luxurious settings such as restaurants, apartments and the streets of Mayfair and shot in 'glorious' Technicolor, it represented optimism for both London and Britain's future prosperity and an end to austerity.[1] The film was notable for its witty script and fantasy sequences; the most significant of these scenes saw mannequins, dressed by the members of the Incorporated Society, step out of the front covers of *Vogue* and *Harper's Bazaar* each emblazoned with the name of the couturier (figure C.1). This film demonstrates that Mayfair had retained its cultural currency as the epicentre of creative British fashion. It is also a clear example of the hierarchical position these ten couturiers had achieved. They now had a clear professional identity and occupied an enviable position that separated their specific businesses from other fashion producers. By 1949, these were the 'Top Ten' of British fashion, a nomenclature used not only in the fashion press, but also at the BBC, in government departments and even by the designers themselves. London not only had a couture industry, but this industry had a clear definition with professional boundaries set by membership of the Incorporated Society of London Fashion Designers.

This book has focused on the role designer collaboration played in the construction and maintenance of the London couture industry throughout the 1930s and 1940s. Through a series of case studies of collaborations and related events it has revealed how these activities validated and supported this field of design. From the emergence of young dressmakers with

Figure C.1
Still from *Maytime in Mayfair* (director: Herbert Wilcox, 1949). *Source:* Mary Evans.

stylistic confidence to couturiers with a specific professional identity, it has
shown how a number of interrelated economic, social and cultural factors
created a supportive network, which gave form to London's identity as a
centre for creative fashion. In particular, this has exposed the interaction
of commercial forces and governmental policy within this process of identity formation and professionalisation. In so doing, the analysis has uncovered many examples of the interconnected networks that were constructed
within Britain's creative economy to offer a nuanced interpretation of how
one specific hierarchy was forged within the fashion system.

It has shown that the London-based dressmakers' initial accreditation as
couturiers was based on the careful manipulation of a specific social and
commercial arena and a design process that came from originality rather
than adaptation. National and international recognition of their design
practice was also the result of trade protectionism and covert political propaganda, particularly in the 1930s, when as a seemingly apolitical form the
creativity of London's couturiers was harnessed to project Britain as a stable

but also modern society. At the same time, in America, trade protectionism underlay a concerted effort to dismantle the hegemony of Parisian design within the fashion system. The promotion of New York, Los Angeles and London as alternate fashion centres was part of a strategy to demonstrate that France was not the only nation that could forecast the future direction of fashion.

The mechanisms of propaganda continued to support the London couture industry throughout the war, whether as part of a campaign to demonstrate that Britain could still 'deliver the goods' or as an ideological and morale-boosting component of the 'People's War'. During the conflict, as the elitism inherent in couture production placed it in a precarious position, it was rendered more egalitarian and therefore acceptable as it was recast through engagement with the government's export campaign and Utility Scheme. This saw the construction of a protective narrative that reached back to historical arguments that promoted elite society's consumption of luxury as good for the nation. After the war, as the reconstruction of the economy became one of the government's key concerns, the recognition of the trade benefits of fashion-centre status ensured that the couturiers continued to be part of national projection.

In 1936, a government policy to increase the dissemination of propaganda fortuitously coincided with the creation of the Fashion Group of Great Britain, which as a branch of an American organisation saw the commercial dictates of this transatlantic market play an integral role in the identity and practice of London couture. In America the deficiencies in demand that accompanied the economic depression led to innovations that played a role in the mechanisms of fashion dissemination and consumption. Most importantly, these recognised the need for the diffusion of information amongst competitors to facilitate better trade practice. The Fashion Group of Great Britain drew on this American idea and constructed a network of creative practitioners as a route to the nation's economic security. In the Fashion Group's twice-yearly collaborative showcase of London couture, particularly in the synchronisation of design and colour, the impact of the commercial dictates of the American fashion industry were made most visible. This coordination was indicative of the manipulations of design practice, by bodies such as the Fashion Group and the British Colour Council, undertaken to control creativity in order to bring stability to the wider industry and its pursuit of stylistic change. The collaborative shows were implemented not only to harness the couturiers' creativity to benefit other fashion producers in Britain by raising design standards but also to regulate supply and demand as part of a wider transatlantic network. It has therefore been argued that much of the support for the professionalisation of the London couture industry was offered not to these individual businesses but as part of a process of control and authentication of design within a period of rising mass consumption.

Almost all of the examples of designer collaboration were undertaken to increase British exports, often specifically to the North American market. Whilst in the interwar period the internationalism of the London couturiers supported the city's recognition as a fashion centre, intermediaries within the fashion system used collaboration to construct a binary understanding for the separate couture industries. This saw London cast as the centre for 'hard' tailored couture and Paris as the destination for 'soft' feminine fashions. This challenged the idea of universality within the fashion-centre system in order to create a specific external identity for British fashion. A response to the American market's need for product differentiation, this abbreviated narrative of London couture production was cultivated by the Fashion Group of Great Britain in the 1930s. The identity of London as the centre for conservative, well-tailored suits was then consolidated in the war, as practicality became a social necessity. In America this understanding of London couture was heightened by the stipulations of the Lend-Lease Agreement, which ensured that between 1941 and 1945 it only imported British woollen goods. During and immediately after the war as conspicuous consumption became economically, socially and politically problematic, the tailored suit was a further indication of the fashion authority of London's couturiers. The promotion of the practicality of this form of dress adhered to the needs for consumer abstinence, and this restrained aesthetic saw the couturiers positioned as official tastemakers who could offer sanctioned guidance to the market.

Tracing the development of the narrative of London as the centre for hard couture demonstrates how the industry operated between the desire to be international and the commercial need to represent the nation. For the London couturiers this design consensus created unity but was also a recurrent point of tension as it affected their subjectivity and creative autonomy. Both the narrative and production of restrained, conservative tailored couture were particularly supportive for the London couturier's practice, but not for the authentication of creative fashions. After 1947, America's demand for both a new, softer, feminine silhouette and fashions that would stimulate the market was met by Parisian couturiers such as Christian Dior. Financed by a wealthy textile company, Maison Dior was able to create extravagant models that gave the international fashion industry the guidance it demanded. Dior, which was started with a business manager and financial partner who provided F5 million francs, became 'the paradigm of the new business model of haute couture'.[2] Before the war, couture firms, in both Paris and London, were generally owned by the designer, initiated with small sums of investment and focused on the creation of made-to-measure clothing. In the post-war period many French couture firms came to adhere to a different form of fashion organisation, reliant on substantial financial investment and commercial expertise. The fundamental impetus of Dior's business model, which depended on the creation of licensing agreements rather than bespoke clothing, began a process that would alter the very nature of couture production. As many Parisian couturiers began to 'shift the authenticity of their work from the design to the brand', their undercapitalized London counterparts continued to create wearable clothing that would sell to their clients.[3] By the end of the 1940s, as the industry began to shift from material to symbolic production, the INC-SOC members remained dependent, for both domestic and export success, on wearable quality clothes, what Hardy Amies, who operated the most commercially astute London house, called the production of 'Fords with a Rolls Royce finish'.[4] During the time frame of this study, the national identity of 'hard' London couture was constructed as a reaction to specific social and commercial dictates and was successful because it adhered to the requirements of the market. However, as the needs of the broader fashion system transformed as it entered a period of affluence and higher quality mass production, the narrative constructed around this type of clothing ultimately lost its agency and power.

After the precarious nature of the previous decades, the 1950s were a 'golden age' for the INCSOC when its members became recognizable household names throughout Britain and beyond.[5] Despite this they continued to operate within an economically fragile business model, as the need to maintain a Mayfair address was expensive, its production processes costly and time consuming, and staff and capital shortages were a perennial problem.[6] To supplement their business and offset these rising costs, many of the couturiers opened boutiques. These acted as a bridge between couture and ready-to-wear where they sold, alongside knitwear and accessories, less formal and less expensive clothing that was made to order but required only one fitting.[7] A number of INCSOC members also pursued licensing agreements, but in comparison to Parisian couturiers few were successful, except Amies, who extended into menswear, and Hartnell, who by 1973 had sixty-six trademarked licences in his name.[8] A number of the members designed lines for ready-to-wear companies.[9] For Digby Morton, couture proved too precarious, and in 1957 after twenty-four years in the business he moved fully into ready-to-wear and design consultancy. In the main, however, the London couturiers continued to remain reliant on made-to-measure clothing as their main product and source of income.

The rise of a recognisable London couture in the 1930s had been dependent on a developed platform for sartorial display and a client base that had a lifestyle that demanded specific clothing and the time and money to lavish on their wardrobes. After the war this began to dissipate as disposable incomes were reduced, social etiquette receded and traditions such as the Season became increasingly irrelevant. In 1958, for instance, the end of debutante presentations to the Queen was particularly detrimental to demand for formal court dressmaking. Throughout the 1950s the number of clients who bought made-to-measure clothing steadily decreased and the market for couture contracted not only in Britain but also in France.[10] In Paris, the decade witnessed the number of couture businesses decline from sixty to thirty-six and many pre-war establishments cease trading (Lelong in 1948; Molyneux in 1950; Piguet in 1951; Rochas in 1952; Schiaparelli in 1954).[11] In comparison, the majority of the INCSOC houses remained open and did not begin to close until the following decade (Victor Stiebel in 1963; Michael Sherard in 1964; Angele Delanghe in 1966; Worth in 1967; John Cavanagh Couture in 1967; Ronald Paterson in 1968; Michael Donnellan in 1971).[12] The London couturiers' resilience throughout the 1950s was due to their focus on a declining but reliable market. This contracted to cater to approximately 500 loyal customers with an average annual spend of 400 pounds.[13] In Hardy Amies' view, by 1953, the wider export market was now important only 'from the prestige point of view, from an international point of view, from every possible patriotic point of view, and, . . . the artistic point of view'.[14] Yet, in terms of couture sales, as he pointed out in a BBC radio broadcast, private customers were the 'backbone' of the business and it was their demand for 'unspectacular buy-ing of unspectacular things' that dominated production.

To stave off liquidation and ensure solvency, the London couturiers responded to the increasingly restrained, discreet and elegant lives of their loyal clientele, a conservative group with similar incomes and lifestyles.[15] The escalating costs of made-to-measure saw these consumers become older and more price conscious. By the late fifties, the epitome of the Lon-don couture client was not a woman of fashion—as in the 1930s—but a 'well-dressed woman', who demanded expertly cut, wearable and flattering garments that were made to last.[16] By 1958, while Victor Stiebel found the fashionable youth styles he observed 'amusing', he acknowledged that they were no longer relevant to his couture clients. Expensive clothes needed to last, and in the pursuit of durability rather than seasonal novelty he claimed to now 'detest' most of his own designs, which he saw as 'almost fancy dress . . . [or] old-fashioned before they are made'.[17] Similarly, by the early 1960s, Norman Hartnell, after forty years in the business, 'wasn't a lead-ing designer from a fashion concept; he was an Establishment designer and those ladies that patronised him . . . were getting an Establishment garment which gave them the confidence for their lifestyle'.[18] In London, the cou-ture businesses that achieved the most longevity were therefore those that embraced their clientele and catered to royal and society patronage; in so doing, Hartnell's couture company operated for sixty-nine years, Amies for sixty-eight and Lachasse for seventy-nine.

In comparison, Parisian couture houses were offered a support structure by their government, textile industry and manufacturers, which allowed their designs to be less reliant on the consumption preferences of their pri-vate clients. After the war, the Chambre Syndicale's new 'Paris-Province' rules had allowed French manufacturers and retailers to enter the Paris shows and to lawfully reproduce or adapt the designs, in return for their pledge to spend a guaranteed minimum in couture purchases.[19] While in London, design had to avoid excess as the garments were produced to be worn by private customers, this ensured that French couture remained more exaggerated to provide inspiration for manufacturers, who would then tone down striking but difficult-to-wear designs.[20] The provision of inspiration for mass manufacturers provided the Parisian couturiers with an important revenue stream and impetus for eye-catching designs that could be adapted and sold at a lower price point. The French government also initiated a programme of financial support provided by a tax on the textile industry. For a decade, from 1951, this provided these private firms with publicly funded subventions as long as they continued to operate according to the principles of craftsmanship dressmaking and use 90 per cent French textiles.[21] With haute couture a rarefied craft with diminishing profitability, Véronique Pouillard has argued it remained operational in France due to this metaphorical 'oxygen tent', without which many establishments would arguably have ceased trading.[22]

In the 1950s the designs produced by the Parisian couturiers therefore retained greater aesthetic and promotional relevance to the broader fashion and textile industry. Whilst similar ambitions had been enshrined in the Incorporated Society's Articles of Association, without comparable support these never really became objectives for its designer-members. They did not see themselves as a 'shop window' for the British textile industry or a creative incubator for the wider fashion industry.[23] In fact, they were often, unsurprisingly, against their cultural and creative capital being used without financial remuneration for the economic benefit of others. This is completely understandable as, apart from a twice-yearly reception paid for by the Board of Trade and small yearly subscription from the textile groups, the INCSOC was financed by the designers themselves. The lack of governmental support offered to the London couturiers remained a source of consternation for the Society's members. In 1958 during a televised debate, when in response to the death of Christian Dior, Sir David Eccles (president of the Board of Trade) suggested that Britain could easily find a designer to replace him in the fashion hierarchy, Victor Stiebel replied, 'Sir David just doesn't know what he is talking about', as London could only become 'a first rate fashion power, if the British Government took the fashion industry more seriously and subsidised it'—a suggestion dismissed by Eccles, who voiced an apparent political attitude, with his swift retort that 'the British Government is not in the business of making clothes'.[24]

Unsurprisingly, the designer-members of the Incorporated Society with no comparable support system and private clients their main source of revenue, rejected the time, effort and expenditure involved in spectacular fashion shows. The salon presentations in Paris and London therefore diverged and the 'atmosphere', as the wholesale designer Michael Guest recalled, 'was different in that a lot of money was spent in Paris. In London it was much cosier, it wasn't such big business'.[25] As a typical newspaper report noted, in

1949, for the INCSOC designers it was 'all strictly business and everyone concerned—the designers, their mannequins and the audience—are doing a job of work, so there are no microphones, no music and no commentators'.[26] Amies claimed to deplore all presentations 'where the audience isn't prepared to buy' and 'purposely' kept his 'showroom as unspectacular as possible' to discourage 'a lot of ladies killing time between lunch and dinner'.[27] This undermined one of the main aims set out in the Incorporated Society's *Articles of Association*, the seemingly innocuous objective 'to organise or hold exhibitions of British fashion'.[28] This rejection of the 'entertainment element' meant that after 1950, the Incorporated Society's members very rarely participated in collective showcases, and when they did it was tokenistic and primarily to ensure the goodwill of the textile industry and particular magazines. In fact, the only joint showcase that received unreserved support from all the Society's members was the instigation, from 1951 onwards, of the annual dress show they presented to the Queen Mother. Over the next decade, the royal family became key to both the prestige and identity of the London couture. So much so, that by 1960 when the INCSOC, at the request of the Fashion Group of America, created a joint collection that toured the United States, it did so under the title 'Tweeds and Tiaras'. The narrative of hard couture and traditional court dress had become ossified around them, an understanding that could not compete with the shifts in fashion towards fast-changing youth style. Whilst beneficial to the couturiers' business model, this narrative was an anathema to the needs of the wider fashion industry, and the press reports of their designs became 'increasingly nostalgic, reactionary, apologetic and ultimately inconsequential'.[29]

The association of the INCSOC with the British establishment was also heightened by the need to construct clear boundaries between itself and the high-level 'wholesale' couture, its unique domestic competitor. Although the London Model House Group, the trade association of this form of ready-to-wear production, was relatively small in terms of the number of firms and employees, by 1950 it had begun, in the view of the Apparel and Fashion Industry's Association, 'to gain an importance to the industry as a whole out of all proportion to its size . . . a style and design source that influenced all grades of manufacture far more than the couture does . . . in many ways, the wholesale couture section of our industry is unique; it has no parallel in any other part of the world'.[30] As the Incorporated Society's

Annual Report from the subsequent year pointed out, this close rivalry had undermined the commercial viability of its members' businesses:

> To make it interesting to a London couturier to continue as a couturier is becoming increasingly difficult. The members, perforce, continue to "throw their bread upon the waters" well aware that a multitude of businesses, small and large, will often benefit more than they can hope to do themselves. The members led the London fashion picture by being the first to group themselves together for export promotion, they were the first to arrange coordinated export collections, the first to arrange official entertainments and the first to have a government reception at Lancaster House. The Wholesale trade has followed and done everything on a much bigger scale. It is probably fair to assume that they have had a correspondingly richer reward. It is the function of the creative mind to stimulate new trends. It is intelligent for an industry to exploit the creative mind but the exploitation must be synonymous with encouragement.[31]

If the government and textile groups had provided the financial support for the Incorporated Society to work more closely with the 'wholesale couture', it arguably could have constructed a differentiation that would have set London as a fashion centre apart from both Paris and New York. Despite requests by an array of intermediaries for the bespoke and wholesale couture to join forces, this form of collaboration was never provided with any concrete financial incentives. It was therefore rejected and it was only ever Hardy Amies who had membership of both the Incorporated Society and the Fashion House Group.[32] The industrial and political network that emerged around the London couture had always been more focused on harnessing the creativity of the designers for the benefit of mass production than in supporting these craft-based private businesses. As clothing codes relaxed and ready-to-wear made gains in quality, design and social acceptance, couture became less desirable and new fashion-conscious designs emerged more readily from manufacturers operating at a lower price point where clothing longevity was less important. This ensured that in 1956, when the Model House Group was liquidated and became the Fashion House Group of London, and the Textile and London Fashion Organization (TALFO) was created to represent its interests, all the textile export groups removed their representatives from their vice-presidential roles of the INCSOC and transposed them to this new body.[33] As the couturiers moved into a period of affluence, ready-to-wear became the norm and made-to-measure production focused on a niche and conservative market, the Incorporated Society therefore lost its relevance to its external networks of support. The unique competition presented by the wholesale couture, the lack of external investment and the difficulty in maintaining labour and business premises explain the structure and professional identity of the INCSOC and particularly its shift towards exclusivity and a closed-shop mentality (figure C.2).

The recognition that the Incorporated Society became a 'closed shop' provides an appropriate conclusion for the concerns of this study. The first references to this idea began to surface in both governmental records and newspaper reports at the end of 1947. The Board of Trade and the Council of Industrial Design even called a meeting with William Haigh (the Society's textile vice president) to discuss this problem, whilst a campaign was

Figure C.2
'The Closed Shop': The Incorporated Society members, October 1949. Standing, from left to right: Michael Sherard, Giuseppe (Jo Mattli), Victor Stiebel and Peter Russell. Seated, from left to right: Hardy Amies, William Haig (National Wool Textile Export Corporation), Colonel Crawford (Bianca Mosca), Mrs Charlotte Mortimer (Worth, London), Viscountess Rothermere (president), Norman Hartnell (chairman), Miss Lilian Hyder (secretary), Sir Raymond Streat (Cotton Board), R. A. G. Barnes (Lace Federation), Digby Morton and Charles Creed. *Source:* Victoria and Albert Museum

launched by five London couturiers not in the Society (Rahvis, Lachasse, Mattli, Strassner and Clive Duncan), which called for it to be abolished and replaced by a national body called the 'British Syndicate of Haute Couture' to which anyone with proven ability could gain entrance.[34] The *Sunday Express* reported their view that 'the Top Ten, with Hartnell as chairman, give the impression that they don't want new members. They represent powerful interests and appear quite happy in the preserve they have created. . . . It is the most exclusive professional body in Britain'.[35] The selection process for new members of the Society was indeed prohibitive as the decision was taken by the designers already included who wanted to protect their own business interests from their competitors. Applications to join were constantly rejected, usually on the basis of lack of design originality or the quality and craftsmanship of their production. This meant that after the war the Society remained small.[36] This exclusivity was entirely understandable as the Incorporated Society was virtually self-appointed and its members were particularly protective of the hierarchical position their collaboration had created.

The recognition that by the end of the 1940s the Incorporated Society had already become a closed shop allows clear conclusions to be drawn about the process of professionalisation of this form of design practice. If a profession is an occupation that has achieved a special level of prestige in society and professionalisation is the process by which high status is attained, the aim, as Geoffrey Millerson has shown, 'is to create exclusiveness, as membership confers status on the individual'.[37] The Incorporated Society was a professional association that operated as a vehicle of separation and distinction from other businesses. It legitimated its members' identity as couturiers and rendered those outside itself as bogus and unprofessional. For the designers, collaboration within the Incorporated Society was essentially a route to business protection and professional prestige rather than to fulfilling the broader aims stated in its constitution. Positioned between craft and commerce, profits and the pursuit of a mass market for their products had never provided the key incentive for this form of business venture. 'Nothing could be further from the truth', as Amies pointed out, than the 'common fallacy' that luxury production would 'make a fortune', as it was 'impossible' in an age of mass production 'to become rich from dealing in anything that is made almost entirely by hand'.[38] In support of his career choice, he turned to the words of Victor Stiebel to highlight the broader function of creative labour: 'we never make any money, but we have a hell of a lot of fun doing it'.[39]

Ultimately, the survival of the London couture industry was set not only by what the designer-members themselves were willing and able to do on their own initiative but also by what social and cultural stipulations, industrial and governmental bodies, 'fashion intermediaries', competitors and their clients (both real and imagined) allowed them to achieve. This small body of London couturiers established and maintained collaborations and created the Incorporated Society in order to successfully navigate a particularly difficult economic period for this field of luxury production. Yet the designers involved were always ambiguous about collaboration and about the altruistic aims set out in the Society's *Articles of Association*. During the time frame of this study (one of economic and political turmoil, austerity and reconstruction), networks were constructed around the London couture industry that ensured its professional recognition. Yet collaboration never achieved the wider relevance expected of it and the Incorporated Society's move towards being a closed shop restricted entry to fresh talent or different business models. Over the next two decades, as the members grew older, retired or continued to tread a well-worn design path, the London couture industry could not compete with the stylistic novelty of young ready-to-wear designers and the symbolic rather than material needs of the international fashion industry.

APPENDIX: MEMORANDUM AND ARTICLES OF
ASSOCIATION OF THE INCORPORATED SOCIETY OF
LONDON FASHION DESIGNERS

(Originally drawn up on 10 November 1941, registered 6 January 1942)

1. The name of the Company (hereinafter called 'the Society') is 'The Incorporated Society of London Fashion Designers'
2. The registered office of the Society will be situated in England
3. The objects for which the Society is established are:—
   a. To maintain and develop the reputation of London as a creative centre of fashion
   b. To collaborate with groups of fabric and other manufacturers, and with companies, firms and individuals, with a view to increasing the prestige of British fashions, and promoting the sales of British dresses, gowns, fabrics and dress accessories in home and overseas markets.
   c. To provide a centre for the collation of fashion articles to create fashion collections, and to promote exhibitions of British fashions at home and abroad.
   d. To assist fashion designers by protecting their original designs, enabling them to exchange information to their mutual advantage, arranging dates for their respective showings, fostering professional and trade interests of persons engaged in creating British fashions, developing the standards of skilled workmanship and representing their views to government and trade bodies and to the press.
   e. To maintain and improve the professional status and standards of conduct of those engaged in the creation of fashions.
   f. To organise or hold exhibitions of British fashions.
   g. Subject to section 14 of the Companies Act, 1929, so far as applicable to purchase, take on lease, or in exchange, hire or otherwise acquire any real or personal property or rights of any kind which may be deemed necessary or convenient with a view to the promotion of the

objects of the Society, and in particular any buildings, or any parts of
the same, or land for the purposes of the erection of buildings
thereon and any furniture, books and other properties.

h. To borrow or raise money, and to issue debentures, debenture stock,
or other securities, and for the purpose of securing any debt or obli-
gation of the Society, to mortgage and charge the undertaking and
all or any part of the property and assets of the Society.

i. To receive donations and contributions from companies, firms and
persons desirous of assisting the work of the Society.

j. To draw, make, accept, endorse, execute and issue bills of exchange,
promissory notes and other negotiable and transferable instruments.

k. To invest and deal with the moneys of the Society not immediately
required in such investments and in such manner as may from time to
time be deemed expedient.

l. To establish, subsidize, promote, take over, co-operate or amalgam-
ate with, or become a member of or affiliated to, or act as trustee or
agent for, or manage or lend money or other assistance to, any organization, association, society or body, corporate or unincorporated,
with objects altogether or in part similar to the objects of this Society, and which is calculated directly or indirectly to advance these
objects or any of them. Provided that it is prohibited by its constitution from distributing its income and property amongst its members
to an extent at least as great as is imposed on this Society by or under
Clause 4 hereof.

m. To sell, lease, grant licences, easements and other rights over, and in
any other manner deal with or dispose of, the property, assets, rights
and effects of the Society, or any part thereof, for such consideration
as may be thought fit, as may be deemed expedient with a view to
promoting the objects of the Society.

n. To undertake and execute any trusts which may seem conducive to
any of the objects of the Society.

o. To procure the registration or incorporation of the Society in or
under the laws of any place outside England.

p. To subscribe or guarantee money for any national, charitable, benev-
olent, or other useful object, or for any purpose which may be considered likely directly or indirectly to further the objects of the
Society.

q. To grant pensions or gratuities to any employees or ex-employees of the Society, or the relations, connections or dependants of any such persons, and to establish or support associations, institutions, clubs, funds and trusts which may be considered calculated to benefit any such persons or advance the objects of the Society.

r. To do all or any of the things and matters aforesaid in any part of the world, and either as principles or agents.

ARCHIVAL SOURCES

BATH MUSEUM FASHION RESEARCH CENTRE

GG Mattli Sketchbooks, 7 boxes dress designs, 8 albums press cuttings, 3 sketchbooks 1948–71, NRA 41279 Fashion.

BBC WRITTEN ARCHIVE CENTRE (CAVERSHAM)

R34/56/2 Policy Advertising in Programmes, Fashions File 2:1947–56.
T14.1101/1 TV Outside Broadcast, Savoy Hotel Fashion Shows, File 1A, 1951.
T14/426/1 Fashions 1951–3.
T14/15 TV Outside Broadcasts Albert Hall, Fashion Parade, 1946.
T16/69/1 Fashion File 1, 1946–1958.
T16/70 TV Policy Fashion, Incorporated Society of London Fashion Designers, File 1, 1954.
T16/7, Fashions: London Model House Group Limited, 1953–4, TV POLICY.
T16/71 TV Policy, Fashions: London Model House Group Limited 1953–4.
T23/3 TV Publicity Advertising in Programmes: Fashion File 1:1950–54.
T31/205 TV Staff Wardrobe, Announcers File 1, 1936–1952.
T31/206/1 TV Staff Wardrobe Department File 1.
T32/154 TV Talks 'Fashions', 1946–1957.
Talks, Hardy Amies, File 1, 1946–62.
Tel/B600/302/798 Betty Spurling, 1939–50.
TV Art 2, Audrey Withers, 1947–59.

BRITISH LIBRARY (96 EUSTON ROAD, LONDON NW1)

National Life Stories/Oral History of British Fashion
Lily Silberberg (C1046/02).
Manny Silvermann, Hartnell Press Cuttings (C1046/11).
Margaret Nicholson (C1046/01).
Michael Southgate (C1046/08).
Michael Talboys (C1046/07).
Percy Savage (C1046/09).

DESIGN ARCHIVE (BRIGHTON UNIVERSITY).

Alison Settle Archive 1929–72 corresp., notes, articles and lectures GB/NNAF/
P44071.
Records of the *Britain Can Make It* exhibition.

FASHION GROUP INTERNATIONAL ARCHIVES
(NEW YORK PUBLIC LIBRARY)

X. SPEECHES AND TRANSCRIPTS
Box 72: 1931–1934.
Box 73: 1938–1941.
Box 74: 1943–March 1948.
Box 75: April 1948–1951.

XI. CONFERENCES, MEETINGS AND SPECIAL EVENTS
Box 94: Fabric Meetings 1940–1959.
Box 101.f.14: Glass in Fashion.
Box 101.f.15: History of Couture.

XII. REGIONAL GROUPS (U.S.) AFFILIATED WITH THE FGI
Box 115.f.5–6: Golden Years Brochure 1955.

XII. REGIONAL GROUPS (ABROAD) AFFILIATED WITH THE FGI
Box 125.f.2–13: London England 1935–1989.
Box 125.f.14–16: Melbourne Australia 1972–1990s.
Box 128.f.1–3: Paris, France.

XIII. FGI FASHION REPORTS AND DIRECTORIES
Box 140: Credit Sheets and News Flashes 1954–1978.

XIV. FGI PRINTED MATERIAL
Box 144: Newsletter Bulletin 1931–1945.
Box 145: Newsletter Bulletin 1946–1956.
Box 151: The FG Presents New York's Fashion Futures with the Collaboration of
the Fashion Originators Guild 1940.

XV. NON-FGI PRINTED MATERIALS

Box 158.f.1: *Fashion Digest Newsletter* Summer 1942 Suits.

Box 159.f.1: Fall–Winter 1947–1948 Fabrics & Colors Woolen Worsted Coats, Suits & Dresses.

Box 159.f.9: Spring 1948 Suits.

Box 160.f.17: *Fashion Scope Newsletter*, Spring 1954 Sportswear.

Box 163.f.10: Agnes Brooks Young, Excerpts from 'Recurring Cycles of Fashion 1927'.

XVI. ADDITIONS. REGIONAL GROUPS (U.S.) AND ABROAD AFFILIATED WITH THE FGI, 1930–2003

Box 182.f.2: Ball Britannica 1960.

CALENDAR OF SPEECHES AND TRANSCRIPTS (BOXES 73–93, 182)

Arthur P. Hirose (Director of Promotion and Market Research for *McCall's* and *Redbook*), *How Will War-Learnt Lessons Affect Postwar Merchandise, Promotions and Distribution in Home Furnishings*, 19 April 1944.

Lucien Lelong, French designer, *Talk Includes Answering Questions from the Audience about Lelong's Perspective on American Fashion*, 22 October 1931.

Paul Bonner, Vice-President of Stehli-Silks, *The Business of Style and Fashions*, 6 May 1931.

Paul Mazur, Lehman Brothers, *The Bankers' Point of View on Fashion*, 7 April 1931.

Zenn Kaufmann (Merchandising Director, Phillip Morris & Co.), *Showmanship in Business*, 17 March 1949.

HARDY AMIES ARCHIVE (14 SAVILE ROW)

Advertising Material 1946–1960.

Designs and Ephemera for the Royal Family.

Weekly Press Books from 1936–1960.

HERIOT-WATT UNIVERSITY (EDINBURGH)

Messrs W and O Marcus Ltd Fashion House Group, Scope and Content
  Design books 1945–1957.
  Loose patterns 1956–1958.
  Unpublished history of the fashion house 1945–1958, ten volumes and two files.

IMPERIAL WAR MUSEUM

Hilda Neal, Diary (Cat. No. 11987, Subject Period 1939–1975).

LONDON COLLEGE OF FASHION LIBRARY
(JOHN PRINCES STREET, LONDON W1)

Victor Stiebel, Sketch book of 1962 and 1963, 741.677 STI.

MASS OBSERVATION ARCHIVE: TOPIC COLLECTIONS
(UNIVERSITY OF SUSSEX)

Personal Appearance and Clothes 1938–54, Box 2: Correspondence and Interviews
    Conducted by PF/TH 1939–40.
    18.2.A: Interviews with people in fashion retail, December 1939–April 1940
      (PF)
    18.2.B: Opinion Forming and the Creative Artist.
    18.2.C–D: Correspondence to/from PF and voluntary contributors, conversa-
      tions with people associated with fashion retail and letters to/from fashion
      business.
    18.2.E: Press cuttings sent to PF March, April and May 1940.
    18.2.F: General Fashion Reports and Ephemera 1939–40.
    Aage Thaarup (Milliner) 6.12.39.
    Ann Seymour (Woman and Beauty) 5.12.39.
    Digby Morton (Designer) 24.4.40.
    Donald Barber (Retail Distribution Association) 4.12.39.
    Elizabeth Wray (*Draper's Record*) 15.12.39.
    H. Scott (Mercia & Co.) 18.12.39.
    James Laver (at the Treasury) 20.2.40.
    Jean Smith (Fashion Group) 29.11.39.
    John Dannhorn (Carot Ltd) 15.12.39.
    Madge Garland (*Vogue*) 15.12.39.
    Margaret Havinden (Crawfords Advertising) 27.2.40.
    Mary Joyce (*Woman's Wear News*) 7.12.39.
    Memo on Present Position: Miss Fox (Courtaulds) 18.12.39.
    Notes and internal memos on fashion in the first two months of the war,
      November 1939–January 1940.
    Press release on clothes study, April 1939.
    R. Driscoll (Kennards) 19.1.40.
    Report on hat wearing, March 1940.
    Resumé 30.4.40.

Statistics on clothes sales 17.2.40.

Victor Stiebel (Designer) 1.12.39.

Miscellaneous. Re. the study of the impact of the war on clothes.

Box 3: Clothes Rationing Questionnaires 1941.

Box 4: The Effects of Clothes Rationing on the Public and Retailers 1941–42,
Includes Interview with

Ann Seymour (Editor of *Woman and Beauty*) 5.3.42.

Digby Morton (Designer) 3.3.42.

JM Payton (Secretary of the Draper's Council of Trade).

Box 5: Press Cuttings 1939–1940.

18.5.A: Press Extracts and Cuttings and Observation: The Effect of War on
Clothing.

18.5.B: Press Cuttings 1939–40.

18.5.C: Press Cuttings 1939–40.

18.5.D: Fashion Adverts.

D. Brinton Lee, 'It Happened like This: A Housewife's Diary of the Blitz' (5262).

Royalty 1942–64 (TC 69).

Box 1: Coronation 1953—Organisation of Study.

Box 2: Coronation 1953—Analysis of National Surveys.

Box 4: Observation of shops, Coronation Decorations and Posters.

Box 5: Pre-Coronation Observations and Accounts.

Box 8: Post-Coronation Accounts, Interviews etc.

Box 11: General Material on Royalty 1942–64.

Box 12: Press Cuttings, 1953 Coronation.

MODERN RECORDS CENTRE (UNIVERSITY OF WARWICK)

Apparel Manufacturers Association, Minutes 1943–45 (MSS.222/1/1).

British Clothing Industry Association Collection.

AFIA Correspondence File MSS. 222/AP/3/1–85.

AFIA Publications MSS. 222/AP/4.

AFIA Other Bodies MSS. 222/AP/5.

Apparel and Fashion Industry's Association (1942–1981).

Autumn 1975 MSS. 222/AP.

Clothing Export Council 1965–1983.

Complete Membership forms MSS. 222/AP/1/2/ii.

Cuttings 58–71 MSS. 222/AP.

Fashions of Today and Tomorrow 1959–67 MSS. 222/AP/4/2/1–29.

London and District Wholesale Clothing Manufacturers Association MSS. 222/
LWC.

Press Cuttings MSS. 222/AP/10.

Spring 1967 MSS. 222/AP/4/1/1.

Wholesale Fashion Trades Association (1933–1955).
Wholesale Fashion Trades Association MSS. 222/APW.
Women's Fashion Export Group: Minutes, Agenda and Accounts 1940–1953
(MSS.22/APX/1).

MUSEUM OF LONDON (LONDON WALL, LONDON EC2)

English Couture Dress Collection 1930–1966.
Recording Project Conducted by the Museum of London with the Fashion House
of Hardy Amies, 1989.

NATIONAL ARCHIVE (KEW)

BT 64: Records of Board of Trade: Industries and Manufactures Department Correspondence and Papers
    BT 64/14 Details of Designation Policies.
    BT 64/201 Post War Planning of the Silk Industry.
    BT 64/213 Removal of Austerity.
    BT 64/307 International Trade Conference 1946–48.
    BT 64/991 Clothing Industry Working Party.
    BT 64/1063 Economic Survey 1950.
    BT 64/3612 What BOT Responsible for in 1944.
    BT 64/3728 Rehabilitation of Cotton Industry 1947.
    BT 64/4092 Plan for BOT Clothing Panels 1943.
    BT 64/4101 Investigation into Reaction to the Clothes Rationing Order 1941.
    BT 64/4194 Clothing Coupons Royal Tour 1946.
    BT 64/4237 Export Wool Goods to Canada 1949–51.
    BT 64/4248–4254 Development Council for the Clothing Industry.
    BT 64/4263 History of Utility Schemes.
    BT 64/4275 Imports of Clothes from US 1949–55.
    BT 64/4361 Promotion of Dollar Exports 1949–50.
    BT 64/5280 Fashion House Group of London Ltd Policy on Acceptance of
        Invitations to Open Fashion Week 1964.
BT 11/1854 Commodities: Apparel and Textiles (Code 3A).
BT 11/4347 Commodities: Apparel and Textiles (Code 3A) Exports to USA 1949.
BT 11/4733 Import and Export Matters (Code 10) Sadler's Wells Ballet Tour of
    USA and Canada Promotion of UK Fashions.
BT 31/35684/313974 Reville School of Fashion Ltd 1936.
BT 31/36505/411857 Fashion Parade Limited 1946.
BT 31/37859/447769 Dissolved Companies—Fashion Industries Club Ltd.
BT 31/45170 Dissolved Companies 1975: The Incorporated Society of London
    Fashion Designers.

BT 31/45224 Dissolved Companies—Combined Fashion Houses Ltd.

BT 61/76/9 British Colour Council Assistance with the South American Fashion Exhibition 1940.

BT 61/78/4 South American Fashion Exhibition: Publicity for London Fashion Collection 1940–1942.

BT 70/102 Wholesale Textile Association.

BT 94/108 Apparel and Textiles: Wholesale Margins.

BT 94/324 Apparel and Textiles: Retail Margin Reductions.

BT 215/1418 Wholesale Fashion Trades Association.

BT 279/222 Trade Fairs and 'British Weeks' Assistance for Fashion Shows 1962–67.

ED 168/879 St. Marylebone, London College of Fashion 1946–55.

FO 837/284 Elsa Schiaparelli.

FS 28/233 Wholesale Fashion Trades Association.

INF 2/44/159 'Printed Silk Scarves' Propaganda Scarves for Export from Jacqmar of Grosvenor Street, London. 5—The Ballet, British Official Photograph 1944.

INF 6/399 Steps of the Ballet (English Ballet) 1948–1950.

INF 6/846 Looking at Britain: Ready to Wear 1962.

INF 6/1237 Mary Quant Fashions 1966.

INF 6/1481 Hardy Amies—Hepworth.

INF 12/792 Film Division—'50 Years of English Fashion' 1959–60.

INF 12/969 Analysis of 60 Years of Fashion 1963.

J13/17317 Victor Stiebel Ltd Companies Winding Up, 1942.

MAF 97/1001 Fashion Show to Promote UK, Exports of Fabrics and Cloth to USA for Dollar Earnings, 1941.

ROYAL COLLECTIONS (ROYAL ARCHIVE, WINDSOR)

Correspondence between the Queen Mother and Lady Pamela Berry (President of the Incorporated Society of London Fashion Designers).

Queen Mother and Princess Margaret Engagement Films for Attendance at the Incorporated Society of London Fashion Designers.

THEATRE MUSEUM ARCHIVE (23 BLYTHE ROAD, LONDON W14)

C. B. Cochran Archive, press cuttings scrapbooks (THM/97).

Emile Littler Collection, letters to Norman Hartnell (THM/144).

VICTORIA AND ALBERT ARCHIVE OF ART AND DESIGN
(23 BLYTHE ROAD, LONDON W14)

Betty Newmarch, designer Horrockes & Dorretta (AAD/1995/16).
Britain Can Make It (AAD/1977/4).
Festival of Britain 1949–51 (AAD/1979/5).
Francis Marshall, fashion & social illustrator, 1920–80 (AAD/1990/2).
Frederick Starke, press cuttings 1949–69 (AAD/2000/10).
Isobel, designer 1925–69 (AAD/1991/12).
John French (AAD/1979/9)
Lachasse Ltd 1930–81 corresp. sales and purchase ledgers (AAD/1989/6).
Michael Sherard, press cuttings albums, 1947–1983 (AAD/2000/6/1–3).
Paper patterns for clothes mainly by Vogue ca. 1957–1980 (AAD/1984/8).
Robina Wallis, second-hand clothes dealer 1927–59 (AAD/1989/8).
Ronald Patterson Press Books.
S. London Ltd, furrier: records, ca. 1920–1968 (AAD/1994/5).
Simone Mirman Albums (AAD/1995/24)
Victor Stiebel Fashion Designer: Press albums 1932–1963 (AAD/1994/1–22).

VICTORIA AND ALBERT MUSEUM—THE FURNITURE, TEXTILES AND
FASHION DEPARTMENT (CROMWELL ROAD, LONDON SW7)

Digby Morton Press Books.
John Cavanagh Archive.
Minutes of the Quarterly Meeting of the Incorporated Society of London Fashion
    Designers 1942–1970.

NOTES

INTRODUCTION

1. See, for example, Mary L. Stewart, 'Copying and Copyrighting Haute Couture: Democratizing Fashion, 1900–1930s', *French Historical Studies* 28, no. 1 (2005): 103–130.

2. For a consideration of the broad range of London's more commercial mass market fashion manufacturers, see Bethan Bide, 'London Leads the World: The Reinvention of London Fashion in the Aftermath of the Second World War', *Fashion Theory* 24, no. 3 (2020): 349–369.

3. For recent scholarship on Paris' position of centrality within the fashion industry, see Valerie Steele, *Paris, Capital of Fashion* (London: Bloomsbury Visual Arts, 2017); Sophie Kurkdjian, 'Paris as the Capital of Fashion, 1858–1939: An Inquiry', *Fashion Theory* 24, no. 3 (2020): 371–391.

4. For further information, see Véronique Pouillard, 'Managing Fashion Creativity: The History of the Chambre Syndicale de la Couture Parisienne during the Interwar Period', *Investigaciones de Historia Economica—Economic History Research* 12, no. 2 (2016): 815–835.

5. From 1956, due to financial instability, the INCSOC allowed fee-paying associate members from auxiliary fashion firms: Aristoc Ltd (hosiery); Berlie Foundations (corsetry); Bolton Leathers, Dumas & Maury (textile merchants); Lilliman & Cox (dry cleaning); Pringle of Scotland (knitwear); Rayne Ltd (footwear); two fur companies: Bradleys and S. London; five milliners: Rudolf, Edelle, Simone Mirman, Aage Thaarup and Vernier; and two hairstylist firms: French of London and Steiner.

6. Havinden operated as the chairman for the first six months when Edward Molyneux replaced her, followed consecutively by Hartnell, then Stiebel, then Amies and finally Edward Rayne (of Rayne Shoes).

7. In 1949 Fellowes was replaced by Viscountess Rothermere (wife of the conservative politician and press magnate Viscount Rothermere, chairman of Associated Newspapers and the Daily Mail & General Trust Ltd). She was followed by Lady Jane Clark (wife of Kenneth Clark, the art historian and museum director) in 1952, who was succeeded by Lady Pamela Berry (wife of Lord Hartnell owner of the *Daily Telegraph* and *Sunday Telegraph*) in July 1954.

8. *Dissolved Companies Record 1975: No of Company 371721 The Incorporated Society of London Fashion Designers*, 26 August 1975 (BT 31/45170). In the 1960s several houses closed: Victor Stiebel (1963), Michael Sherard (1964) and Ronald Paterson (1968).

9. In 1945 the Chambre set out two specific classes of production: Couture and Couture-Création; the distinction between the two was carefully defined and regulated. The latter category was the most prestigious, and only in this class could the titles 'couturier' or 'haute couturier' be used; in the former it was 'artisan maitre couturier', 'couturiere', and 'couture'. The category a house belonged to was decided by a jury of textile representatives and the Chambre's administrative team. For further detail on the operation of the Chambre Syndicale, see Mary Brooks Picken and Dora L. Miller, *Dressmakers of France: The Who, How and Why of French Couture* (New York: Harpers and Bros, 1956), 9–18; Jeannette A. Jarnow and Beatrice Judelle, *Inside the Fashion Business* (New York: John Wiley and Sons, 1965), 89–128; Diana de Marly, *The History of Haute Couture, 1850–1950* (London: B. T. Batsford, 1980), 106–107 and 195–197; Alexandra Palmer, *Couture and Commerce: The Transatlantic Fashion Trade in the 1950s* (Vancouver: University of British Columbia Press, 2004), 14–17.

10. Marjorie Dunton, 'La Chambre Syndicale', in *Couture: An Illustrated History of the Great Paris Designers and Their Creations*, edited by Ruth Lynam (New York: Doubleday and Company, 1972), 40–49.

11. For a consideration of plagiarism within the industry in the interwar years, see Véronique Pouillard, 'Design Piracy in the Fashion Industries of Paris and New York in the Interwar Years', *Business History Review* 85, no. 2 (2011): 319–344.

12. *Memorandum and Articles of Association of the Incorporated Society of London Fashion Designers*, registered 6 January 1942. For full details, see the appendix.

13. Claire Hancock, 'Capitale du Plaisir: The Remaking of Paris', in *Imperial Cities: Landscape Display and Identity*, edited by Felix Driver and David Gilbert (Manchester: Manchester University Press, 1999).

14. See, for example, Amy de la Haye, 'The Fourth Generation', in *A Family of Fashion: The Messels: Six Generations of Dress*, edited by Eleanor Thomson (London: Philip Wilson Publishers, 2006), 92–111 (99). Also, Edwina Ehrman, 'Broken Traditions: 1930–55', in *The London Look: Fashion from Street to Catwalk*, edited by Christopher Breward, Edwina Ehrman and Caroline Evans (London: Yale University Press, 2004), 97–116.

15. Christopher Breward, *Fashioning London: Clothing the Modern Metropolis* (Oxford: Berg, 2004), 126.

16. For the comparison of Stiebel to Balmain, see 'Designer on the Move', *Rhodesia Herald*, 24 December 1957. For Donnellan to Balanciaga, see Claire Wilcox, *The Golden Age of Couture: Paris and London 1947–1957* (London: V & A Publishing, 2007).

17. For an exploration of this aspect of fashion, see Gilles Lipovetsky, *The Empire of Fashion: Dressing Modern Democracy*, translated by C. Porter (Princeton, NJ: Princeton University Press, 1994).

18. Minutes of the Incorporated Society's Designer Meeting, 27 February 1949.

19. 'The World of Creative Fashion', *BBC Radio Debate*, 14 August 1949.

20. Hardy Amies, *Just So Far* (London: Collins, 1954), 166. A reservation in using the terms *couture* and *couturier* is highlighted throughout this autobiography by these terms being placed in italics.

21. Angela McRobbie, *British Fashion Design: Rag Trade or Image Industry?* (London: Routledge, 1998), 64–65. For further discussion of the links between art and fashion, see Nancy Troy, *Couture Culture: A Study in Modern Art and Fashion* (Cambridge, MA: MIT Press, 2003); Chris Townsend, *Rapture: Art's Seduction by Fashion* (London: Thames and Hudson, 2002); Peter Wollen, *Addressing the Century: 100 Years of Art and Fashion* (London: Hayward Gallery Publishing, 1999); Adam Geczy and Vicki Karamina, *Fashion and Art* (London: Berg Publishers, 2012); Nicky Ryan, 'Prada and the Art of Patronage', *Fashion Theory Journal* 11, no. 1 (2007): 7–24.

22. See, for example, Cheryl Buckley and Hazel Clark, *Fashion and Everyday Life: London and New York* (London: Bloomsbury Academic, 2017); Regina L. Blaszczyk and Véronique Pouillard, *European Fashion: The Creation of a Global Industry* (Manchester: Manchester University Press, 2018); Bide, 'London Leads the World', 349–369.

23. For a selection of academic response to these contemporary challenges, see Zeynep Ozdamar Ertekin, Bengu Sevil Oflac and Cemre Serbetcioglu, 'Fashion Consumption during Economic Crisis: Emerging Practices and Feelings of Consumers', *Journal of Global Fashion Marketing* 11, no. 3 (2020): 270–288; Alice Payne, 'Fashion Futuring in the Anthropocene: Sustainable Fashion as "Taming" and 'Rewilding', *Fashion Theory Journal* 23, no. 1 (2019): 5–23; Annamma Joy, John Sherry, Alladi Venkatesh, Jeff Wang and Ricky Chan, 'Fast Fashion, Sustainability, and the Ethical Appeal of Luxury Brands', *Fashion Theory* 16, no. 3 (2012): 273–295; Nathaniel Dafydd Beard, 'The Branding of Ethical Fashion and the Consumer: A Luxury Niche or Mass-Market Reality?', *Fashion Theory* 12, no. 4 (2008): 447–467; Rachel Taylor, 'Invent Your Own Fashion Economy: Post-Growth Cultures', *Fashion Practice* 11, no. 3 (2019): 397–416; Lynda Grose, 'Fashion and Sustainability: Where We Are and Where We Need to Be', *Fashion Practice* 11, no. 3 (2019): 291–301; Kedron Thomas, 'Cultures of Sustainability in the Fashion Industry', *Fashion Theory* 24, no. 5 (2020): 715–742.

24. Marcus Fairs, '"It's the end of fashion as we know it" says Li Edelkoort', *Dezeen*, March 2015.

25. For further detail, see Pierre-Yves Donze and Ben Wubs, 'LVMH: Storytelling and Organizing Creativity in Luxury and Fashion', in Blaszczyk and Pouillard, *European Fashion*, 63–85.

26. The ethical problems of this model, which often uses offshore labour to produce branded goods at premium prices, has been documented in Dana Thomas, *Deluxe: How Luxury Lost Its Luster* (New York: Penguin, 2007), and Peter McNeill and Georgio Riello, *Luxury: A Rich History* (New York: Oxford University Press, 2016). For a consideration of the spectacularisation of late capitalist catwalk shows, see Caroline Evans, *Fashion at the Edge: Spectacle, Modernity and Deathliness* (New Haven, CT: Yale University Press, 2007); here she draws on Guy Debord, *Society of the Spectacle* (Detroit, MI: Black and Red, 1984).

27. Hayley Maitland, 'Remembering Norman Hartnell, the Fashion Designer behind Princess Beatrice's Vintage Wedding Dress', *Vogue.co.uk*, 19 July 2020.

28. Before 2001, London couture was discussed in three essays which focused on government-led initiatives rather than the Society or the couturiers: David Tomlinson, *British Cotton Couture 1941–1961* (Exhibition Catalogue, Gallery of English Costume, Platt Hall, Manchester, 1985); Anthea Jarvis, 'British Cotton Couture: British Fashion and the Cotton Board, 1941–1969', *Costume: The Journal of the Costume Society*, no. 31 (1997): 92–99; Helen Reynolds, 'The Utility Garment: Its Design and the Effect on the Mass-Market 1942–45', in *Utility Reassessed*, edited by Judy Attfield (Manchester: Manchester University Press, 1999), 125–142. It is also notable that only three of the London couturiers published autobiographies of their careers: Charles Creed, *Maid to Measure* (London: Jarrolds, 1961); Norman Hartnell, *Silver and Gold* (London: Evans Brothers, 1955); and Hardy Amies, *Just So Far* (London: Collins, 1954) and *Still Here: An Autobiography* (London: Weidenfeld and Nicolson, 1985). Of the Incorporated Society's seventeen members, only Sir Norman Hartnell, the 'royal-couturier' who designed for the wardrobe of Queen Elizabeth II, was a recipient of a museum exhibition. 'Hartnell: Clothes by the Royal Couturier, 1930s–60s', March 1985 to February 1986, Museum of Costume, Bath, with an accompanying exhibition catalogue *Norman Hartnell, 1901–79, the Royal Pavilion Art Gallery and Museums* (Brighton, 1985).

29. Amies' company did however stay open in Savile Row after his death, but focused on menswear; it collapsed into administration in March 2019. Whilst Hartnell and Amies were both acquired as part of the London fashion portfolio of the Hong Kong–based venture capital Fung Group, these two 'sleeping beauties' were not resurrected as legacy luxury brands. The term 'sleeping beauty' is used to describe a Parisian haute couture house that was internationally recognised but has become dormant that is reintroduced as a luxury brand in the contemporary market. For an exploration of this practice, see Johanna Zanon, 'Reawakening the "Sleeping Beauties" of Haute Couture: The Case of Guy and Arnaud de Lummen', in Blaszczyk and Pouillard, *European Fashion*, 86–118.

30. Amy de la Haye, *The Cutting Edge of Fashion, 1947–1997* (London: V & A Publications, 1998), 18. For consideration of documentation of the next generation of London designers, see, for example, Judith Watt, *Ossie Clark 1965–74* (London: V & A Publications, 2003); Shawn Levy, *Ready Steady Go: Swinging London and*

the Invention of Cool (London: Fourth Estate, 2003); Claire Wilcox, *Vivienne Westwood* (London: V & A Publications, 2005); Sinty Stemp and Felicity Green, *Jean Muir: Beyond Fashion* (Woodbridge: Antique Collectors Club, 2006); Christopher Breward, David Gilbert and Jenny Lister, *Swinging Sixties* (London: V & A Publications, 2006); Alwyn Turner, *Biba: The Biba Experience* (Woodbridge: Antique Collectors Club, 2007); Richard Lester and Marit Allen, *John Bates Fashion Designer* (Woodbridge: Antique Collectors Club, 2008); Ian R. Webb, *Foale and Tuffin: The Sixties a Decade of Fashion* (Woodbridge: ACC Editions, 2009); Jenny Lister, ed., *Mary Quant* (London: V & A Publications, 2019).

31. For example, see Francois Baudot, *A Century of Fashion* (London: Thames and Hudson, 1999). This text, whilst documenting twentieth-century fashion, makes no mention of London's couture industry and only mentions English fashion design from 1960 onwards. Charlotte Seeling, *Fashion: The Century of the Designer, 1900–1999* (Cologne: Konemann, 1999), includes a section on 'British Fashion' which only considers the post-war period; it has two pages on Norman Hartnell and Hardy Amies which focus on their role as 'royal couturiers'.

32. In terms of the rise in national studies of fashion between 2000 and 2009, see Nicola White, *Reconstructing Italian Fashion* (Oxford: Berg, 2000); Christopher Breward, Becky Conekin and Caroline Cox, eds., *The Englishness of English Dress* (Oxford: Berg, 2002); Breward, *Fashioning London*; Alexandra Palmer, *Fashion, a Canadian Perspective* (Toronto: University of Toronto Press, 2004); Yuniya Kawamura, *The Japanese Revolution in Paris Fashion* (Oxford: Berg, 2004); Norma Rantisi, 'The Ascendance of New York Fashion', *International Journal of Urban and Regional Research* 28, no. 1 (2004): 86–106; Alison Goodrum, *The National Fabric: Fashion, Britishness, Globalisation* (Oxford: Berg, 2005); Christopher Breward and David Gilbert, eds., *Fashion World Cities* (Oxford: Berg, 2006); Javier Gimeno Martínez, 'Selling Avant-Garde: How Antwerp Became a Fashion Capital (1990–2002)', *Urban Studies* 44, no. 12 (2007): 2449–2464; Marlis Schweitzer, 'American Fashions for American Women: The Rise and Fall of Fashion Nationalism', in *Producing Fashion: Commerce, Culture and Consumers*, edited by Regina Blaszczyk (Philadelphia: University of Pennsylvania Press, 2008): 130–149; Rebecca Arnold, *The American Look: Fashion, Sportswear and the Image of Women in the 1930s and 1940s* (New York: I. B. Tauris, 2009); Agnes Rocamora, *Fashioning the City: Paris, Fashion and the Media* (London: I. B. Tauris, 2009); Jennifer Craik, 'Is Australian Fashion and Dress Distinctively Australian?', *Fashion Theory* 13, no. 4 (2009): 409–442; Alison Goodrum, 'True Brits? Authoring National Identity in Anglo-Japanese Fashion Exports', *Fashion Theory* 13, no. 4 (2009): 461–480.

33. This was initiated by Gavin Waddell, 'The Incorporated Society of London Fashion Designers: Its Impact on Post-War British Fashion', *Costume: The Journal of the Costume Society*, no. 35 (2001): 92–115. Followed by two essays in Breward, Conekin and Cox, *The Englishness of English Dress* in 2002: Amy de la Haye, 'Gilded Brocade Gowns and Impeccable Tailored Tweeds: Victor Stiebel (1907–76) a

Quintessentially English Designer', 133–146, and Edwina Ehrman, 'The Spirit of
English Style: Hardy Amies, Royal Dressmaker and International Businessman',
147–160. Three London-based exhibitions in the middle of the decade were also
formative in stimulating research and addressing the marginalisation of London-
based couture. Museum of London's *The London Look*, exhibition October 2004–
May 2005 accompanied by Breward, Evans and Ehrman, *The London Look*. London's
Victoria and Albert Museum then held *Swinging Sixties*, curated by Christopher
Breward, David Gilbert and Jenny Lister. This exhibition was completed as part of
the ESRC/AHRC 'Cultures of Consumption' Programme, June 2006–February
2007. The *Golden Age of Couture: Paris and London 1947—1957* exhibition at the
Victoria and Albert Museum, September 2007 to January 2008. Wilcox, *Golden Age
of Couture*. This catalogue included Amy de la Haye, 'Material Evidence London
Couture 1947–57', 89–107. The designers also became the focus of PhD research:
Jane Hattrick, 'The Life and Work of the London Couturier Norman Hartnell:
Issues of Design, Business, Royal Patronage and Consumption 1924–1979' (PhD
thesis, University of Brighton, 2012); Caroline Ness, 'The Recovery of the Career
of the London Dress Designer Jo Mattli, His Contribution to the British Fashion
and Textile Industry during the Mid Twentieth Century' (PhD thesis, University
of Glasgow, 2014). Caroline Ness and Mary M. Brooks, 'Rediscovering Mattli: A
Forgotten 1950s London Couturier', *Costume* 45, no. 1 (2011): 85–100; Michael
Pick, *Be Dazzled! Norman Hartnell, Sixty Years of Glamour and Fashion* (New York:
Pointed Leaf Press, 2009); Michael Pick, *Hardy Amies* (Suffolk: Antique Collectors Club Editions, 2012); *Hartnell to Amies: Couture by Royal Appointment*, curated
by Dennis Northdruft and Michael Pick, Fashion and Textile Museum, London,
November 2012–February 2013.

34. See, for instance, Troy, *Couture Culture*; Mary Lynn Stewart, *Dressing Modern
French Women: Marketing Haute Couture 1919–1939* (Baltimore, MD: Johns Hopkins University Press, 2008); Lourdes Font, 'International Couture: The Opportunities and Challenges of Expansion, 1880–1920', *Business History* 54, no. 1 (2012):
30–47; Palmer, *Couture and Commerce*; Alexandra Palmer, 'Inside Paris Haute
Couture', in Wilcox, *Golden Age of Couture*, 63–83; Véronique Pouillard, 'In the
Shadow of Paris? French Haute Couture and Belgian Fashion between the Wars',
in Blaszczyk, *Producing Fashion*, 62–81; Steele, *Paris, Capital of Fashion*; Sophie
Kurkdjian, 'The Cultural Value of Parisian Haute Couture', in Steele, *Paris, Capital
of Fashion*; Sophie Kurkdjian, 'The Emergence of French Vogue: French Identity
and Visual Culture in the Fashion Press, 1920–1940', *International Journal of Fashion
Studies* 6, no. 1 (2019): 63–82.

35. Jennifer Kaufmann-Buhler, Victoria Pass and Christopher Wilson, eds., *Design
History Beyond the Canon* (London: Bloomsbury Publishing, 2019), 7. For a discussion of Design History's 'Great Men Narratives', see Hazel Conway, *Design History: A Students' Handbook* (London: Harper Collins, 1987); Peter Hall, 'Narratives
of History', paper given at the *Narratives and Design Studies: A Task of Translation*

Symposium at Parsons the New School of Design (New York, March 2014). Both authors trace this tradition within design history to the 1936 seminal work of Nicolas Pevsner, *Pioneers of Modern Design: From William Morris to Walter Gropius* (Bath: Palazzo Editions, 2011).

36. For an interesting exploration of this movement away from the 'cult of personality' towards an examination of the collective and cumulative dimension of design, see Jan Michl, 'On Seeing Design as Redesign—An Exploration of a Neglected Problem in Design Education', *Scandinavian Journal of Design History* 12 (2002): 7–23.

37. Kaufmann-Buhler, Pass and Wilson, *Design History beyond the Canon*, 15.

38. Charlotte Fiell and Peter Fiell, *The Story of Design: From the Paleolithic to the Present* (New York: Monacelli Press, 2016), 7.

39. See, for example, Fiona MacCarthy, *All Things Bright and Beautiful: Design in Britain 1830 to Today* (London: Allen & Unwin, 1972); Noel Carrington, *Industrial Design in Britain* (London: Allen & Unwin, 1976); Richard Stewart, *Design and British Industry* (London: John Murray, 1987); Jonathan Woodham, *The Industrial Designer and the Public* (London: Pembridge, 1983).

40. Jonathan M. Woodham, 'Britain Can Make It and the History of Design', in *Design and Cultural Politics in Post-war Britain: The Britain Can Make It Exhibition of 1946*, edited by Patrick J. Maguire and Jonathan M. Woodham (London: Leicester University Press, 1997), 18. For examples of this area of Woodham's research, see his 'The Design Archive at Brighton: Serendipity and Strategy', *Art Libraries Journal* 29, no. 3 (2004): 15–22; 'The Festival of Britain and the Council of Industrial Design: Educating the Consumer in Postwar Britain', *Crafts Magazine*, September/October 2001; 'Managing British Design Reform I: Fresh Perspectives on the Early Years of the Council of Industrial Design', *Journal of Design History* 9, no. 1 (1996): 55–65; 'Managing British Design Reform II: The Film—An Ill-Fated Episode in the Politics of "Good Taste"', *Journal of Design History* 9, no. 2 (1996): 101–115.

41. Grace Lees-Maffei, 'Introduction: Professionalization as a Focus in Interior Design History', *Journal of Design History* 21, no. 1 (2008): 1–18.

42. For a small example, see Jill Seddon and Suzette Worden, eds., *Women Designing: Redefining Design in Britain between the Wars* (Brighton: University of Brighton, 1994); Cheryl Robertson, 'From Cult to Profession: Domestic Women in Search of Equality', in *The Material Culture of Gender*, edited by Katherine Martinez and Kenneth Ames (Delaware: Henry Francis DuPont Winterthur Museum, 1997), 89; Pat Kirkham, ed., *Women Designers in the USA 1900–2000: Diversity and Difference* (New Haven, CT: Yale University Press, 2000); Suzette Worden and Jill Seddon, 'Women Designers in Britain in the 1920s and 1930s: Defining the Professional and Redefining Design', *Journal of Design History* 8, no. 3 (1995): 177–193; Jill Seddon, 'Mentioned, but Denied Significance: Women Designers and the

"Professionalization" of Design in Britain, c. 1920–1951', *Gender & History* 12, no. 2 (2000): 425–447; Penny Sparke, *Elsie de Wolfe: The Birth of Modern Interior Decoration* (New York: Acanthus, 2005); Michelle Jones, 'Design and the Domestic Persuader: Television and the British Broadcasting Corporation's Promotion of Post War "Good Design"', *Journal of Design History* 16, no. 4 (2003): 307–318; Michelle Jones, 'Design in the Monochrome Box: The BBC Television Design Department and the Modern Style, 1946–1962', in *Design and Popular Entertainment*, edited by Christopher Frayling and Emily King (Manchester: Manchester University Press, 2009), 161–179; Philip Pacey, '"Anyone Designing Anything?" Non-Professional Designers and the History of Design', *Journal of Design History* 5, no. 3 (1992): 217–225; Barbara Burman, ed., *The Culture of Sewing: Gender, Consumption and Home Dressmaking* (Oxford: Berg, 1999); Jo Turney, 'Here's One I Made Earlier: Making and Living with Home Craft in Contemporary Britain', *Journal of Design History* 17, no. 3 (2004): 267–282; Roni Brown, 'Identity and Narrativity in Homes Made by Amateurs', *Home Cultures* 4, no. 3 (2007): 213–238, especially 265–266; Gerry Beegan and Paul Atkinson 'Professionalism, Amateurism and the Boundaries of Design', *Journal of Design History* 21, no. 4 (2008): 305–313.

43. For this shift within fashion studies, see Leah Armstrong and Felice McDowell, eds., *Fashioning Professionals: Identity and Representation at Work in the Creative Industries* (London: Bloomsbury Publishing, 2018). Within design history, also see Leah Armstrong, 'Steering a Course between Commercialism and Professionalism: The Society of Industrial Artists Code of Conduct for the Professional Designer in Britain', *Journal of Design History* 29, no. 2 (2016): 161–179; Leah Armstrong, 'A New Image for a New Profession: Self Image and Representation in the Professionalisation of Design in Britain 1945–1960', *Journal of Consumer Culture* 19, no. 1 (2017): 104–124. For an earlier British analysis of professionalisation, see Harold Perkin, *The Rise of Professional Society: England since 1880* (London: Routledge, 1989) and *The Third Revolution: International Professional Elites* (London: Routledge, 1996).

44. Jeffrey L. Meikle, 'Material Virtues: On the Ideal and the Real in Design History', *Journal of Design History* 11, no. 3 (1998): 194.

45. Pamela Walker Laird, *Pull: Networking and Success since Benjamin Franklin* (Cambridge, MA: Harvard University Press, 2006), 2.

46. Patrick J. Maguire, 'Introduction: Politics and Design in Post-War Britain', in Maguire and Woodham, *Design and Cultural Politics*, 3.

47 This aligns with design history's embrace of Bruno Latour's *actor–network theory* demonstrated at the discipline's annual conference in 2008. Fiona Hackney, Johnathan Glynne and Viv Minton, eds., *Networks of Design, Proceedings of the Annual International Conference of the Design History Society* (UK) (University College Falmouth, 2008). The range of interdisciplinary inquiry at this event, whilst eclectic, encouraged design historians to think more carefully about the impact of networks on design practice.

48. For the development of this term, see Regina L. Blaszczyk, *Imagining Consumers: Design and Innovation from Wedgwood to Corning* (Baltimore, MD: Johns Hopkins University Press, 2000). For the interest of business history in fashion, see Katrina Honeyman and Andrew Godley, 'Introduction: Doing Business with Fashion', *Textile History* 34, no. 2 (2003): 101–106. This edition stemmed from a conference at Reading University in December 2001, which for the first time brought together economic and business historians of the clothing industry with fashion and design historians. Similar interdisciplinary approaches were apparent in 'Fashions: Business Practices in Historical Perspective', Joint Meeting of the Business History Conference and the European Business History Association, Bocconi University, Milan, June 2009.

49. Blaszczyk, *Imagining Consumers*, 12.

50. Blaszczyk and Pouillard, *European Fashion*, 6. Also see Blaszczyk, *Producing Fashion*, and R. L. Blaszczyk, *The Color Revolution* (Cambridge, MA: MIT Press, 2012).

51. Per H. Hansen, 'Networks, Narratives, and New Markets: The Rise and Decline of Danish Modern Furniture Design, 1930–1970', *Business History Review* 80 (Autumn 2006): 449–483 (483).

52. Per H. Hansen, 'Business History: A Cultural and Narrative Approach', *Business History Review* 86, no. 4 (Winter 2012): 693–717 (696).

53. This understanding is similar to Lenora Auslander's analysis of the complexities of the work of 'taste professionals' that emerged in the nineteenth century in the French furniture industry. Leora Auslander, *Taste and Power: Furnishing Modern France* (Berkeley: University of California Press, 1996).

54. Hansen, 'Networks, Narratives, and New Markets', 449–483.

55. Grace Lees-Maffei, 'The Production—Consumption—Mediation Paradigm', *Journal of Design History* 22, no. 4 (2009): 351–376; Grace Lees-Maffei, 'Studying Advice: Historiography, Methodology, Commentary, Bibliography', *Journal of Design History* 16, no. 1 (2003): 3.

56. Lees-Maffei, 'The Production—Consumption—Mediation Paradigm', 351–376.

57. Hansen, 'Business History', 711.

58. The prohibition of advertising is recognized as essential to the maintenance of professional integrity; for example, the architects RIBA's Code of Conduct (1929) states: 'an architect must not publicly advertise'. This rejection of commercialism within the construction of professional identity is explored in Alexander M. Carr-Saunders and Paul A. Wilson, *The Professions* (London: Clarendon Press, 1933).

59. It is often the constant comparison to France, America and Italy that has defined London's boundaries as a fashion centre, particularly the products and structure of

its couture industry; see, for example, Bettina Ballard, *In My Fashion* (C. Tingling & Co., 1960); Colin McDowell, *Forties Fashion and the New Look* (London: Bloomsbury, 1997); Wilcox, *Golden Age of Couture*; Breward, *Fashioning London*.

60. To clarify the use of the terms 'English' and 'British' in relation to the London couture, there is a general consensus that throughout the period of this study whilst Englishness and Britishness were often fused, the British were usually seen as 'English in their culture'. Whilst English is therefore understood as a cultural term, its nature is geographically and socially specific. As the political historian Richard Johnson has suggested, British society should be viewed 'as a series of concentric circles' with a centre (based in London and the Home Counties) that defines the whole. The networks surrounding the London couture, the environment in which it operated, its elite made-to-measure garments and the clients it catered to placed its practice firmly at the centre of English culture. Therefore, London couture in its practice and its cultural connotations will be read as English. For a further exploration of the definition of English and British, see Richard Johnson, *The Politics of Recession* (London: Macmillan, 1985), 234–235.

61. This approach aligns with recent consideration of the national implication of other couture groups; see Pouillard, 'In the Shadow of Paris?', 62–81; Alexandra Palmer, 'The Association of Canadian Couturiers', in Palmer, *Canadian Perspective*, 90–109. An important text is also Agnes Rocamora's *Fashioning the City: Paris, Fashion and the Media* (London: I. B. Tauris, 2009), which demonstrates how the representation of Paris in the fashion press naturalized that city's claim to fashion authority, particularly as embodied in the fashionable feminine symbol of the Parisienne.

62. For example, see Javier Gimeno-Martínez, *Design and National Identity* (London: Bloomsbury Publishing, 2016); Elke Gaugele and Monica Titton, *Fashion and Postcolonial Critique* (Cambridge, MA: MIT Press, 2020); Patrizia Casadei and David Gilbert, 'Unpicking the Fashion City: Global Perspectives on Design, Manufacturing and Symbolic Production in Urban Formations', in *Creative Industries and Entrepreneurship: Paradigms in Transition from a Global Perspective*, edited by Luciana Lazzeretti and Marilena Vecco (Cheltenham: Edward Elgar, 2018), 79–103; Wessie Ling and Simone Segre Reinach, eds., *Fashion in Multiple Chinas: Chinese Styles in the Transglobal Landscape* (London: Bloomsbury Publishing, 2018); Frederik Godart, 'The Power Structure of the Fashion Industry: Fashion Capitals, Globalization and Creativity', *International Journal of Fashion Studies* 1 (2014): 39–55; David Gilbert, 'A New World Order? Fashion and Its Capital in the Twenty-First Century', in *Fashion Cultures Revisited: Theories, Explorations and Analysis*, edited by Stella Bruzzi and Pamela Church Gibson (London: Routledge, 2013), 11–30; Lisa Skov, 'Dreams of Small Nations in a Polycentric Fashion World', *Fashion Theory* 15, no. 2 (2011): 137–156; Carla Jones, Ann Marie Leshkowich and Sandra Niessen, eds., *Re-Orienting Fashion: The Globalization of Asian Fashion* (Oxford: Berg 2003), 215–243.

63. A fashion centre was also different as it was based firmly in its production capacity, whereby it was a 'centre' not only of designer activity and authority but also of manufacture and production. In comparison the contemporary fashion *capital* or *city* is a product of post-industrial concerns that reflects the symbolic development of fashion design as a central component within the global branding industry.

64. Kjetil Fallan and Grace Lees-Maffei, eds., *Made in Italy: Rethinking a Century of Italian Design* (London: Bloomsbury Publishing, 2013), 29. For the continued relevance of national studies of European fashion, see Silvia Roses Castellsaguer, 'Spanish Couture: In the Shadow of Cristobal Balenciaga', *Fashion Theory* (2020), DOI: 10.1080/1362704X.2020.1770399.

65. Kelly Lim, 'The Chinese Designers of Haute Couture: Three Designers Helping Redefine the Term "Made in China"', *Vogue* (Hong Kong), 24 October, 2019.

66. Lees-Maffei and Fallan, *Made in Italy*, 2.

67. Lou Taylor and Marie McLoughlin, *Paris Fashion and World War Two: Global Diffusion and Nazi Control* (London: Bloomsbury Visual Arts, 2020).

68. For research into the broader markets for London couture, see Palmer, *Couture and Commerce*; Beatrice Behlen, 'London and UK', Alexandra Kim, 'United States & Canada' and Angela Lassig, 'Australia and New Zealand', in *London Couture: 1923–1975: British Luxury*, edited Amy de la Haye and Edwina Ehrman (London: V & A Publishing, 2015), 203–246.

69. Alex Cairncross, *The British Economy since 1945* (London: Wiley Blackwell, 1995); B. W. E. Alford, *British Economic Performance 1945–1975* (Cambridge: Cambridge University Press, 1995); *Exports to Canada: Report to the President of the Board of Trade of the United Kingdom Clothing Mission* (His Majesty's Stationary Office, 1949). For the importance of the American market for French couture, see Schweitzer, 'American Fashions', 130–149.

CHAPTER 1

1. 'London Launches a Mode', *British Vogue*, 23 January 1935.

2. 'The Pulse of Fashion', *Harper's Bazaar*, February 1935.

3. Ann Archer, 'British Threaten French Corner on Style Rule', *United Press Red Letter*, New York, 6 October 1933.

4. Hartnell, *Silver and Gold*, 106.

5. See Jonathan M. Woodham, *The Industrial Designer and the Public* (London: Pembridge, 1983).

6. 'These Four Young Men Dictate Designs for Women: Hartnell, Stiebel, Russell, Symonds', *Sunday Referee*, March 1936.

7. This number of attendees was repeated throughout a range of newspaper reports held in the Stiebel Press Books (AAD/1994).

8. Harry Yoxall, *A Fashion of Life* (New York: Taplinger Publishing, 1996), 67–70.

9. Breward, *Fashioning London*, 100.

10. Charles Eyre Pascoe, *London of To-day: An Illustrated Handbook for the Season* (Boston: Roberts Brothers, 1890); Amy de La Haye, 'Court Dressmaking in Mayfair from the 1890s to the 1920s', in de la Haye and Ehrman, *London Couture*, 11–27.

11. Pascoe, *London of To-day*.

12. Andrew Godley, 'The Development of the UK Clothing Industry, 1850–1950: Output and Productivity Growth', *Business History* 37, no. 4 (1995): 33.

13. See, for example, Erica Rappaport, *Shopping for Pleasure: Women and the Making of London's West End* (Princeton, NJ: Princeton University Press, 2000).

14. Bronwyn Edwards, 'We Are Fatally Influenced by Goods Brought in Bond Street: London, Shopping and the Fashionable Geographies of 1930s Vogue', *Fashion Theory* 10, nos. 1–2 (2006): 73–96.

15. *Post Office London Directory* (London Metropolitan Archives, Ref 3.4).

16. Christopher Breward, 'Fashion's Front and Back: Rag Trade Cultures and Cultures of Consumption in Post-War London', *The London Journal* 31, no. 1 (2006): 15–40.

17. For further detail, see Clive Warwick, 'French Haute Couture Houses in London', in de la Haye and Ehrman, *London Couture*, 197–202.

18. Molyneux was British; Schiaparelli, Italian; Dilkusha, British (Princess Dilkusha de Rohan raised in India); Karinska, Ukrainian; Piguet, Swiss; only Heim was French. Many of these couturiers who came to Britain placed specific emphasis on designing sportswear in their London houses.

19. Didier Grumbach, *Histories de la Mode* (Paris: Editions de Seuil, 1993), 32–33.

20. For a detailed consideration of these changes, see Walter, A. Morton, *British Finance 1930–1940* (London: Arnos Press, 1978), 169.

21. Pouillard, *In the Shadow of Paris*, 68.

22. The designers were Madam Alexedis, Hardy Amies (Lachasse), Henry Bridburg, Richard Busvine (Viola Redfern Ltd) Madam Champcommunal (Reville-Terry then Worth) Robert Douglas, Matilda Etches, Genne Glenny, Norman Hartnell, Sophia Harris (Motley), Isobel, Charles James, Alex Lord (Leathercraft), Eva Lutyen, Giuseppe Mattli, Winifred Mawdsley, Ronald Morrel, Digby Morton, Lydia Moss (who produced mainly lingerie but also a range of tea dresses), Guy Olliver, the Rahvis Sisters, Peter Russell, Victor Stiebel, Edward H. Symonds (Reville), Rose Taylor and Teddy Tinling, Ulrich Ltd, Madame Enos, Peggy

Moffat, and Eileen Idare. Of these only seven were to become part of the Incorporated Society of London Fashion Designers.

23. Hartnell, *Silver and Gold*, 30.

24. Neil Taylor, 'Molyneux', in de la Haye and Ehrman, *London Couture*, 107.

25. 'Grosvenor-Street Mayfair—London's Most Famous Fashion Street: Isobel Leaving Regent Street', *Evening News*, 25 June 1936.

26. Paul Cohen-Portheim, *Spirit of London* (London: J. Lippincott, 1930), 41–47.

27. Taylor, 'Molyneux', 101.

28. *Vogue*, 22 July 1936, 68.

29. Yoxall, *A Fashion of Life*, 71.

30. Margaret, Duchess of Argyll, *Forget Me Not* (London: Wyndham Publications, 1977), 35.

31. Pascoe, *London of To-day*.

32. Yoxall, *A Fashion of Life*, 69–70.

33. Amies, *Just So Far*, 17.

34. Hartnell, *Silver and Gold*, 27 and 44.

35. Victor Stiebel, 'Unpublished Memoirs', Adrian Woodhouse archive.

36. The milliner Aage Tharrup, in an interview with Mass Observation in October 1939, gave the figure 'of a yearly income of at least £3,000'. Mass Observation Archive (henceforth MO), MO/TC 18—Box 2.

37. 'Dress Designing as a Career for Women', script to program written by Isobel for the BBC, 31 May 1928.

38. Hartnell, *Silver and Gold*, 40.

39. Jane Gordon, 'Speeding-Up on 1933 Fashion: British Dress Designers Two Weeks Ahead of Paris', *Daily Express*, 23 January 1933.

40. The *New York Times* quoted in 'These Four Young Men Dictate Designs for Women: Hartnell, Stiebel, Russell, Symonds', *Sunday Referee*, March 1936.

41. Pascoe, *London of To-day*, 134.

42. Breward, *Fashioning London*, 113.

43. Prior to the 1930s only a handful of London-based designers, such as Lucile and Redfern, gained recognition as innovators of styles. Yet their design authority was based in part on the development of branches of their business in Paris and New York. For further details, see Valerie Mendes and Amy de la Haye, *Lucile Ltd: London, Paris, New York and Chicago, 1890s–1930s* (London 2009); Susan North, 'John Redfern and Sons, 1847 to 1892', *Costume* 35 (2005): 4–27.

44. Michael Pick, 'Gerald Lacoste', *Thirties Society Journal*, no. 3 (1982): 12–16.

45. 'Dress Designing Triumphs', *Modern Weekly*, 14 May 1932.

46. For a consideration of the Georgian Revival, see Elizabeth Mackellar, 'Representing the Georgian: Constructing Interiors in Early Twentieth Century Publications, 1890–1930', *Journal of Design History* 20, no. 4 (2007): 325–342; M. Rosso, 'Georgian London Revisited', *London Journal* 26 (2001): 35–50.

47. Peter Mandler, *Fall and Rise of the Stately Home* (New Haven, CT: Yale University Press, 1999), 279.

48. Stewart, *Dressing Modern French Women*, 35.

49. Yoxall, *A Fashion of Life*, 67–70.

50. In 1932 the main shows for creative fashion design were presented equally by male and female designers, by Victor Stiebel, Glenn Glenny, Reville, Hartnell, Lachasse, Worth, Molyneux, Peter Russell, Jane Munns, Isobel, Paulette, Eileen Idare, Helen Chandler and Peggy Morris; by 1936 seventeen of the twenty-seven main showings were male. The future Incorporated Society was also a male-dominated trade group, with only two businesswomen (Bianca Mosca and Angele Delaughne and one female in-house designer, Madam Champcommunal, at Worth [London]).

51. *Sunday Referee*, 26 March 1936.

52. Valerie Steele, *Women of Fashion: Twentieth Century Designers* (New York: Rizzoli International Publications, 1991).

53. Suzette Worden and Jill Seddon, 'Women Designers in Britain in the 1920s and 1930s: Defining the Professional and Redefining Design', *Journal of Design History* 8, no. 3 (1995): 177–193.

54. Lady Elizabeth Murray, 'London Is the World's Fashion Centre', *Daily Mail*, 17 February 1937, 124.

55. Statistics on the number of staff Stiebel employed taken from American *Fashion Group Bulletin*, 1934. Fashion Group International Records (hereafter FGIR), Box 144.F.6. Claims that his business was fully established taken from Ann Perkins, 'London's Dressmaking World', *Women's Wear Daily*, July 1936.

56. Ross McKibbin, *Classes and Cultures: England 1918–1951* (Oxford: Oxford University Press, 1998), 31.

57. Barbara Cartland, *The Isthmus Years 1919–1939* (London: Hutchinson, 1945), 12.

58. McKibbin, *Classes and Cultures*, 2.

59. David Cannadine, *The Decline and Fall of the British Aristocracy* (New Haven, CT: Yale University Press, 1990), 342.

60. Cathy Ross, *Twenties London: A City in the Jazz Age* (London: Philip Wilson Publishers), 35.

61. 'An Englishman's Idea: Victor Stiebel, Here on a Visit, Says That Modern Style Is International', *New York Times*, 18 November 1934.

62. 'An Englishman's Idea', 1934.

63. FGIR, Box 72.

64. Caroline Seebohm, *The Man Who Was Vogue: The Life and Times of Condé Nast* (New York: Viking Press, 1982), 142.

65. Seebohm, *The Man Who Was Vogue*, 142.

66. Kerstan Cohen, *International Directory of Corporate Histories* (Condé Nast Publications Inc. Gale Virtual Reference Library, 2004).

67. Seebohm, *The Man Who Was Vogue*, 120.

68. Cynthia, L. White, *Women's Magazines 1693–1968* (London: Michael Joseph, 1970), and Seebohm, *The Man Who Was Vogue*, 120.

69. Howard Cox and Simon Mowatt, 'Creating Images of Fashion: Consumer Magazines and American Competition in Britain, 1910–1940', *Business and Economic History Online*, January 2009.

70. 'Victor Stiebel's Midnight Party, 22 Bruton Street', British *Vogue*, April 1933, 78.

71. Kristen Hoganson, 'The Fashionable World: Imagined Communities of Dress', in *After the Imperial Turn: Thinking with and through the Nation*, edited by Antoinette Burton (Durham, NC: Duke University Press, 2003), 260–278 (265).

72. Seebohm, *The Man Who Was Vogue*, 77.

73. Ross, *Twenties London*, 41.

74. Paul Cohen-Portheim, *England the Unknown Isle* (New York: E. P. Dutton & Co., 1931), 113.

75. Juliet Gardiner, *The Thirties: An Intimate History* (Harper Collins, 2010), 623.

76. Duchess of Argyll, *Forget Me Not*, 46.

77. Stiebel, 'Unpublished Memoirs'.

78. 'Almost in Confidence', *Sunday Dispatch*, 26 February 1933.

79. *Bystander* article quoted in Duchess of Argyll, *Forget Me Not*, 46.

80. Stiebel, 'Unpublished Memoirs'.

81. *The Sun*, December 1932.

82. Stiebel, 'Unpublished Memoirs'.

83. McKibbin, *Classes and Cultures*, 2. For further information on the commercial stimulus provided by a growth in extravagant parties, see Susan Shephard, *The Surprising Life of Constance Spry* (London: Pan Books, 2011), 127.

84. Shephard, *Surprising Life*, 119.

85. Constance Spry, *Fashion Group Bulletin*, May 1939.

86. Spry claimed that the 'Flowers and Clothes' show was a 'huge success with an attendance of nearly 800 people'. This event led to British *Vogue*'s 'Flower Edition', 20 March 1935.

87. Shephard, *Surprising Life*, 183.

88. Ross, *Twenties London*, 40.

89. 'Which Period Do You Prefer?', *The Bystander*, 13 December 1933.

90. 'Back to Victoria', *Yorkshire Post*, 7 April 1934.

91. Cynthia Cooper, 'Dressing Up: A Consuming Passion', in *Fashion: A Canadian Perspective*, edited by Alexandra Palmer (Toronto: University of Toronto Press, 2004), 43.

92. Alexandra Harris, *Romantic Moderns: English Writers, Artists and the Imagination from Virginia Woolf to John Piper* (London: Thames and Hudson, 2010).

93. Harris, *Romantic Moderns*, 75.

94. For further information of the importance of this commission for Beaton, Hartnell and the visual representation of the Queen, see Hugo Vickers, *Elizabeth, the Queen Mother* (London: Arrow Books, 2006), 178.

95. Harris, *Romantic Moderns*, 96.

96. This mixture of the past and present was also seen in the work of Paris-based couturiers such as Schiaparelli, Vionnet, Maggy Rouff and Mainbocher. Yet this hybridity can be seen as particularly English. For example, see the work of design historians who highlight the Janus-faced nature of British aesthetic modernism. For example, David Matlass, 'Ages of English Design: Preservation, Modernism and Tales of Their History, 1926–1939', *Journal of Design History* 3, no. 4 (1990): 203–212, shows the clear sense of continuum between the past and present in British design, while Cheryl Buckley points to the number of 'modernisms' within British design in the 1930s and shows that modernity was not deferred but renegotiated in a number of ways. Cheryl Buckley, *Designing Modern Britain* (London: Reaktion Books, 2007), 83.

97. Stiebel was fortunate that one of his first clients was C. B. Cochran's wife, who endorsed his letter of introduction to her husband. A letter Cochran sent back to Stiebel stated, 'I had no idea that it would interest you to do costumes, although I am certain you would do them very successfully. Next time I am doing a play, which calls for them I shall ask you to try your hand'. Charles B. Cochran, letter to Victor Stiebel, 11 October 1933 (property of Adrian Woodhouse).

98. 'Fashion Calling . . . A Few Camera Studies of Victor Stiebel's Striking Clothes Designed for "Music in the Air"', *The Bystander*, 24 May 1933.

99. For a discussion of the importance of the Letty Lynton dress within fashion history, see Christopher Breward, *Fashion* (Oxford: Berg 2005), 136–138.

100. Melville-Brown, 'Most Interesting Man I Ever Met', *Manchester Daily Sketch*, January 1938.

101. Grace Thorncliffe, 'Notes in Diary of a Fashion Model', *Moundsville Journal* (Marshall, WV), 20 April 1937.

102. James Laver, 'Fashion—The English Contribution', *The Studio*, November 1934.

103. By 1937 this instability was compounded by Mussolini's Abyssinian War (September 1935–May 1936), Nazi Germany's Reoccupation of the Rhineland (March 1936), the Spanish Civil War (July 1936) and the Formation of the Axis (November 1936).

104. Philip M. Taylor, *The Projection of Britain: British Overseas Publicity and Propaganda 1919–1939* (Cambridge: Cambridge University Press, 1981), 132.

105. The British Council's original Mission Charter is set out on its website at http://britishcouncil.org. For further details of the utilization of Tallents' ideas, see Taylor, *The Projection of Britain*, 123.

106. Rex Leeper, 'British Culture Abroad', *Contemporary Review*, February 1935, 200–210.

107. Taylor, *The Projection of Britain*, 20.

108. *Department of Overseas Trade Memorandum on Interdepartmental Publicity Committee*, 28 March 1931, quoted in Taylor, *The Projection of Britain*, 106.

109. Stephen Tallents, *The Projection of England* (London: Olen Press, 1932), 7.

110. Taylor, *The Projection of Britain*, 67.

111. Taylor, *The Projection of Britain*, 67.

112. Stiebel, Unpublished Memoirs.

113. See, for example, Andrew Godley, Anne Kershen and Raphael Shapiro, 'Fashion and Its Impact on the Economic Development of London's East End Womenswear Industry, 1929–62: The Case of Ellis and Goldstein', *Textile History* 34, no. 2 (2003): 214–228. This article demonstrates that consumption rose steadily and the fashion content of demand across a broad market was higher in the 1930s than in the 1950s. For a consideration of wider areas of growth, see Derek H. Aldcroft, *The Interwar Economy: Britain 1919–1939* (London: Batsford, 1970), 44. This shows that between 1934 and 1937 real income increased by 19 per cent.

114. 'As Hard as Selling Coals to Newcastle? Norman Hartnell—Famed Dress Designer—Leaves by Air with British Mannequins to Sell British Frocks in Paris— The 'Home of Fashion', Pathé film (1932). https://www.britishpathe.com/video /as-hard-as-selling-coals-to-newcastle.

115. The Empire Marketing Board was set up in 1926. It was established as a substitute for trade tariff reform and protectionist legislation and was abolished in 1933. Its aim was to promote trade throughout the Empire and to promote the consumption of Empire goods.

116. Stephen Constantine, 'The Buy British Campaign of 1931', *European Journal of Marketing* 21, no. 4 (1987): 44–59.

117. J. H. Thomas *The Times*, 14 November 1931, quoted in Constantine, 'Buy British Campaign', 44–59.

118. Constantine, 'Buy British Campaign', 44–59.

119. Constantine, 'Buy British Campaign', 44–59.

120. Deirdre Murphy, 'Couture and the British Court', in de la Haye and Ehrman, *London Couture*, 254.

121. 'Buying an Exclusive Frock from London', *London Evening News*, 6 February 1932.

122. Murray, 'London Is the World's Fashion Centre'.

123. Alex K. Cairncross and Barry J. Eichengreen, *Sterling in Decline: The Devaluations of 1931, 1949 and 1967* (Oxford: Basil Blackwell, 1983).

124. Murray, 'London Is the World's Fashion Centre'.

125. Leslie Hannah, Peter Temin and Steve Toms, 'Long-Term Supply-Side Implications of the Great Depression and 1930s Micro-Economic Policies: Anglo-American Reflections', conference paper, 'Lessons from the Great Depression for the Making of Economic Policy', British Academy, 16–17 April 2010. The British tariff thus rapidly led to the Ottawa Agreement of 1932, in which Empire countries agreed to preferential tariffs among themselves and a correspondingly tougher policy toward non-British exporters.

126. Stewart, *Dressing Modern French Women*, 84.

127. Pouillard, *In the Shadow of Paris*, 72.

128. Geoffrey Jones, *The Evolution of Multinational Business: An Introduction* (London: Routledge, 1996), 9 and 27.

129. Large fashion-only retailers, such as William Filene's Sons Company in Boston, Henri Bendel, Saks, Bergdorf Goodman and Lord & Taylor in New York, were a distinctive American phenomenon. These American speciality stores dominated the fashion scene until the late twentieth century. For further information, see Regina L. Blaszczyk, 'The Rise and Fall of European Fashion at Filene's in Boston', in Blaszczyk and Pouillard, *European Fashion*, 170–200.

130. For research into the role of the Fashion Group in the development of the American fashion industry, particularly in New York, see Arnold, *American Look*, 93–101.

131. Approximately 1,500 industry representatives attended the first *Fashion Futures* (FGIR, Box 73.F.1).

132. 'New York Models the Perfect Fall-Winter Wardrobe: Fashions Exhibited Represent Exciting Style Symposium', *Miami News*, 16 September 1935.

133. The French couturiers represented in *Fashion Futures* for fall/winter 1935, which took place at the Astor Hotel in New York, were Alix, Chanel, Creed, Heim, Lanvin, Lelong, Louiseboulanger, Mainbocher, Molyneux, Patou, Piguet, Marcel Rochas, Maggy Rouff, Schiaparelli and Vionnet. The English couturiers were Glen Glenny, Digby Morton, Hartnell, Isobel, Madame Enos, Victor Stiebel and Lanz of Salzburg. The American designers were Louise Barnes, Clare Potter, Helen Cookman, Fiffi, and Muriel King, whilst Adrian, Travis Banton, Howard Greer, Orry Kelly and Bernard Newman represented Hollywood.

134. In Stiebel's case this was B. Altman in New York, Marshall Field in Chicago and I. Magnin in San Francisco.

135. 'Society to See Victor Stiebel's English Fashion Creations', *Chicago Illustrated*, 30 November 1934.

136. 'Victor Stiebel Hopeful of Establishing London as a Couture Centre for the U.S.', *Women's Wear Daily*, New York, 3 January 1935.

CHAPTER 2

1. Alison Settle, 'The Story of the British Fashion Group: Women's Whims Bring Work', *Tit-Bits Magazine*, 12 December 1936.

2. The London dress creators cooperating in the Queen Mary showcase were Reville Ltd, Hardy Amies at Lachasse, Digby Morton, Peter Russell, Victor Stiebel, Robert Douglas, Norman Edwards, Charles James, Winifred Mawdsley and Ronald Morrel. Norman Hartnell was unable to participate due to the pressures of court dress needed after the funeral of King George V.

3. 'British–U.S. Interchange of Abilities Urged: Great Possibilities in Relationships of American Ready to Wear and British Styles and Fabrics, says E. H. Symonds', *Women's Wear Daily*, June 1936.

4. 'London Collections Reviewed', *Draper's Record*, October 1936.

5. Troy, *Couture Culture*, 4.

6. Rob Schorman, *Selling Style: Clothing and Social Change at the Turn of the Century* (Philadelphia: University of Pennsylvania Press, 2003), 51–57.

7. For a consideration of the development of this attitude to standardisation, where industrial 'standards' came to denote efficiency, production control and quality, see Blaszczyk, *The Color Revolution*, 78.

8. 'Review of Mr. Victor Stiebel's lecture at the Women's Service Hall', *Nursery World*, April 1937.

9. *Fashion Group Bulletin*, Luncheon at the Ritz Carlton Hotel New York, 20 November 1934.

10. Stewart, *Dressing Modern French Women*, 80.

11. 'British—U.S. Interchange of Abilities Urged'.

12. By 1920 the United States had a population of 106 million, whereas Britain had a population of approximately 40 million. After the First World War America was the world leader in banking and industry and had the largest consumer market.

13. The Made-to-Measure Dressmakers involved with the Fashion Group were Hardy Amies (Lachasse, 9 Farm Street, W1), Norman Hartnell (26 Bruton Street, W1), Mattli (6 Yeoman's Row, SW3), Digby Morton (63 Grosvenor Street, W1), Victor Stiebel (22 Bruton Street, W1), Madame Alexedis (21 Grosvenor Street, W1), Richard Busvine (Viola Redfern Ltd, 21 Hanover Square, W1), Madame Champcommunal (Worth, 50 Grosvenor Street, W1), the Hon. Mrs. Cripps (Robert Douglas Ltd, 21 New Bond Street, W1), Dennis Glenny (Genne Glenny, 64 Grosvenor Street, W1), Sophia Harris (Motley, Garrick Street, WC1), Alex Lord (Leathercraft Ltd, 42 Berkeley Street, W1), Dora and Raemonde Rahvis (19 Upper Grosvenor Street, W1), Schiaparelli (6 Upper Grosvenor Street, W1), Rose Taylor (60 Grosvenor Street, W1), Teddy Tinling (8 Hanover Street, W1) and Mrs Guy Olliver (73 Grosvenor Street, W1). Information from the Hardy Amies Archive, Savile Row (HAA).

14. Elizabeth Wilson and Lou Taylor, *Through the Looking Glass: A History of Dress from 1860 to the Present Day* (London: BBC Books, 1989), 123.

15. Edwina Ehrman, 'Supporting Couture', in de la Haye and E. Ehrman, *London Couture*, 34.

16. Amies, *Just So Far*, 9.

17. Digby Morton, Mass Observation Interview, 3 March 1942 (MO Archive, TC 18—Box 4).

18. Colin McDowell, *Forties Fashion and the New Look* (London: Bloomsbury, 1997) 22, 40 and 183; Edwina Ehrman, 'Broken Traditions', 111; Ehrman, 'Supporting Couture', 34; Robert O'Byrne, *Style City: How London Became a Fashion Capital* (London: Frances Lincoln, 2009), 10–11.

19. O'Byrne, *Style City*, 10. The justification for this assertion, however, is limited. O'Byrne draws this conclusion from the fact that Norman Hartnell, the most successful English couturier at that time, did not participate in the joint shows the Group held for American buyers. This summation is based on the brief account of the Group in Colin McDowell's *Forties Fashion and the New Look* (London: Bloomsbury, 1997).

20. Alison Settle, Transcript of Speech at the London Fashion Group Inaugural Lunch, 31 October 1935 (FGIR, Box 125.F.2).

21. *Fashion Group Bulletin*, 20 November 1934 (FGIR, Box 125.F.2).

22. The inaugural lunch took place on 31 October 1935; there were sixty members and eighty guests present. Alongside the seventeen dress designers and those mentioned in the above text the members also included Mrs Bembaron, Lady Earle, Alistair Morton, Betty Penrose, Derek Patmore, Renee Scudamore, Harry Yoxall, Princess Dilkusha de Rohan, Mrs A. Vick of Rodier Limited, Mary Joyce of Century Press and Charles Rayne of Rayne Shoes. Telegrams were received from the architect Oliver Hill about the Paris international exhibition of 1937, Sir William Crawford (founder of the Crawford's Advertising Agency), Lady Earle, Schiaparelli, the illustrator Edmund Dulac, Mary Brooks Picken (chairman of American fashion group) Alice Perkins (chairman of the Paris Fashion Group), Colonel Styles (Head of Horrocks fabrics), Elizabeth Arden, James Laver and Lady Lee of Total Broadhurst. Other non-Fashion Design Members present were from many different fields, i.e., architecture (Ralph Tubbs), buyers (Fortnum & Mason, Miss Nina LeClercq, and Harrods (Miss E. Richards), carpets (Crossley and Sons Ltd), cosmetics (Elizabeth Arden, Cyclax), corsets (Berlei, Warner Bros), dress houses (Jaeger Co. Ltd), executives (Lady Chamberlain, Miss Florence Sangster of W. S. Crawford, Mrs. Oliver Strachey of the Women's Employment Federation), fabrics (Donald Bros, Campbell Fabrics, Arthur Coles, Courtaulds, Warner & Son, Edinburgh Weavers, William Hollins, Ramsden Wood Print Works, Stevenson & Sons Ltd, Morton Sundour Fabrics, Munro & Co., British Celanese Ltd, Kays of Shetland, Cumberland Mills), fashion school (Peter Holliss Reville School, 15 Hanover Square), flowers (Constance Spry), furs (The National Fur Co.), gloves, hairdresser (Mr. Raymond), hats (Scotts, Aage Thaarup), interior decoration (John Fowler, Sibyl Colefax Ltd, Mrs & Mr Hayes Marshall of Fortnum and Mason, Mollo and Egan Ltd) and journalists (Alison Settle, Madge Garland). Information taken from FGIR, Box 125, F2.

23. Morgan was the chairman of Smith's Crisps and a key member of the Travel Association that promoted Britain as a tourist destination. He wrote influential texts on business management and efficiency in both production and retail. See H. E. Morgan, *Business Organisation* (London: Eveleigh Nash Company, 1917), and *Retailers Compendium: A Complete and Practical Guide to Successful Shopkeeping Enterprise* (1923). It was Morgan who in the First World War coined the motto 'business as usual'.

24. Frank Mort, 'The Commercial Domain: Advertising and the Cultural Management of Demand', in *Commercial Cultures: Economies, Practices, Spaces*, edited by Peter Jackson, Michelle Lowe, Daniel Miller and Frank Mort (Oxford: Berg, 2000), 35–53 (36).

25. Mort, 'The Commercial Domain', 36.

26. Settle, Transcript of Inaugural Lunch Speech.

27. The import figure for American dresses is taken from data from 1939 included in J. M. Brewster, 'Imports from USA of Made Up Garments General Correspondence: Summary of the Export Industry', *Board of Trade Memo*, 15 July 1954 (BT64/4275).

28. For further details, see M. D. C. Crawford, *The Ways of Fashion* (New York: Fairchild Publishing, 1948), 220.

29. Before the First World War 80 per cent of the cotton industry's output was exported and made up 25 per cent of British exports; the country held 65 per cent of world trade in cotton textiles. By 1938 this was more than halved by the development of industries in former markets and competition in third markets such as Japan. For further details, see D. H. Aldcroft, *The Inter-war Economy: Britain 1919– 1939* (London: Batsford, 1970), 156. Also see Dorothy Fox, 'Fashion Is Not All Spinach: Research Findings of the Man-Made Fibres Federation', *Fashion Group Quarterly*, Autumn 1939, 5–6.

30. Fox, 'Fashion Is Not All Spinach', 6; and Aldcroft, *The Inter-war Economy*, 156.

31. British histories of design recognise the influence of the American consultant designer on British design practice in the 1930s. See, for example, Penny Sparke, *Consultant Design: The History and Practice of the Designer in Industry* (London: Pembridge Press, 1983), and Sparke, *Introduction to Design and Culture 1900 to the Present* (London: Routledge, 2004).

32. Settle, 'The Story of the British Fashion Group'.

33. For an exploration of scientific management also called 'Taylorism', see Gregory Votolato, *American Design in the Twentieth Century* (Manchester: Manchester University Press, 1998), 78, 143 and 166. For Hoover's role in the implementation of the American system of progressive democracy, see Blaszczyk, *Color Revolution*, 167.

34. Blaszczyk, *Color Revolution*, 86.

35. Blaszczyk, *Color Revolution*, 86.

36. Transcript of Settle's article for the Fashion Group Quarterly, January 1936 (ASA/GB/NNAF/P44076).

37. For example, by March 1936 the American Fashion Group *Bulletin* started its regular 'News from England' section.

38. Fashion Group *Bulletin*, January 1936 (FGIR, Box 125F.2).

39. For an exploration of the concept of Americanisation which underpinned these anxieties, see, for example, Neil Campbell, Jude Davis and George McKay, *Issues in Americanisation and Culture* (Edinburgh: Edinburgh University Press, 2004). In terms of worries about the destruction of civilisation, see Richard Overy, *The Morbid Age* (London: Allen Lane, 2009).

40. Settle, 'Story of the British Fashion Group'.

41. Margaret Havinden, 'Greetings to Our Associate Members', *Fashion Group Circular*, May 1939 (HAA).

42. Havinden, 'Greetings'.

43. Settle, Transcript of Inaugural Lunch Speech.

44. See, for example, Janice Winship, 'Culture of Restraint: The British Chain Store 1920–39', in Jackson et al., *Commercial Cultures*, 15–34; Sally Alexander, *Becoming a Woman, and other Essays on 19th and 20th Century Feminist History* (London: Virago, 1994); Mica Nava, 'Modernity Tamed? Women Shoppers and the Rationalisation of Consumption in the Interwar Period', *Australian Journal of Communication* 22, no. 2 (1995): 1–19.

45. There was a considerable flourishing of interest in design for industry. The Design and Industries Association (DIA) was founded in 1915; inspired by the German Deutscher Werkbund, it promoted design understanding between designers, manufacturers, retailers and the general public. The British Institute of Industrial Art (BIIA) set up in 1920 by the Board of Trade was conceived to raise standards of industrial design and public taste in design. The Society of Industrial Artists (SIA), created in 1930, was also concerned with the professionalisation of design. In 1936 a National Register of Industrial Art Designers was established and in 1937 the Royal Society of Arts established its Designers for Industry. For further details, see Michael Farr, *Design in British Industry: A Mid Century Survey* (London: Cambridge University Press, 1952), 139–281; Leah Armstrong, 'Steering a Course between Commercialism and Professionalism: The Society of Industrial Artists Code of Conduct for the Professional Designer in Britain', *Journal of Design History* 29, no. 2 (2016): 161–179.

46. The Council of Art and Industry was established in response to the Gorell Report of 1932, which examined how to raise the level of Britain's industrial art. The Council was the coordinating body set to stimulate the development of good design. It produced many reports, which included *Designer in Industry* (1937), *The Working Class Home: Its Furnishings and Equipment* (1937) and *Design and the Designer in the Dress Trade* (1939; the publication of this was postponed by the start of war). It organised the exhibitions *British Industrial Art in Relation to the Home* (1933) and *British Art in Industry* (1935).

47. Frank Pick, *Report of the Dress Committee of the Council for Art and Industry: Design and the Designer in the Dress Trade* (London: His Majesty's Stationery Office, 1939), 3.

48. Members of the Dress Committee were Sir Frederick Marquis (chairman; he was a businessman, politician and statesman and in 1936 was the chairman of Lewis's Ltd Liverpool), Lady Ivy Chamberlain (vice chairman; she was also president of the Fashion Group), A. Baylis Allen (principle of the Bromley School of Art),

Rebecca Compton (occasional inspector and examiner to Board of Education), A. S. Hopkins (assistant secretary at the Board of Trade), James Laver (keeper, Victoria and Albert Museum), Joyce Reynolds (editor of *Harper's Bazaar*), Alison Settle (fashion advisor), Dr May Smith (investigator, Industrial Health Research) and Mr R. Tomlinson (senior inspector of Art London County Council).

49. Julian Holder, 'Design in Everyday Things: Promoting Modernism in Britain, 1912–1944', in *Modernism in Design*, edited by Paul Greenhaulgh (London: Reaktion Books, 1990), 123–145.

50. Buckley, *Designing Modern Britain*, 81.

51. Buckley, *Designing Modern Britain*, 81.

52. Sparke, *Introduction to Design and Culture*, 49. This teaming of commerciality with refined taste is particularly noticeable in the work of Crawford's Advertising Agency, which under the guidance of Havinden and her husband Ashley developed a reputation for a tasteful stylish art-directed approach to advertising. For further detail on Crawford's, see Frank Mort, 'The Commercial Domain: Advertising and the Cultural Management of Demand in Post-War Britain', in *Moments of Modernity: Reconstructing Britain, 1945–1964*, edited by Becky Conekin, Frank Mort and Chris Waters (London: Rivers Oram Press, 1999), 44.

53. Alison Settle set up her 'Advisory and Efficiency Service' in 1936. This work took many forms: some organisations had a contract, paying a retaining fee so as to be able to command expert advice throughout the year. Others paid a preliminary consultation fee and obtained a written report on the present state of the fashion market. Others had a short consultancy, extending over one or two months of the designing season.

54. The most famous example of an American fashion consultancy is Tobé Associates (established in New York in 1928 at the same time as the American Fashion Group), which tracked fashion trends, particularly from Paris, and through its regular 'Reports' disseminated these as clearly defined guidelines for manufacturers and retailers across the country. For further information, see Véronique Pouillard, 'The Rise of Fashion Forecasting and Fashion Public Relations: The History of Tobe and Bernays', in *Globalizing Beauty: Consumerism and Body Aesthetics in the Twentieth Century*, edited by Hartmut Berghoff and Thomas Kühne (New York: Palgrave Macmillan, 2013), 151–169.

55. Letter sent from Josiah Wedgwood, Director of Josiah Wedgwood & Sons Ltd, Etruria, Stoke-on-Trent, to Mrs Alison Settle, 13 November 1936. Settle became their fashion advisor from 1936 until the outbreak of war, for '£50 per year plus expenses'.

56. Wedgwood to Settle letter, November 1936.

57. 'Colour Report' sent to Mr Josiah Wedgwood from Alison Settle, 22 April 1938.

58. See, for example, Victoria Chappelle, 'The Group Presents Fashion Notes on the January Dress Show', *Fashion Group Bulletin*, January 1938.

59. Chappelle, 'Group Presents', January 1938. In December 1937 the Fashion Group created a Dress Fabric Subcommittee as an honorary panel of advisers for the textile trade; this included members from the textiles subcommittee: E. W. Goodale, Anthony Hunt, Holbrook Jackson, Hayes Marshall and Alistair Morton and four members from the Dress Subcommittee: Madge Garland, Norman Hartnell, Victor Stiebel and Teddy Tinling.

60. *Fashion Group Bulletin*, January 1938.

61. Isobel, 'Dress Designing as a Career for Women', *BBC Radio Script*, 31 May 1928.

62. Ehrman, 'Broken Traditions', 111.

63. *Fashion Group Bulletin*, January 1936.

64. The English firms cooperating in the 'Calendar of Events' were Norman Hartnell, Reville (Edward Symonds), Victor Stiebel, Reville-Terry, Ronald Morrel, Digby Morton, Genne Glenny, Peter Russell, Eva Lutyens, Matilda Etches, Henry Bridburg, the milliners Aage Thaarup, and Derek Skeffington.

65. *Notes on the First Fashion Group of Great Britain Dress Subcommittee Meeting*, November 1935.

66. 'New York Becomes the Natural Fashion Centre of the World', *Tobé Fashion Reports*, 3 October 1940, 18.

67. Caroline Reynolds Milbank, *New York Fashion: The Evolution of American Style* (New York: Harry N. Abrams, 1989), 105.

68. Phillida, 'London Dressmakers Will Catch the U.S. Buyers', *Sunday Dispatch*, January 1936.

69. King George V died on 20 January 1936; the shows were scheduled to start three days later.

70. Anne Jeffery, 'From the British Fashion Front', *Radio Pictorial*, London, March 1936.

71. *Fashion Group Bulletin*, January 1936.

72. The designers/dress houses involved were Hardy Amies at Lachasse, Mattli, Digby Morton, Victor Stiebel, Richard Busvine at Viola Redfern, Lady Earle at Winifred Mawdsley, the Hon. Mrs Cripps at Robert Douglas, Genne Glenny, Motley, Alex Lord at Leathercraft, Rahvis, Rose Taylor, Teddy Tinling and the milliner Aage Thaarup, who acted as the Dress Subcommittee's chairman. *Fashion Group Bulletin*, March 1937.

73. Jane Gordon, 'London's New Fashions: Review of Models Sponsored by London Fashion Group', *News-chronicle*, London, 9 February 1937.

74. 'London Fashion Group Show Starts Talk of Still Better Exhibition for Next July', *Women's Wear Daily*, 3 February 1937.

75. 'London Designers Confirm Plans for American Showings in July', *Women's Wear Daily*, 15 February 1937.

76. Blaszczyk, *Color Revolution*, 174.

77. Herbert Blumer, 'Fashion: From Class Differentiation to Collective Selection', *The Sociological Quarterly* 10, no. 3 (1968): 275–291 (278).

78. Blumer, 'Fashion', 278.

79. 'London Collections Reviewed', *Draper's Record*, October 1936.

80. Mr A. Hoskins, Board of Trade Letter to the Office of the High Commissioner for Canada, 20 November 1936. (BT64).

81. 'B.C.C.s Scoop for Spring, Chinese Colours: "We Are the First to Produce These Colours," says Mr. R. F. Wilson', *Draper's Record*, 2 November 1935.

82. Blaszczyk, *Color Revolution*, 39.

83. 'Coordinating a Color Chart' talk given by the manager of the merchandising division of the National Retail Dry Goods Association at the New York Fashion Group's monthly meeting, 20 January 1932.

84. 'Fashion Opinion Forming', Mass Observation documentation of phone conversation with Donald Barber, Retail Distribution Association, 10 March 1940.

85. Alan Saville, 'Recollections of the Silk Trade, 1930–1940', *Costume: The Journal of the Costume Society*, no. 27 (1993): 86–91.

86. By the end of that year the Council's activities were mentioned in over 700 articles in the British daily press and trade and fashion journals, and in nearly 100 foreign publications. See *Annual Report of the Board of Management of the British Colour Council*, presented to the Members of the Council at the Fifth Annual General Meeting held on 14 May 1936 (BT64).

87. Dyeing establishments grew up in response to the McKenna Duties, which since the First World War imposed an import tax of 33 per cent on luxury goods; as undyed fabrics received a lower import tax companies were encouraged to have imported fabrics dyed in England.

88. *Annual Report*, 14 May 1936. Lord Derby, colloquially known as the 'King of Lancashire', was a Conservative politician and diplomat. He was Secretary of State during the First World War and British Ambassador to France between 1918 and 1920. He was also patron of the Cotton Board, British Colour Council, Travel Association of Great Britain and the original vice president of the Incorporated Society of London Fashion Designers. For further details, see Randolph S. Churchill, *Lord Derby 'King of Lancashire': The Official Life of Edward, Seventeenth Earl of Derby, 1865–1948* (London: Heinemann, 1959).

89. *Annual Report*, 14 May 1936. Also see Mr. A. Hoskins, Board of Trade letter to the Office of the High Commissioner for Canada, 20 November 1936.

90. 'The White City, British Industries "Show the World": The Duchess of York Sees All-British Fashion Parade, Mannequins, Materials & Models That Paris—At Her Best—Could Not Excel', Pathé film (1933), https://www.britishpathe.com /video/british-industries-show-the-world.

91. *Annual Report,* 14 May 1936.

92. Robert Wilson based the reports on a council press release entitled 'Immediate & Future Trends in Colour: British Colour Council Press Release in Response to the Death of the King', 30 January 1936, and the Board of Trade Archive holds versions of it in *The Times* and *Draper's Record*.

93. 'Fabricana', *Vogue*, London, 19 February 1936, 24.

94. Fashion Group International Archive, Box 72 F.6.

95. M. Corey, 'Fall Fashions in High Style from London', *Journal* (Providence, RI), 1 August 1937; 'London as a Fashion Centre: American Buyers No Longer Go Direct to Paris. They See London Collections First', *The Sphere*, 14 August 1937.

96. 'English Designers Show Attractive Sports Clothes', *New York Times*, 23 August 1937.

97. *Fashion Group Bulletin*, December 1937.

98. Sara Pennoyer (the publicity director of Bonwit Teller department store), *Fashion Group Bulletin*, August 1937. For further information on how elite taste rejected bright colours, see David Batchelor, *Chromophobia* (London: Reaktion Books, 2000). For a discussion of colour in British tweed that reflected the rural landscape and a brightening of tweed colours in the 1920s, see Fiona Anderson, *Tweed* (London: Bloomsbury Publishing, 2016), 107.

99. Blaszczyk, *Color Revolution*, 40–41.

100. 'Her [Schiaparelli's] Purple and Pink Palette', *Vogue: Paris Fashions 2*, 15 September 1937.

101. 'London Fashions via the Queen Mary: British Dress Houses Submit Models to America', *The Sun*, Baltimore, June 1936.

102. 'London Fashions via the Queen Mary'.

103. Phillida, 'London Dressmakers Will Catch the U.S. Buyers', *Sunday Dispatch*, January 1936.

104. 'British–U.S. Interchange of Abilities Urged'.

105. See, for example, Edward Symonds, 'Who Creates Fashions?', *The Strait Times*, 8 July 1933, 15.

106. *The Fashion Group Bulletin* 2, no. 6 (June 1936): 2. For an example of how Reville promoted British fabric, see 'The Latest in Afternoon Gowns by Reville', Pathé film (15 June 1933), https://www.britishpathe.com/video/the-latest-in-afternoon-gowns-by-reville.

107. King George V died on 20 January 1936, and his oldest son ascended to the throne as King Edward VIII; during the period of mourning he was not crowned. He remained king for 235 days, abdicating on 11 December 1936, to marry the twice-divorced American Wallis Simpson. His brother, whose coronation as King George VI took place on the 12 May 1937, succeeded him.

108. Modestina, 'London Steals a March on Paris', *The Daily Sketch*, January 1937.

109. 'Peeresses Welcome Coronation Dress Plan', *Daily Mail*, October 1936.

110. 'London Designers Confirm Plans for American Showings in July', *Women's Wear Daily*, 15 February 1937.

111. 'London Designers Confirm Plans'.

112. 'Styles American Buyers Want at West End', *Drapers' Record*, 24 July 1937.

113. 'London as a Fashion Centre: American Buyers No Longer Go Direct to Paris'.

114. 'Fitted Jacket Suits with Related Topcoats Bought by English Socialites and American Trade Buyers', *Women's Wear Daily*, 15 September 1937.

115. ''Bulkies' Hip Length Tweed Coats over Suits, News at Lachasse', *Women's Wear Daily*, 14 July 1937.

116. For further details of the importance of the ensemble wardrobe in America in the interwar period, see Blaszczyk, *Color Revolution*, 172.

117. 'Coordinating a Color Chart' talk given by the manager of the merchandising division of the National Retail Dry Goods Association at the New York Fashion Group's monthly meeting, 20 January 1932.

118. 'Coordinating a Color Chart' talk.

119. For an exploration of the manner in which fashion relies on both standardisation and novelty, see, for example, Joanne Finkelstein, *The Fashioned Self* (Cambridge: Polity Press, 1991), 130.

120. Lipovetsky, *The Empire of Fashion*, 131.

121. Useful texts on the social and political history of objects are Leora Auslander, *Taste and Power: Furnishing Modern France* (Berkley: University of California Press, 1996); Arjun Appadurai, ed., *The Social Life of Things* (Cambridge: Cambridge University Press, 1986); William M. Reddy, *The Rise of Market Culture: The Textile Trade and French Society* (Cambridge: Cambridge University Press, 1987); Annie Phizacklea, *Unpacking the Fashion Industry: Gender, Racism and Class in Production* (London: Routledge, 1990). Also helpful on taste are Terry Eagleton, *The Ideology*

of the Aesthetic (Oxford: Wiley Blackman, 1990), and Pierre Bourdieu, *Distinction: A Social Critique of the Judgement of Taste* (London: Routledge, 2010).

122. Auslander, *Taste and Power*, 3.

123. Auslander points out women as the main consumers were expected to find 'the *juste milieu* between idiosyncrasy and conformity'. Auslander, *Taste and Power*, 401. The paradox of the pressure on women both to adhere to fashion and yet to be individual can also be seen in Adrian Forty, *Objects of Desire: Design and Society since 1750* (London: Thames and Hudson, 1986) 107.

124. Simmel takes this opposition and outlines two types of individualism: the first is equal to equality where people are free to dress like each other as they are freed from the constraints of social constructs and hierarchies. The second form relates to modern life where individuality is seen as being unique and appearing different from others. Simmel posits these ideas of individuality as succeeding historical developments. There is a cultural expectation to look individual; yet in practice how people choose to dress is often very similar. For further exploration of this idea, see Sophie Woodward, *Why Women Wear What They Wear* (Oxford: Berg, 2007), 3, 7, 9, 27–28, 120, 122 and 137.

125. *Vogue: London Modes and Motors Edition*, 13 October 1937, 30.

126. Madge Garland, 'Fashion Group Show—A Preview', *Vogue*, 19 January 1938, 19.

127. 'Review of Mr. Victor Stiebel's Lecture at the Women's Service Hall', *Nursery World*, April 1937.

128. Here I draw on Benedict Anderson's concept of the 'imagined community' coined to discuss nationalism. The creation of imagined community was facilitated by the rise of 'print capitalism'. The concept is particularly pertinent to understand how separate nations frame and reimagine their identity. Benedict Anderson, *Imagined Communities: Reflections on the Origin and Spread of Nationalism* (London: Verso Books, 2006).

129. Arnold, *American Look*, 28. Sportswear had three subcategories: those actually designed for sports such as tennis and golf, resort wear to both travel in and wear on holiday, and town and country wear—most specifically tweed suiting.

130. 'These Four Young Men Dictate Designs for Women', *Referee Magazine*, London, March 1936.

131. For further detail, see Alun Hawkins, 'The Discovery of Rural England', in *Englishness: Politics and Culture 1880–1920*, edited by Robert Colls and Philip Dodd (London: CroomHelm, 1986), and Alex Potts, 'Constable Country between the Wars', in *Patriotism*, vol. 3, edited by Raphael Samuel (London: Routledge, 1989), 168.

132. For a consideration of how these ideas were utilised particularly in the British ceramic and furniture industry, see Buckley, *Designing Modern Britain*, 67–68.

133. Harris, *Romantic Moderns*, 47.

134. Kingsley Martin, *A Second Volume of Autobiography 1931–45* (London: Hutchinson, 1968), 209.

135. *Fashion Group Bulletin*, 1937.

136. For the development of women's tailoring, see Lou Taylor, 'The Wardrobe of Mrs Leonard Messel', in Breward et al., *Englishness of English Dress*, 118. For the impact of the English suit in the interwar American market, see Arnold, *American Look*, 27–29.

137. Ann Archer, 'British Threaten French Corner on Style Rule', *United Press Red Letter*, New York, 6 October 1932.

138. 'As They Wear It—The French—The Britishers', *Vogue*, January 1932, 40–41.

139. Ehrman, 'Broken Traditions', 107.

140. 'Daylong Frocks Seen as Style Emancipator', *United Press*, 26 February 1933.

141. Amies, *Just So Far*, 38.

142. Blumer, 'Fashion', 278.

143. It also operated as a promotion for the Linton Tweed Mills in Cumberland, as Agnes Linton had provided financial support for Amies' business. Amies, *Just So Far*, 50.

144. 'One Design Each at Fashion Group Party', *Draper's Record*, 16 July 1938.

145. Havinden, 'Greetings to Our Associate Members'.

CHAPTER 3

1. Ehrman, 'Broken Traditions', 106.

2. Margaret Havinden, Mass Observation interview (MOI), 27 February 1940.

3. 'London Delivers the Goods', *Vogue*, UK, September 1940, 27.

4. Edna Woolman-Chase, *Always in Vogue: An Autobiography of Vogue's Famous Fashion Editor and the Story of Fashion in America through the Past Sixty Years* (New York: Doubleday and Company, 1954), 332.

5. A tailored suit could require up to five fittings, although a house such as Lachasse had already, by the late thirties, taken its fittings to as few as two to cater to its many out-of-town clients of the 'racing set'. Information taken from 'Much Too Expensive for Me: A Sisterly Essay for Frightened People', *Eve's Journal*, January 1939, 86–88 (87).

6. 'Personal Appearance and Clothes: Correspondence and Interviews' 1939–40/ Interviews with People in Fashion Retail December 1939–April 1940', conducted

by Thomas Harrison (Mass Observation Archive, University of Sussex, TC18 /2/A).

7. Margaret Havinden (in her capacity as chairman of the Fashion Group of Great Britain), MOI, 27 February 1940.

8. 'Brisk Action on the Mayfair Front', *Vogue*, London, November 1939, 26–27.

9. Jean Smith (secretary of the Fashion Group of Great Britain), MOI, 29 November 1939. Also reported in 'Travelling Dress Show', *Birmingham Mail*, 4 December 1939.

10. 'London Dressmakers Plan Provincial Selling Tour', *Women's Wear Daily*, 19 October 1939.

11. Stephen Broadberry and Peter Howlett, 'Blood, Sweat and Tears: British Mobilisation for World War II', in *A World at Total War: Global Conflict and the Politics of Destruction, 1939–45*, edited by Roger Chickering and Stig Föster (Cambridge: Cambridge University Press, 2002), 157–176.

12. 'Gossip on Fashion Dictators', *The Northern Whig*, Belfast, 21 November 1952. For further information of Stiebel's war activity, see Shephard, *Surprising Life*, 233.

13. Interview with Brenda Naylor (Hartnell employee), 13 February 2012.

14. Peter Day, 'How Secret Agent Hardy Stayed in Vogue during the War', *The Telegraph*, 29 April 2003. For Amies' description of his war activity, see Amies, *Just So Far*, 72–78. For the covert nature of Amies' war-time role, see David Lister, 'Queen's Tailor Hardy Amies Was a Wartime Hitman', *The Independent*, 24 August 2000, and *Episode II—Secret War: Hardy Amies and Operation Ratweek*, directed by Martin J. O. Hughes, Acorn Media (2011).

15. Charles Creed, *Maid to Measure* (London: Jarrolds, 1961), 132.

16. Victor Stiebel, 'Company Liquidation Notice', *The London Gazette*, 10 September 1940.

17. This pooling of resources and space was facilitated by the government's relaxation of restrictions on the number of employees allowed in the workrooms.

18. Madge Garland, MOI, 15 December 1939.

19. Victor Stiebel, MOI, 1 December 1939. Similar views were also reported in 'Fashions on Tour', *Birmingham Post*, 16 October 1939, and Joanne Chase, 'Dress House Goes on Tour', *Overseas Daily Mail*, 21 October 1939.

20. Stiebel, MOI, 1 December 1939.

21. Garland, MOI, 15 December 1939.

22. Stiebel, MOI, 1 December 1939.

23. Aage Tharrup, MOI, 6 December 1939.

24. Ann Seymour (wife of Digby Morton), fashion editor of *Woman & Beauty*, MOI, 6 December 1939.

25. Mary Joyce (editor of *Woman's Wear News*), MOI, 7 December 1939.

26. Donald Barber (secretary of Retail Distributor's Association) and J. M. Paynton (secretary of Draper's Chamber of Trade), MOI, November 1939. Similar observations were made by a number of industry observers for Mass Observation.

27. 'Dress Down to Dress Up', *Vogue*, UK, December 1939, 44–45.

28. Victor Stiebel, MOI, 1 December 1939.

29. J. M. Paynton, MOI, November 1939.

30. 'Mayfair Plans Cycling Skirts', *Daily Mail*, 19 September 1939; 'Frocks for Early Evening Air Raids', *The Star*, 11 October 1939; 'What the Fashions Will Be This Winter', *Draper's Organiser*, October 1939.

31. 'Fashion Marches on Programme', 12 December 1939.

32. Programme Introduction to the Fashion Gala, Grosvenor House (In Aid of Frances Day's Penny Fund), 2 December 1939, 'General Fashion Reports and Ephemera 1939–40' (18/2/F Mass Observation Archive).

33. For similar ideas in an American context, see Charles F. McGovern, *Sold American: Consumption and Citizenship, 1890–1945* (Chapel Hill: University of North Carolina Press, 2006). Also in relation to the charitable fashion shows produced by the English designer Lucile in the First World War, see Marlis Schweitzer, 'Patriotic Acts of Consumption: Lucile (Lady Duff Gordon) and the Vaudeville Fashion Show Craze', *Theatre Journal* 60 (2008): 585–608.

34. For an example of this advertising campaign see *Vogue*, UK, December 1939.

35. For an example of the Schiaparelli and Viyella advert, see *Vogue*, 18 August 1937. There was one short-lived exception when Viyella used Norman Hartnell in one set of adverts; see *Vogue*, March 1936.

36. For details of Schiaparelli's forced removal from Britain, see 'Elsa Schiaparelli File', National Archive, FO 837/284.

37. Stiebel, MOI, 1 December 1939.

38. As mentioned in chapter 1 the previous title of this column was 'Our Lives from Day to Day'.

39. 'Our Lives in Wartime London', *Vogue*, UK, November 1939, 34.

40. Arthur Marwick, *Class: Image and Reality in Britain, France and the USA since 1930* (London: Collins, 1980), 219.

41. The main objectives of the voluntary support that could be offered are set out by the Home Office in *Air Raid Precautions, What You Can Do* (London: HMSO, 1938).

42. Later in the war as membership expanded many less-wealthy members of the Service undertook their work whilst simply wearing a WVS badge on their lapels.

43. Brinton-Lee, diary entry for 17–23 August 1940 (Imperial War Museum, Cat. No. 9761, August 1940–May 1941).

44. Nathan Joseph, *Uniforms and Nonuniforms: Communication through Clothing Contributions in Sociology* (Westport, CT: Greenwood Press, 1986), 61.

45. Jenny Hartley, 'Warriors and Healers, Impostors and Mothers: Betty Miller's "On the Side of the Angels"', in *Dressing Up for War: Transformations of Gender and Genre in the Discourse and Literature of War*, edited by Aranzzu Usandizaga and Andrew Monnickendam (Amsterdam: Rodopi B.V., 2001), 180.

46. Charles Graves, *Women in Green: The Story of the WVS* (London: Heinemann, 1948), 31.

47. The colours of the WVS uniform adhered to the British Colour Council's trend predictions and had been used throughout Morton's couture collection of June 1939.

48. Graves, *Women in Green*, 38.

49. For a perceptive analysis of this occurring in men's service dress, see John Berger, *About Looking, Writers and Readers Cooperative* (London: Bloomsbury Publishing, 1980), 30–31.

50. Lachasse Ltd, ladies dressmakers, milliners and tailors: records, ca. 1930–1981.

51. Peter McNeil, '"Put Your Best Face Forward": The Impact of the Second World War on British Dress', *Journal of Design History* 6, no. 4 (1993): 283–299.

52. Anne Seymour, MOI, 6 December 1939.

53. Digby Morton, MOI, 24 April 1940.

54. Hilda Neal, diary entry, 18 September 1940 (Imperial War Museum, Cat. No. 11987, Subject Period 1939–1975).

55. Malcolm McMillian, MP for the Western Isles, House of Commons Debate: CLAUSE 18—Charge and Commencement of Purchase Tax, 8 August 1940, http://hansard.millbanksystems.com/commons/1940.

56. Mr. Barnes, MP for East Ham South, House of Commons Debate, 8 August 1940.

57. House of Commons Debate, 8 August 1940.

58. As the Chancellor pointed out, the exclusion of clothing would have meant the exemption of 'a taxable field of over £315,000,000', House of Commons Debate, 8 August 1940.

59. 'Tailored Tradition', *Vogue*, UK, December 1940, 32.

60. War Cabinet Office, 'Urgent Economic Problems', 1940, quoted in W. K. Hancock and M. M. Gowing, *British War Economy* (London: HMSO, 1949), 210.

61. The separate export groups were created to represent the cotton, wool, rayon, lace, silk, hosiery and hat industries.

62. For details of the fragmented nature of the textile industry prior to the war, see Board of Trade, *An Industrial Survey of the Lancashire Area* (London: HMSO, 1932); Alan Fowler, 'Lancashire Cotton Trade Unionism in the Inter-war Years', in *Employers and Labour in the English Textile Industries, 1850–1939*, edited by J. A. Jowitt and A. J. McIvor (London: Routledge, 1988).

63. For further consideration of the economic implications of the change in the war effort, see Hancock and Gowing, *British War Economy*, 118–120.

64. 'Exports—From Zero to £500,000', *Harper's Bazaar*, UK, February 1941, 9. For clarity: in the 1930s Molyneux opened a house in London but remained based in Paris; during the war he moved himself and his full operation to London.

65. W. M Hill (Department of Overseas Trade), Board of Trade Memo on letter from Captain Molyneux, 16 January 1941.

66. Edward Molyneux, quoted in 'Exports—From Zero to £500,000', 9.

67. 'Fashion and Fabrics Tour of South America 1941', Board of Trade file (BT61/78/4).

68. The Board of Trade records do not mention which three languages these were. The lack of thorough research undertaken by the Board of Trade into the actual workings of the separate markets in the different countries of South America, alongside the lack of documentation or analysis of the exports generated by the campaign, suggest that, rather than a revenue-raising venture, the government was more interested in this export collection as propaganda to demonstrate that Britain could pay its debts.

69. 'Fashion and Fabrics Tour of South America 1941'.

70. W. M Hill (Department of Overseas Trade), letter to F. Hollings (Board of Trade), 1 January 1941 (BT61/78/4).

71. Robert Williamson (Industrial Publicity Unit of the Ministry of Information), letter to W. M. Hill (Department of Overseas Trade), 4 June 1941 (BT61/78/4).

72. 'Fashion and Fabrics Tour of South America 1941'.

73. For the impact of WWI on the textile industry, see Alan Fowler, 'British Textile Workers in the Lancashire Cotton and Yorkshire Wool Industries', in *The Ashgate Companion to the History of Textile Workers, 1650–2000*, edited by Lex Heerma Van Voss, Els Hiemstra-Kuperus and Elise Van Nederveen Meerkerk (Surrey: Ashgate Publishing, 2010), 231–252. Also John Singleton, 'The Cotton Industry and

the British War Effort, 1914–1918', *Economic History Review* 47 (1994): 601–618, and J. Jewkes, 'The Post-war Depression in the Lancashire Cotton Industry', *Journal of the Royal Statistical Society* 91 (1928): 156–158, 162–163.

74. Sir Cecil Weir, 'British Fashions for South America', *Harper's Bazaar*, March 1941, 27.

75. 'Fashion and Fabrics Tour of South America 1941'.

76. This was in despite of the Colour Council contacting an array of export groups for womenswear in Nottingham, Manchester, Bradford, Stockport and Leicester. Robert Wilson (British Colour Council) letter to the Controller General of the Board of Overseas Trade, 4 June 1941 (BT61/78/4).

77. 'Fashion and Fabrics Tour of South America 1941'.

78. 'Exporting British Fashions: Lord Derby's Interest', *Melbourne Argus*, 22 July 1941.

79. Hartnell, *Silver and Gold*, 103.

80. Susan Brewer, *To Win the Peace: British Propaganda in the United States during World War II* (Ithaca, NY: Cornell University Press, 1997), 200. Until America entered the war, with the bombing of Pearl Harbor in December 1941, it maintained a policy of neutrality as a non-belligerent ally.

81. Robert Wilson, letter to the Controller General of the Board of Overseas Trade, 4 June 1941.

82. Margaret Dupree, ed., *Lancashire and Whitehall: The Diary of Sir Raymond Streat* (Manchester: Manchester University Press, 1987), 26–27.

83. 'Fashion and Fabrics Tour of South America 1941'.

84. File: 'South American Fashion Exhibition: Publicity for London Fashion Collection April 1941–April 1942' (BT61/78/4).

85. 'Fashion and Fabrics Tour of South America 1941'.

86. 'Artists and Dressmakers Collaborate in Contemporary Designs Exhibit', *Women's Wear Daily*, 15 May 1937.

87. Digby Morton, MOI, 3 March 1942.

88. Fox, 'Fashion Is Not All Spinach', 5–6.

89. Fox, 'Fashion Is Not All Spinach', 5–6. See also Frank Pick, *Report of the Dress Committee of the Council for Art and Industry to the Right Honourable Oliver Stanley, President of the Board of Trade: Design and the Designer in the Dress Trade* (London: His Majesty's Stationery Office, 1939), and Hugh Dalton, *Industrial Design Memorandum by the President of the Board of Trade, for the War Cabinet Reconstruction Committee, Ministerial Committee on Industrial Problems*, 20 June 1944.

90. Fox, 'Fashion Is Not All Spinach', 5–6.

91. Dupree, *Diary of Raymond Streat*, 76.

92. 'Fashion and Fabrics Tour of South America 1941'.

93. To pay the designers the Colour Council raised £1,100 from the Cotton Export Group, £800 from the Wool Export Group, £700 Rayon Export Group, £250 from the Lace Export Group, £160 from the Silk Export Group, £100 from the Hosiery Export Group (knitwear) and £50 from the Hat Export Group (BT61/78/4).

94. See *Report of the Dress Committee of the Council for Art and Industry*.

95. *Queen Cotton*, directed by Cecil Musk (British Council Films, 1941), http:// film.britishcouncil.org/queencotton.

96. Government Cinematograph Advisor, complaint about British Council films quoted by D. W. Ellwood, 'Showing the World What It Owed to Britain: Foreign Policy and "Cultural Propaganda", 1935–45', in *Propaganda Politics and Film, 1918–45*, edited by Nicholas Pronay and D. W. Spring (London: Macmillan, 1982), 50–71.

97. *Queen Cotton*.

98. Dupree, *Diary of Raymond Streat*, 76.

99. *Queen Cotton*.

100. *Gone with the Wind* (director: Victor Fleming; Metro Goldwyn Mayer, 1939). This film won ten academy awards in 1940.

101. *Vogue*, UK, May 1941. The appetite for Paris couture was difficult to dispel, however; for an exploration of this, see Claudia de Oliviera, 'The Diffusion, Reception and Use of Paris Style Information by the Press and *Haute Couture* Salons in Rio de Janeiro, Brazil, 1939–45', in Taylor and McLoughlin, *Paris Fashion and World War Two*.

102. Sir Cecil Weir, 'British Fashions for South America', *Harper's Bazaar*, UK, March 1941, 27.

103. 'British Design Group to Visit U.S. in October', *Women's Wear Daily*, 10 July 1941. Bianca Mosca left Paquin shortly after completing the designs for the South American showcase. She then set up under her own name at Jacqmar alongside Stiebel.

104. 'Fashion "Aces" Get Leave—To Design for U.S.', *Sunday Referee*, 17 August 1941. This temporary release was secured by the Board of Trade through negotiation with the army authorities. Stiebel was given seven days and Amies a number of free afternoons.

105. 'British Design Group to Visit U.S. in October', *Women's Wear Daily*, 10 July 1941.

106. 'Fashion Show for U.S. Cancelled', *News Chronicle*, 13 September 1941.

107. 'American Designers and the Future of American Fashion', *Tobé Fashion Reports*, 16 July 1940, 16.

108. Victoria Pope, 'True U.S. Couture Emerges in Shows', *New York Times*, 5 September 1940. This was in response to the efforts of six Fifth Avenue retailers who held invitation-only catwalk shows for American high society. These shows featured 800 original custom-made American designs 'in the French tradition'.

109. Sandra Stansbery Buckland, 'Promoting American Fashion 1940 through 1945: From Understudy to Star' (PhD thesis, Ohio State University, 1996).

110. When the tour was cancelled the Cotton Board's Colour, Design and Style Centre bought the couturiers' cotton models. These are now in the possession of Platt Hall, Gallery of English Costume in Manchester and were featured in the gallery's 1985 exhibition entitled *British Cotton Couture, 1941–1961*.

111. Amies, *Just So Far*, 84.

112. Sidney Pollard, *The Development of the British Economy, 1914–1990* (London: Arnold, 1992), 177.

113. Letter from Mr. Eden To Sir R. Campbell, 30 August 1941.

114. Internal government letter from Sir R. Campbell to Mr. Eden, 5 September 1941 (MAF 97/1001).

115. Sir R. Campbell to Mr. Eden, 5 September 1941.

116. Alan P. Dobson, *U.S. Wartime Aid to Britain, 1940–46* (London: Croom-Helm, 1986), 16.

117. Brewer, *To Win the Peace*, 205.

118. Hancock and Gowing, *British War Economy*, 243.

119. R. G. D. Allen, 'Mutual Aid between the US and the British Empire, 1941–45', *Journal of the Royal Statistical Society* 109 (1946): 243–271.

120. P. J. Wiles, 'Pre-war and War-time Controls', in *The British Economy 1945–1950*, edited by G. D. N. Worswick and P. H. Ady (Oxford: Oxford University Press, 1952), 125–158.

121. *Directorate of Civilian Clothing Functions and Establishment*, 30 July 1941.

122. Digby Morton, MOI, 3 March 1942.

123. Angus Calder, *The People's War: Britain 1939–45* (London: Pimlico, 1992), 406.

124. Morton, MOI, 3 March 1942.

125. 'Third Year of War Finds London Dress Designers Still Carrying On', *Women's Wear Daily*, 4 November 1941.

126. 'London Couture Engaged in "Reconfection" Quality Apparel to Remove "Frills"', *Women's Wear Daily*, 28 March 1942.

127. While the decrease across the whole country left only a quarter of the industry in operation. London was particularly hard hit. In terms of actual statistics, the 1935 *Census of Production* recorded that there were 2,347 London companies that had more than ten employees each and employed 126,808 workers. By 1942 a Board of Trade Survey demonstrates that concentration had now left only forty-five establishments, based mainly in the East End of London, that were all much larger, each with more than 200 employees now employing approximately 35,000 workers.

128. Alan Dobson, 'The Export White Paper, 10th September 1941', *Economic History Review* (1986): 59–76 (63).

129. For further details of this scheme, see Christopher Sladen, *The Conscription of Fashion: Utility Cloth, Clothing and Footwear, 1941–52* (London: Scolar Press, 1995).

130. Mr Kahn (Board of Trade), letter to Mr. R. M. Gould (Ministry of Labour and National Service), 26 August 1941 (BT64/3579).

131. Mr. Gould, letter to Mr. Kahn, 1 September 1941 (BT64/3579).

132. *Memorandum and Articles of Association of the Incorporated Society of London Fashion Designers*, Registered 6 January 1942 (Board of Trade Records BT64). For full details, see the appendix.

133. Geoffrey Millerson, *The Qualifying Associations* (Abingdon: Routledge, 1964), 8.

134. Millerson, *Qualifying Associations*, 14.

135. Ehrman, 'Broken Traditions', 106.

136. 'Colour, Design, and Style Centre', *The Textile Weekly*, 16 January 1942.

137. *Minutes of the Incorporated Society's Designer Meeting (MISDM)*, 6 January 1942.

138. *MISDM*, 6 January 1942.

139. *MISDM*, 6 January 1942.

140. *MISDM*, 21 January 1942.

141. 'Well Known London Dressmakers Still Operate', *Women's Wear Daily*, 11 May 1944.

142. To facilitate the formation of the Incorporated Society, Thow Munro (vice president of the National Wool Textile Export Corporation) obtained a grant of £1,000 from its members to enable the designers to start the necessary proceedings for incorporation.

143. *MISDM*, 21 January 1942.

144. Buckland, 'Promoting American Fashion', 134.

145. 'Incorporated Society Delegate Meeting with Sir Thomas Barlow, at the Board of Trade', 21 January 1942. For full details of this scheme, see Geraldine

Howell, *Wartime Fashion: From Haute Couture to Homemade, 1939–1945* (Oxford: Berg, 2012), and Sladen, *The Conscription of Fashion*.

146. Helen Reynolds, 'The Utility Garment: Its Design and the Effect on the Mass-Market 1942–45', in *Utility Reassessed*, edited by Judy Attfield (Manchester: Manchester University Press, 1999), 125–142 (137).

147. For complaints lodged against the Utility Regulations, see Reynolds, 'The Utility Garment', 125–142.

148. *MISDM*, 21 January 1942.

149. *MISDM*, 21 January 1942.

150. *MISDM*, 21 January 1942. Eight of the designers made garments for the Utility scheme: Hardy Amies, Digby Morton, Bianca Mosca, Peter Russell, Worth, Stiebel, Creed and Molyneux.

151. *Incorporated Society Delegate Meeting with Sir Thomas Barlow, at the Board of Trade I.C.I. House Millbank*, 27 January 1942.

152. *Delegate Meeting with Sir Thomas Barlow*.

153. 'Fashion Experts Come to Northampton For Ideas', *Northampton Chronicle & Echo*, May 1942.

154. 'No Wish to Be Fashion Dictator, Says British Board of Trade Issuing Latest Clothing Dictum', *Women's Wear Daily*, 1 June 1942.

155. 'War-Time Clothes for Women: Expert Fashion Designers to Prepare Models', *The Times*, 12 May 1942.

156. Attfield, *Utility Reassessed*, 1–10.

157. Attfield, *Utility Reassessed*, 2.

158. *Minutes of Couturier Scheme Delegate Meeting*, 27 January 1942.

159. 'Brisk Action on the Mayfair Front', *Vogue*, UK, November 1939.

160. *MISDM*, 8 October 1942.

161. *MISDM*, 8 October 1942.

162. Tom Heron, *Board of Trade Memo*, 6 July 1944 (BT64/3579).

163. Heron, *Board of Trade Memo*.

164. 'Utility by Mayfair Designers . . . Trade Adaptations', *Draper's Record*, 26 September 1942; 'Britain's Austerity-Utility Clothes: British Garment Manufacturers Not Impressed with B.O.T. Designs', *Women's Wear Daily*, 13 October 1942; 'Madam Will Be Well-Dressed by Spring Utility Fashions', *Daily Sketch*, 23 September 1942.

165. Reynolds, 'The Utility Garment', 137.

166. Heron, *Board of Trade Memo*.

167. Heron, *Board of Trade Memo*.

168. 'Britain's Austerity-Utility Clothes'.

169. Heron, *Board of Trade Memo*.

170. For further information, see Amanda Durfee, 'Utility Futility: Why the Board of Trade's Second World War Clothing Scheme Failed to Become a Fashion Statement', *Penn History Review* 25, no. 2 (2019).

171. For a full exploration of the idea, see Angus Calder, *The People's War: Britain 1939–45* (London: Pimlico, 1992).

172. Geoff Ely, 'Finding the People's War: Film, British Collective Memory, and World War Two', *American Historical Review* 105, no. 5 (2001): 821.

173. Sonya Rose, *Which People's War? National Identity and Citizenship in Wartime Britain* (Oxford: Oxford University Press, 2003), 31.

174. Rose, *Which People's War?*, 67.

175. Martin Francis, 'Cecil Beaton's Romantic Toryism and the Symbolic Economy of Wartime Britain', *Journal of British Studies* 45, no. 1 (2006): 90–117 (95–96).

176. 'Up at 7 . . . Out at 8', *Vogue*, UK, February 1943, 18–19.

177. *Ship with Wings*, directed by Sergei Nolbandov (Ealing Studios, 1942).

178. Anthony Aldgate and Jeffrey Richards, *Britain Can Take It: British Cinema in the Second World War* (London: I. B. Tauris, 2007), 317.

179. Tom Harrison, 'Films and the Home Front—The Evaluation of the Effectiveness by Mass-Observation', in *Propaganda, Politics and Film, 1918–45*, edited by Nicholas Pronay and D. W. Spring (London: Macmillan, 1982), 234–245.

180. 'Well Known London Dressmakers Still Operate', *Women's Wear Daily*, 11 May 1944.

CHAPTER 4

1. Mildred Smolze, Tobé Fashion Report Representative's Speech at the New York Fashion Group Luncheon, 25 October 1944 (Fashion Group Archive, Box 75).

2. Buckland, 'Promoting American Fashion'.

3. Smolze, Tobé Fashion Report Representative's Speech.

4. Hugh Dalton, Extract from the House of Commons Report, vol. 406, no. 12, 19 December 1944 (National Archive, CAB 124/513).

5. Hugh Dalton, *Industrial Design Memorandum by the President of the Board of Trade, for the War Cabinet Reconstruction Committee, Ministerial Committee on Industrial Problems*, 20 June 1944 (CAB 124/513).

6. Peter Hennessy, *Never Again Britain 1945–51* (London: Penguin, 1992), 380.

7. Paddy Maguire, 'Designs on Reconstruction: British Business, Market Structures and the Role of Design in Post-War Recovery', *Journal of Design History* 4, no. 1 (1991): 15–30 (18).

8. Lord Woolton, letter to Hugh Dalton, 3 February 1944 (BT 64/3579).

9. Hugh Dalton, letter to Lord Woolton, 21 March 1944 (BT 64/3579).

10. Ruth Emily McMurry and Muna Lee, *The Cultural Approach: Another Way in International Relations* (Chapel Hill: University of North Carolina Press, 1947), 34.

11. Brewer, *To Win the Peace*, 217.

12. Alec Cairncross, *The British Economy since 1945* (Oxford: Blackwell Publishers, 1995), 45.

13. Cairncross, *British Economy*, 50. North America was Britain's major source of raw materials and foodstuffs, supplying a little over one fifth of British imports in 1938 and nearly one third in 1946.

14. For details of the problems encountered by British exporters across many areas of manufacture, see Maguire, 'Designs on Reconstruction', p. 15.

15. *Internal Board of Trade Memo*, 7 October 1946 (BT 64/4146).

16. Amies, *Just So Far*, 107.

17. 'Customer Record—Mrs Backhouse: Countess Gurowska', Lachasse Ltd Ladies Dressmakers, Milliners and Tailors Records, ca. 1930–1981 (AAD/1989/6).

18. *MISDM*, 21 October 1946.

19. *MISDM*, 21 October 1946. Although Molyneux relocated to Paris, the London branch of Molyneux remained a member of the Incorporated Society under the guidance of Molyneux's sister Kathleen Lumley. The London branch remained until September 1951 when Molyneux retired due to ill health and Jacqmar took over his workroom.

20. For details of these measures, see the AFIA's, *Report on the Present Position of the Apparel and Fashion Industry Prepared as a Basis for Guiding its Future Progress, 1950* (BT 94/324).

21. The AFIA's *Report on the Present Position of the Apparel and Fashion Industry*, blamed this on the government policy of 'full employment and the raising of the school leaving age'. The wages the couture houses could offer, which did not have the economies of scale of industrial production, also remained an obstacle to recruitment.

22. Leonard Tivey and Ernest Wohlgemuth, 'Trade Associations as Interest Groups', *The Political Quarterly* 29, no. 1 (January 1958): 59–71.

23. Tivey and Wohlgemuth, 'Trade Associations'. They show that governments became more important within the economic and social sphere as the result of changes in the structure of industry, patterns of international trade, intensification of internal and external competition, the effect of slumps and the demands of modern war, thereby increasing the need for and influence of trade associations.

24. *MISDM*, 13 February 1946.

25. At the request of the government the couturiers extended these tours to northern mill towns to support recruitment into the textile industry. These recruitment drives were not only an immediate post-war event but continued into the 1950s.

26. *MISDM*, 13 February 1946.

27. Michael Talboys, 'Interview', in British Library, Oral History of British Fashion (2004) C1046/07.

28. For example, after Molyneux retired in September 1951, his 'famous tailor' Rossi was swiftly taken on by Hartnell, whilst Stiebel at Jacqmar commandeered three principal saleswomen, one tailor and one fitter each with their entire workroom staff. For further detail, see Alison Settle, 'From a Woman's Viewpoint', *The Observer*, 28 January 1951. This practice also supported the creation of new couture members; for example, John Cavanagh set up his new house with many of Molyneux's former staff, and when Peter Russell moved to Australia, in 1953, Michael Donnellan took over his staff and premises at Carlos Place.

29. Tivey and Wohlgemuth, *Trade Associations*, 59–71.

30. *MISDM*, 9 September 1945. For a similar attitude in a wider range of industries, see Patrick J. Maguire, 'Patriotism, Politics and Production', in *Design and Cultural Politics in Post War Britain: The Britain Can Make It Exhibition of 1946*, edited by Patrick J. Maguire and Jonathan M. Woodham (London: Leicester University Press, 1997), 37.

31. *MISDM*, 9 September 1945.

32. Cairncross, *British Economy*, 70. This continued until 1948 when Britain received Marshall Aid. Clothes rationing and the Utility Scheme also continued beyond this until 1949 and 1952, respectively.

33. *MISDM*, 12 December 1946.

34. *MISDM*, 1 April 1947.

35. Elsa Shelley, 'British Fashions Wish Them Luck', *Women's Journal*, May 1946.

36. Sheryl Kroen, 'Negotiations with the American Way', in *Consuming Cultures, Global Perspectives: Historical Trajectories, Transnational Exchanges*, edited by John Brewer and Frank Trentmann (Oxford: Berg, 2006), 251–278 (269).

37. 'Haute Couturiers' Magnificent Effort in Country's Year of Need', *Women's Wear Daily*, 7 August 1947.

38. British *Vogue*, February 1946.

39. 'Week of Fashion Parades', *Birmingham Post*, 4 February 1946.

40. *MISDM*, 20 February 1946.

41. Amies' American visit was undertaken between 30 April and 16 May 1946. The fifteen-day trip was taken at the request of Marshall Field's department store and overseen by the American Marketing Corporation. He toured New York, Pittsburgh, Chicago, Detroit and Boston.

42. Hardy Amies, *Report on the American Market*, presented at an informal meeting of the Incorporated Society, 29 May 1946.

43. Montagu-Pollock (head of British Council Cultural Relations Department), *The Case for Cultural Publicity*, 30 May 1945.

44. Amies, *Report on the American Market*.

45. 'Fashion Shows in Paris Will Be Opened Today', *New York Times*, 26 February 1945.

46. 'Schiaparelli Emphasises Color in Fashions Draped Print Dresses Feature Paris Show', *New York Times*, 16 March 1946.

47. Amies, *Report on the American Market*.

48. The predominance of this practice was highlighted in an article in *Women's Wear Daily*, which also illustrated the commercial viability of London originals; see 'WWD Foresees British Styles Taking Hold in America', *Women's Wear Daily*, 12 June 1946. Hardy Amies also declared at a press conference in July 1946 that 'there was a ready market for the London couture product in America with day suits made by London couturiers selling for more than they cost in the home market'; see 'London Fashion Parade Week', *Daily Telegraph*, 26 July 1946.

49. *Women's Wear Daily*, 12 June 1946.

50. Amies, *Report on the American Market*.

51. Alison Settle, 'London: Can It Become a World Fashion Centre?', *Picture Post*, 6 September 1945.

52. Melita Spraggs, 'English Collections Are Much More Elaborate but Are Still Suitable for Practical Wear', *Christian Science Monitor*, 2 February 1946.

53. For further examination of this idea, see Becky E. Conekin, 'Lee Miller: Model, Photographer and War Correspondent in Vogue, 1927–1953', *Fashion Theory* 10, nos. 1–2 (2006): 97–125 (106).

54. Hardy Amies, 'Fashion and Beauty, the Art of Good Dressing', *Radio Broadcast for the BBC Home Service*, London, 13 June 1946, 4:00–4:15.

55. *Hardy Amies, Autumn and Winter Collection Programme*, 1946 and Programme of B. Altman & Co., Fifth Avenue, New York Couture Showing, 2 October 1946.

56. Programme of B. Altman & Co., Fifth Avenue, New York Couture Showing, 2 October 1946.

57. Virginia Pope, 'Twelve English Models Go on View Here', *New York Times*, 2 October 1946.

58. Notes of meeting between the Board of Trade Representatives and Captain Molyneux, 4 December 1942 (AAD/2011/14).

59. Notes of Meeting between the Board of Trade Representatives and Captain Molyneux.

60. Eileen Ashcroft, 'London, 1946, Brings Back Crinolines and the Wasp Waist', *Transatlantic Daily Mail*, 13 February 1946.

61. Joyce Mather, 'Fashion Displays by Molyneux and Digby Morton', *Yorkshire Post*, 1 August 1946.

62. Jane Austin, 'Joyful British Dresses Are Shown to the World', *The Recorder*, 2 February 1946, 5.

63. 'London Fashion Shows', *The Times*, 6 February 1946.

64. Mather, 'Fashion Displays by Molyneux and Digby Morton'.

65. See, for example, 'Non-Austerity Fashion: World Buyers at London Shows', *Yorkshire Post*, 29 January 1946; 'The London Shows—Couture', *Draper's Record*, March 1946; Victoria Chappelle, 'London Fashion Trends', *Johannesburg Star*, May 1946; Gordon Beckles, 'These Men Have a Flair', *Strand Magazine*, June 1946.

66. *A Question of Taste*, Scottish Committee of the Council of Industrial Design and Pathé Documentary Unit 1946 (Design Council Archive Brighton); *Fashion Fantasy* (director: Richard Grey; Condor Film Productions, 1946). BFI Films.

67. Scripted commentary, *A Question of Taste*.

68. 'Clothes for Teen-age Girl', *Weekly Scotsman*, 6 November 1947.

69. Scripted commentary, *A Question of Taste*.

70. Mathew Hilton, *Consumerism in 20th Century Britain* (Cambridge: Cambridge University Press, 2003), 163.

71. For a discussion of the attitude to luxury and necessity, see Ina Zweiniger-Bargielowska, *Austerity in Britain: Rationing, Controls and Consumption 1939–1955* (Oxford: Oxford University Press, 2002). This was a continuation of the debate that surrounded the condemnation of luxury, which had raged since the eighteenth century and was strongly gendered as a 'female vice'.

72. The use of a Wren is important, for as Antonia Lant points out, the Women's Royal Navy Service had 'an upper class aura'. *Blackout: Reinventing Women for Wartime British Cinema* (Princeton, NJ: Princeton University Press, 1991), 202. Also see J. B. Priestley, *British Women Go to War* (London: Collins, 1944), 49. This

upper-class aura would have made her future employment as a Mayfair fashion mannequin more plausible.

73. Commentary for *Fashion Fantasy*.

74. Richard Dyer, 'Entertainment and Utopia', in *Movies and Methods*, vol. 2, edited by Bill Nicholls (Berkeley: University of California Press, 1985), 220–232.

75. Kroen, 'Negotiations with the American Way', 266.

76. Labour Party, *Let Us Face the Future* (London, 1945) 2. For further discussion of the basics of Labour Party ideology, see Martin Francis, *Ideas and Politics under Labour 1945–1951: Building a New Britain* (Manchester: Manchester University Press, 1997).

77. Zweiniger-Bargielowska, *Austerity in Britain*.

78. Zweiniger-Bargielowska, *Austerity in Britain*, 79–96.

79. This was an expectation that any political party was unwise to ignore. It is Zweiniger-Bargielowska's contention that a key element within the Conservative party's return to office in 1951 (as its policy of market liberalisation was equated with a return to unrestrained consumerism) was the thwarted consumer desire for material goods. See Ina Zweiniger-Bargielowska, 'Exploring the Gender Gap: The Conservative Party and Women's Vote, 1945–1964', in *The Conservatives and British Society, 1880–1990*, edited by Martin Francis and Ina Zweiniger-Bargielowska (Cardiff: University of Wales Press, 1996), and 'Rationing, Austerity and the Conservative Party After 1945', *Historical Journal* 37, no. 1 (1994): 173–197.

80. Commentary to *Fashion Fantasy*.

81. This understanding is indebted to historical analysis, which can be seen as part of the third phase within the post-war history of British national identity and character during the Second World War. The first phase was underpinned by the idea of the post-war consensus and the 'People's War' and 'People's Peace'. The second phase came in the 1970s and 1980s and can be seen in work such as Correlli Barnett, *The Audit of War: The Illusion and Reality of Britain as a Great Nation* (London: Macmillan, 1986), and Patrick Wright, *On Living in an Old Country* (London: Verso Books, 1985), 83–87, where the idea of the People's War was situated as a conservative myth, not as a falsified narrative but in the sense that it had sustained an aura of nostalgia and complacency. The third phase that began in the 1990s is seen in work such as Zweiniger-Bargielowska, *Austerity in Britain*; Pam Cook, *Fashioning the Nation: Costume and Identity in British Cinema* (British Film Institute, 1996); and Sonya Rose, *Which People's War? National Identity and Citizenship in Wartime Britain* (Oxford: Oxford University Press, 2004), which has uncovered the subversive elements of the national character unleashed by war, ones that triggered subsequent anti-establishment, feminist and multicultural rebellions. An influential essay was also Josephine Dolan, 'Post-war Englishness: Maytime in Mayfair, utopian visions

and consumer culture', in *Englishness: Diversity, Differences and Identity*, edited by Christopher Hart Kingswinford (Midrash Publishing, 2007).

82. *Notes for Guidance to Selectors* (ID/352/14A).

83. *Summer Exhibition 1946*, note from Stafford Cripps, Board of Trade to C. S. Leslie CoID, 10 August 1945 (ID/312). Of the 127 women's garments in the exhibition, the made-to-measure dressmakers contributed twenty-eight, mainly evening, dinner, debutante and cocktail dress. The wholesale model houses provided sixty-one garments, mainly daywear.

84. See, for example, Penny Sparke, ed., *Did Britain Make It? British Design in Context 1946–86* (London: Design Council, 1986), and Jonathan M. Woodham and Patrick J. Maguire, eds., *Design and Cultural Politics in Post-war Britain: The Britain Can Make It Exhibition of 1946* (London: Leicester University Press, 1997).

85. For example, Woodham and Maguire, in *Design and Cultural Politics*, do not refer to the dress section at all except in a brief reference when discussing the textile exhibits. Although Sparke's *Did Britain Make It?* includes an essay by Anne Gardner on fashion retailing, this does not mention the fashion exhibit at BCMI.

86. Raymond Mortimer, 'Britain Can Make It!', *New Statesman & Nation*, 28 September 1946, 220.

87. 'Giles Velarde Interviews James Gardner', in Sparke, *Did Britain Make It?*, 9–19 (11). Also see James Gardner, *The ARTful Designer: Ideas off the Drawing Board,* (James Gardner, 1993), 127–143.

88. Jonathan M. Woodham, 'Design Promotion 1946 and After', in Sparke, *Did Britain Make It?*, 23–38 (25).

89. Penny Sparke, *As Long as It's Pink: The Sexual Politics of Taste* (London: Pandora/Harper Collins, 1995), 105 and 222.

90. Although the theatre designer Oliver Messel was the original choice to create three fashion sets for the Women's clothing display of 'country, evening (ballroom and restaurant) and possibly a London Street', the display section of the fashion court was given over to the exhibition designer James Bailey. *MISDM*, 28 March 1946.

91. Sparke, *As Long as It's Pink*, ix.

92. Sparke, *As Long as It's Pink*, 54–55. As Sparke (pp. 56–57) points out, 'women and their tastes—their preoccupation with surface rather than substance, with ephemerality rather than universality, with appearance rather than with utility, and with the inessential rather than the essential—provided a broad cultural frame for the criticisms of nineteenth-century reformers'.

93. *MISDM*, 28 March 1946.

94. *Britain Can Make It Exhibition Catalogue*, Group M—Fashions—Couturiers, 182–187. The couture garments that were noted for the use of British fabric were

Russell's dinner gown with fabric by Silkellal, Amies' dinner dress with fabric by John Knox, Molyneux's morning dress with fabric by Dobroyd and Delanghe's debutante dress with fabric produced by students of Bromley School of Art. None of the wholesale dressmaking houses documented their fabric sources.

95. Maguire and Woodham, *Design and Cultural Politics*.

96. The demographic of the exhibition attendees is demonstrated in the Mass Observation survey of the event, which documented 2,523 interviews and 1,000 overheard comments.

97. Report by Mass Observation during their survey of BCMI (ID/903), final total of attendees at BCMI: 1,432,546. For statistics, see *Report by the Director to the Meeting of the Council of Industrial Design*, 10 January 1947.

98. Margot Lawrence, 'Clothes Go Abroad but Ideas Stay Home', *Reynolds News and Sunday Citizen*, 3 February 1946.

99. From: Head of T. S (Norman Collins) to Tel P. D. Subject FASHION (1st Jan. 1948), *Fashion File 1 1946–1958* (T16/69/1).

100. Woodham, 'Design Promotion 1946 and After', 27.

101. Maguire and Woodham, *Design and Cultural Politics*, 119.

102. For a detailed consideration of this group, see Elizabeth Tragenza, 'London before It Swung: British Ready-to-Wear under the Model House Group and Fashion House Group 1946–1966' (thesis, Royal College of Art, 2014).

103. Richard Collier, 'The Fashion Story (2)', *Housewife*, June 1952, 50–53 (51).

104. Arnold, *American Look*, 33.

105. The term 'femme d'intérieur' is difficult to translate by a single phrase: roughly 'homemaker', literally 'woman of indoors/inside', she is an important component in the understanding of femininity in the nineteenth century and the theory of the separation of the spheres. See, for example, Leonora Davidoff and Catherine Hall, *Family Fortunes: Men and Women of the English Middle Class, 1780–1850* (London: Hutchinson, 1987).

106. *MISDM*, 28 March 1946.

107. The Guild of British Creative Designers included twenty-two limited companies all with a W1 address: Acquer, Arthur Banks, Baroque, Mary Black, Samuel Bloom & Co., Fischelis, Harvey & Clark, Madame Hayward, Elizabeth Henry, Lady in Black Fashions, Doree Leventhal, Mercia & Co., Vivian Porter & Co., Reissman & Chaim, Selincourt & Sons, Travella & Selita E. Seton, Cotterill & Co., J. S. Sharpe, B. & M. Simmone, C. R. Welford & Co., Louis Levy and Martha Hill of Leicester.

108. 'Mayfair Modes: Albert Hall Fashion Shows Couture Ball, Guild of British Designers', Pathé film (1946), www.britishpathe.com/video/mayfair-modes /query/design.

109. TV Outside Broadcast, *Albert Hall Fashion Parade*, 2 October 1946 (BBC Written Archive, T14/15/1); this exhibition is briefly mentioned in Palmer, *Couture and Commerce*, 26. In November when it arrived in Canada it was presented at Eaton's department store in Toronto.

110. Andrea Stuart, *Showgirls* (London: Jonathan Cape, 1996), 1–2.

111. Lant, *Blackout*, 79.

112. Script for BBC Programme, TV Outside Broadcast, *Albert Hall Fashion Parade*.

113. Audrey Withers, 'Fashion, Dress, Fabrics and Accessories', in *Design 46: A Survey of British Industrial Design as Displayed in the Britain Can Make It Exhibition Organised by the British Council of Industrial Design* (London: His Majesty's Stationary Office, 1946), 45–61 (47).

114. The impact on the fashion industry is well documented. For example, see Véronique Pouillard, 'Keeping Designs and Brands Authentic: The Resurgence of the Post-War French Fashion Business under the Challenge of US Mass Production', *European Review of History* 20, no. 5 (2013): 815–835.

115. *Victor Stiebel Export Collection, Press Release*, January 1947 (property of Adrian Woodhouse).

116. Cairncross, *British Economy*, 37. For a detailed consideration of the crippling effect the weather had on Britain's industry and economy, see Alex Robertson, *The Bleak Midwinter 1947* (Manchester: Manchester University Press, 1987).

117. *MISDM*, 17 September 1947.

118. Michael Batterberry and Ariane Batterberry, *Mirror, Mirror: A Social History of Fashion* (New York: Holt, Rinehart and Winston, 1977), 348.

119. Farid Chenoune, *Dior* (New York: Assouline, 2007), 20.

120. Alison Settle, *Wool as a Fashion Fabric: The Wool Education Society Lecture at the Royal Society of Arts* (London: Department of Education of the International Wool Secretariat, 1950).

121. Quoted by Grace Garner in 'Now London Copes with "The New Look"', *Saturday Night*, Toronto, 15 November 1947.

122. See, for example, 'Battle of the Long Skirt Is On: Cripps Takes a Hand', *The Recorder*, 3 August 1947; 'New York Wanted the New Look . . . So You, Milady, Will Have to Grin and Wear It!', *Bristol Evening News*, January 1948; 'Battle of the New Look', *Bournemouth Times and Directory*, January 1948.

123. 'Battle of the Long Skirt Is On'.

124. Victor Stiebel, 'Fashion and Beauty: About Clothes', *BBC Radio Home Service London* (transmitted 23 October 1947, 4:45 5:00).

125. Zweiniger-Bargielowska, for example, claims the rapid adoption of the New Look, particularly by the adaptation of old clothing, is indicative of 'the depth

of female disaffection' and therefore was an aesthetic embodiment of the 'postwar world the British Labour administration had promised but failed to deliver'. For a full consideration of the sociology of the New Look, see Jessica Schwartz, 'Skirting the Issue: Interweaving Dress into Sociopolitical Histories' (thesis, Columbia University, 2011), and for its adaptation within British working-class dress, see Angela Partington, 'Popular Fashion and Working Class Affluence', in *Chic Thrills: A Fashion Reader*, edited by Juliet Ash and Elizabeth Wilson (London: Pandora Press, 1992). For the New Look's effect on the Australian fashion market, see Margaret Maynard, '"The Wishful Feeling about Curves": Fashion, Femininity and the New Look in Australia', *Journal of Design History* 8, no. 1 (1995): 43–59.

126. Dora Matthews, 'Unpublished Memoirs', Royal Ontario Museum, quoted in Palmer, *Couture and Commerce*, 23. For a corresponding description of London evening wear, see Bettina Ballard, *In My Fashion* (London: Secker and Warburg, 1960), 227.

127. 'A Modern Man's Ideas on Modern Women', *Modern Woman*, January 1948.

128. Digby Morton, 'Royal Wedding Opportunities: Is the King Badly Advised?', *The Recorder*, 18 October 1947.

129. 'Trade: Trousseau Trouble', *Fashion and Fabrics*, 25 October 1947.

130. For example, the propaganda disseminated by the Ministry of Information throughout the war presented the notion of Britain as ruled by moral righteousness and united across class and gender. For further detail, see Richard Overy, *Why the Allies Won* (New York: W. W. Norton, 1995).

131. 'Great Britain Rich Fabrics, Simple Styles for Wedding Guests', *Women's Wear Daily*, 3 November 1947.

132. M. M. Johnstone, *Board of Trade Internal Memo*, 15 December 1947 (B.T. 64/1026).

133. T. P. Harvey (private secretary to the Queen) letter to Harold Wilson, 10 December 1947 (B.T. 64/1026).

134. Harvey to Wilson, 10 December 1947. These trade figures were also reported in Alison Settle, 'The Paris Shows: "New Look" Established', *The Observer*, 7 February 1948.

135. Maynard, 'The Wishful Feeling about Curves', 45.

136. Yoxall, *A Fashion of Life*, 51.

137. Alison Settle, 'Economics of the New Look: French Campaign to Make Dollars out of Textiles', *Yorkshire Post*, 18 February 1948.

138. Patricia Lennard, 'London Breaks with Paris', *Evening Standard*, 4 February 1947.

139. Alexandra Palmer, 'Inside Paris Haute Couture', in *The Golden Age of Couture: Paris and London 1947–57*, edited by Claire Wilcox (London: V & A Publishing, 2007), 63–83.

140. Amies, *Just So Far*, 176.

141. By the 1950s, as Alexander Palmer has shown, each season, even moderate-sized Paris houses such as Griffe and Dessès designed over double the garments of a London couture house. 'Griffe and Dessès designed around 110–170 garments a season, while Dior presented between 230–250 of which approximately 48 would eventually be eliminated'; Palmer, 'Inside Paris Haute Couture', 63–83.

142. Tomoko Okawa, 'Licensing Practices at Maison Christian Dior', in *Producing Fashion: Commerce, Culture and Consumers*, edited by Regina L. Blaszczyk (Philadelphia: University of Pennsylvania Press, 2008), 82–110 (84).

143. Okawa, 'Licensing Practices at Maison Christian Dior', 88. At its launch in October 1946, Maison Dior was capitalized at old F5 million (about $42,000).

144. Okawa, 'Licensing Practices at Maison Christian Dior'.

145. For a detailed consideration of the process that saw French couture houses turned into brands, see Pouillard, 'Keeping Designs and Brands Authentic', 815–835.

146. Even by 1951, with the textile industry operating under fewer restrictions the contributions to the society remained similar: £250 from the International Wool Secretariat, £300 from the National Wool and Textile Export Corporation, £250 from the Cotton Board, £300 from the British Rayon Federation, then £100 each from the Silk and Rayon Users Association, the Irish Linen Guild and the Federation of Lace and Embroidery Employers Associations. It also received £1,050 from its designer–members' subscriptions. Its expenditure for the year was £2,895 with £467 spent on entertaining and travelling; the rest was spent on the administration and running costs of the office, clerical staff salaries, printing and stationery, postage and telegrams, etc. Details taken from *Incorporated Society of London Fashion Designers Income and Expenditure Account for the Year Ended 31 December 1951*.

147. The couturiers' use of French fabric generated a substantial amount of press commentary. See, for example, 'French Influence on Fashion', *Yorkshire Observer*, January 1947, and Alison Settle, 'From a Woman's Viewpoint', *The Observer*, 2 February 1947.

148. Settle, 'From a Woman's Viewpoint'.

149. Settle, 'From a Woman's Viewpoint'.

150. Minutes of Meeting held at the British Rayon Centre, 18 January 1950.

151. Minutes of Meeting held at the British Rayon Centre, 18 January 1950. For a similar analysis, see Marguerite Dupree, ed., *Lancashire and White Hall: The Diary*

of Raymond Streat, vol. 2: 1939–1987 (Manchester: Manchester University Press, 1987), xvii.

152. *MISDM*, 2 March 1948.

153. The Marshall Plan (the European Recovery Program) was a system of American economic aid to Western Europe given between 1948 and 1951. This money, $3.297 billion, was not a loan and did not need to be repaid. This money was mostly used for the purchase of goods from the U.S.

154. *Reynolds News*, 1 February 1948.

155. Lucie Noel, 'London Styles Complement the Efforts of Paris Couture', *New York Herald Tribune*, 25 January 1949.

156. Cecil Beaton, *The Happy Years: Diaries 1944–48* (London: Weidenfeld and Nicolson, 1972), 54.

157. See the appendix and the discussion of these aims in the introduction.

CONCLUSION

1. For an interesting exploration of this film, see Laura Crossley, 'Get the London Look: Anna Neagle as the Emblem of British Fashion and Femininity in Maytime in Mayfair', *Film, Fashion & Consumption* 4, no. 1 (2015): 57–73 (17).

2. Pouillard, 'Recasting Paris Fashion', 39; Diana De Marly, *Christian Dior* (London: B. T. Batsford, 1990), 17–18.

3. Pouillard, 'Keeping Designs and Brands Authentic', 815.

4. 'Hardy Amies Leader of Fashion Says: "Be True to Ourselves and the World Will Buy"', *British Rayon and Silk Journal*, April 1949, 36.

5. See Wilcox, *Golden Age of Couture*.

6. The investment capital for these companies remained small; for instance, the Minutes of Incorporated Society Meeting, 31 March 1949, show that when Michael Sherard joined in 1949 he had only £1,500 of capital.

7. For example, boutiques were set up by Creed in 1949, Amies in 1950, Worth in 1957 and John Cavanagh in 1959.

8. For further detail, see Jane Hattrick, 'Norman Hartnell', in de la Haye and Ehrman, *London Couture*, 56–58. From 1945 Norman Hartnell developed a successful range of licensed goods, which saw his name on perfumes, toiletries, jewellery, stockings, lingerie and make-up. One of his most successful was his perfume 'In Love', released in 1953 to coincide with the coronation.

9. Sherard launched a ready-to-wear line in 1953; by 1957, Morton is engaged solely in producing ready-to-wear. Cavanagh, Paterson, Amies and Mattli were

all designing some ready-to-wear for mid prices by the early 1960s; for example, Cavanagh designed for the wholesaler firms Berg of Mayfair and Burberrys.

10. For example, in 1955 Dior at its height had 25,000 clients; by 1989 together Dior and Yves Saint Laurent had 200 clients. See Diana Crane, *Fashion and Its Social Agendas: Class, Gender and Identity in Clothing* (Chicago: University of Chicago Press, 2000), 142.

11. Didier Grumbach, *Histories de la Mode* (Paris: Seuil, 1993), 49.

12. When the Incorporated Society was finally dissolved in August 1975, the directors were Hardy Amies, Norman Hartnell, Rahvis and Edward Rayne. Hartnell remained open until 1992, continuing for thirteen years after the death of its founder. Amies maintained his house until 2008, a business model reliant on impeccable tailoring, grand ballgowns and elegant occasion wear.

13. Edwina Ehrman, 'Digby Morton', in de la Haye and Ehrman, *London Couture*, 126.

14. Hardy Amies, 'Taking Stock: Flair and Fashion', *BBC Home Service*, broadcast 7:30–8:15, 19 February 1953. Edgar Lustgarten (as chair), panel: Hardy Amies, Ewan McNairn (Scottish tweed manufacturer), Alys Ziegler (export buying agent for the Henri Bendel department store in New York) and Cleveland Bell (director of the Design Centre of the Cotton Board).

15. Ernestine Carter, '. . . A Longer Line in London', *Sunday Times*, 26 July 1959.

16. 'The Incorporated Society of London Fashion Designers Winter Collections', *The Ambassador*, September 1959.

17. 'Stiebel's on His Own Again', *Sydney Morning Herald*, 24 December 1958.

18. Michael Talboys (designer at Hartnell in the 1960s), *British Library Oral History of British Fashion*, interviewed by Linda Sandino, tape 3 (F14680), side A, 5 February 2004.

19. Véronique Pouillard, 'Recasting Paris Fashion: Haute Couture and Design Management in the Postwar Era', in Blaszczyk and Pouillard, *European Fashion*, 35–62 (37).

20. 'Britain Dresses Up for the Queen: Clothes for the Coronation Year Are Rich, Regal and Reserved', *Life*, New York, 30 March 1953.

21. Pouillard, 'Recasting Paris Fashion', 47.

22. Despite financial subventions over the next decade, until they were curtailed, the French couture houses receiving them decreased in size, from forty-five firms in 1952 to twenty-four in 1960.

23. This is noted throughout meetings documented in the Incorporated Society's Minutes.

24. *This Week: Panorama*, ITV Television Broadcast, 8:30, 6 February 1958. After the war it was not until eminent figures in the fashion industry lobbied the British government for support for the British fashion industry that the British Fashion Council was created in 1983, with a focus on ready-to-wear; this was chaired first by Edward Rayne, the last chairman of the INCSOC.

25. Michael Guest, interview with the author, 19 December 2007.

26. 'Around the Salons of Mayfair', *Bristol Evening Post*, 25 July 1949.

27. Amies, *Just So Far*, 201–202.

28. See the appendix.

29. Jonathan Faiers, 'Reporting London Couture 1940–72', in de la Haye and Ehrman, *London Couture*, 301.

30. *A Report on the Present Position of the Apparel and Fashion Industry Prepared as a Basis for Guiding Its Future Progress*, Apparel and Fashion Industry's Association, 1950 (BT 94/324), 14–15.

31. *Incorporated Society of London Fashion Designers Annual Report for 1950*, 7 June 1951.

32. For further detail on the wholesale couture, see Tragenza, 'London before It Swung'.

33. Roma Fairley, *A Bomb in the Collection: Fashion with the Lid Off* (London: Clifton Books, 1969), 45.

34. *MISDM*, 8 September 1947.

35. 'Paradise (W1) Has Trouble', *Sunday Express*, 12 October 1947.

36. It did not accept any new members until Giuseppe Mattli in 1948, when Angele Delanghe resigned, followed by Michael Sherard in 1949. The house of Lachasse then joined in October 1950 after Bianca Mosca's resignation and subsequent death. After Molyneux retired and both his London and Paris houses closed in September 1951, it was then another year until the Paris-trained couturier John Cavanagh was granted membership, followed in 1953 by Michael Donnellan and Ronald Patterson and finally Clive Evans in 1962.

37. Millerson, *The Qualifying Associations*, 10.

38. Amies, *Just So Far*, 197.

39. Amies, *Just So Far*, 197.

INDEX